Essentials of Modeling and Analytics illustrates how and why analytics can be used effectively by loss prevention staff. The book offers an in-depth overview of analytics, first illustrating how analytics are used to solve business problems, then exploring the tools and training that staff will need in order to engage solutions. The text also covers big data analytical tools and discusses if and when they are right for retail loss prevention professionals, and illustrates how to use analytics to test the effectiveness of loss prevention initiatives. Ideal for loss prevention personnel on all levels, this book can also be used for loss prevention analytics courses.

David B. Speights, Ph.D., is the Chief Data Scientist for Appriss, which provides proprietary data and analytics solutions to address risk, fraud, security, safety, health, and compliance issues. He has 20 years of experience developing and deploying analytical solutions for some of the world's largest corporations, retailers, and government agencies. Speights was formerly first vice president of Mortgage Credit Risk Modeling at Washington Mutual and chief statistician at HNC Software. He holds a Ph.D. in Biostatistics from the University of California, Los Angeles, and has several patents.

Daniel M. Downs, Ph.D., is the Senior Statistical Criminologist at Appriss and has spent the last 5 years focusing on predictive modeling. He is an author, presenter, and researcher, and has a vast background in loss prevention and criminology. Downs was a research coordinator for the Loss Prevention Research Council, where he engaged in fact-based research to develop loss control solutions to positively affect the retail industry. He received his Ph.D. in Criminology from the University of Illinois and his M.A. in Experimental Psychology from California State University, San Bernardino.

Adi Raz, MBA, is the Senior Director of Data Sciences and Modeling at Appriss and has over 15 years of experience developing analytics solutions and modeling for the retail and financial services industries. Raz has spent many years developing predictive and analytical solutions for over 30 national retailers. She manages a data sciences and modeling team and is also responsible for analytical research and development. She received her B.S. in Economics and Statistics from James Madison University and her MBA from Pepperdine University, and is currently a Business Administration doctoral candidate.

Essentials of Modeling and Analytics

Retail Risk Management and Asset Protection

David B. Speights, Ph.D.
Daniel M. Downs, Ph.D.
Adi Raz, MBA, DBA Candidate

Routledge
Taylor & Francis Group

LONDON AND NEW YORK

First published 2018 by Routledge

2 Park Square, Milton Park, Abingdon, Oxfordshire OX14 4RN
52 Vanderbilt Avenue, New York, NY 10017

Routledge is an imprint of the Taylor & Francis Group, an informa business

First issued in paperback 2019

Library of Congress Cataloging-in-Publication Data
Names: Speights, David B., author. | Downs, Daniel M., author. | Raz,
  Adi, author.
Title: Essentials of modeling and analytics : retail risk management and asset
  protection / David B. Speights, Ph.D., Daniel M. Downs, Ph.D., Adi Raz,
  MBA, DBA Candidate.
Description: New York, NY : Routledge, 2017. | Includes bibliographical
  references.
Identifiers: LCCN 2017005828 | ISBN 9781498774024 (hardback)
Subjects: LCSH: Retail trade—Security measures. | Retail trade—Risk
  management. | Retail trade—Statistical methods. | Theft—Prevention.
Classification: LCC HF5429.265 .S74 2017 | DDC 658.8/700681—dc23
LC record available at https://lccn.loc.gov/2017005828

ISBN: 978-1-4987-7402-4 (hbk)
ISBN: 978-0-367-87880-1 (pbk)

Typeset in Bembo Std
by Apex CoVantage, LLC

Contents

Contents

David B. Speights, Ph.D.
Chief Data Scientist, The Retail Equation (A Division of Appriss)

Dr. David Speights is the chief data scientist for Appriss. He has 20 years of experience developing and deploying analytical solutions for some of the world's largest companies. Throughout his career, he has managed massive amounts of data using big data tools. Currently, he is responsible for analytical modeling and managing point-of-sale data from more than 25 national retailers (equating to more than 100 million rows of new data daily). He joined Appriss through the acquisition of The Retail Equation in 2015. He has been with The Retail Equation since 2000. Prior to joining the company, Speights was first vice president of Mortgage Credit Risk Modeling at Washington Mutual and chief statistician at HNC Software. He is often asked to consult on projects within a number of industries. Speights holds a Ph.D. in Biostatistics from the University of California, Los Angeles, and has several patents.

Daniel M. Downs, Ph.D.
Senior Statistical Criminologist, The Retail Equation
(A Division of Appriss)

Dr. Downs is the Senior Statistical Criminologist at Appriss and has spent the last 5 years focusing on quantitative research methods and predictive modeling. Dr. Downs is an author, presenter, and researcher, and has a vast background in retail loss prevention and criminology. Downs was a research coordinator for the Loss Prevention Research Council (LPRC), where he engaged in fact-based research to develop loss control solutions to positively affect its members and the retail industry. As an adjunct professor at the University of Florida, Downs taught a course entitled Crime Prevention: Field Research and has taught other courses related to criminology, statistics, and research methods. Downs received his Ph.D. in Criminology from the University of Illinois, and his M.A. in Experimental Psychology and B.S. in Psychology from California State University, San Bernardino.

Adi Raz, MBA, Doctoral Candidate
Senior Director, Data Sciences and Modeling,
The Retail Equation (A Division of Appriss)
Adi Raz is the Senior Director of Data Sciences and Modeling at Appriss and has over 15 years of experience developing analytics solutions and modeling for the retail and financial services industries. She joined Appriss through the acquisition of The Retail Equation, where she has spent the past 12 years developing predictive and analytical solutions for over 30 national retailers. Currently, she is responsible for managing the data sciences and modeling team responsible for all active retail models, handling more than 12 million transactions a day. Adi is also responsible for analytical research and development and has a long track record of improving predictive models to better drive profitable solutions for retailers. Prior to The Retail Equation, Adi was employed at Circuit City, Washington Mutual Bank, and Countrywide in senior analytics roles, developing and deploying predictive solutions. Adi received her Bachelor's degree in Economics and Statistics from James Madison University and her MBA from Pepperdine University, graduating first in her class from both programs. She is currently a Business Administration Doctoral candidate.

The use of data and analytics in retail loss prevention is in the early stages of development and there is limited literature on their application to loss prevention. In other sectors like insurance, finance, health, telecommunications, and even retail marketing, analytics has been used for decades. In loss prevention, analytics has gained popularity and usage over just the last few years. From this period, however, there are a number of examples on how data and analytics have been used by loss prevention teams to save their companies money and apprehend suspicious employees or customers. This book stemmed from the importance and necessity to highlight the uses of analytics and to illustrate how it can be used more effectively in loss and crime prevention.

This particular subject matter is close to us and we advocate an analytical approach to loss prevention owing to our interactions with more than 35 national retailers and more than 40 years of collective experience in applying analytics for over 100 different companies and organizations. In addition to our practical experience, we have experience of teaching courses on statistical methods as well as loss prevention and criminology theory. We were inspired to write this book because we know there is a lack of practical fact-based analytical handbooks in loss prevention.

The purpose of this book is to take the reader through loss prevention analytics with a step-by-step approach. First, we will build a theoretical foundation for criminology and loss prevention. Second, we will describe how companies are using analytics to solve business problems. Third, we will discuss the statistical approaches used to solve the loss prevention problem. Fourth, we will review the tools and training that staff will need to engage in data analytics. Fifth, we will explore the world of big data analytical tools and their application for retail loss prevention. Sixth, we will explain what the analytics infrastructure for a loss prevention department should look like. Finally, we will illustrate how to use analytics to justify and then test the effectiveness of loss prevention investments.

The journey of writing the book has been arduous yet rewarding and will have been worth taking if you garner new insights and knowledge that can be applied to your team or efforts. Overall, our hope is that its contents can benefit and support loss and crime prevention.

Acknowledgments

We thank our employer, The Retail Equation (an Appriss, Inc. company), for providing us with the opportunity to complete this book. A special thanks as well to Vishal Patel, Ph.D., who contributed significantly to Chapter 12. We also thank Tom Rittman, Pete Bradshaw, and Mark Hammond for providing support on the content and editing. Additionally, we thank our spouses, who supported us in this effort and the additional work this required.

Introduction

The explosion of data in the past two decades has transformed our world. According to research done in 2013, 90% of the data in the world at that time had been collected in the prior two years (Dragland, 2013). This explosion of information has created a vacuum for analytics applications. Analytics professionals, computer scientists, and data enthusiasts have quickly moved to fill this void with applications that help us locate our destination, market products to us more efficiently, catch terrorists, track credit card fraud, control the temperature in our house, recommend products, movies, and music, drive our cars, and support retail loss prevention.

Retail loss prevention has adopted many technologies during this information explosion, with such tools as exception reporting, automated fraud detection, predictive models, facial recognition, crime indices, organized retail crime detection, and many more. Even with these advances, retailers are constantly under attack by an ever-evolving population of criminals and unscrupulous employees, and need the latest technology to keep up. Analytics, in all of its varieties, is the engine that helps retailers fight the growing and continuous threats they face every day.

If all occurrences of shoplifting were reported to the police, it would constitute the largest single crime committed in the United States (Bellur, 1981). According to the National Retail Security Survey, in 2015, retail loss totaled $44.2 billion dollars (Moraca *et al.*, 2015). That is more than the gross domestic product of Jamaica, Albania, and Mongolia combined. Why is retail loss so large? Well, for two reasons: there will always be opportunities for crime and people willing to commit those crimes. That being said, retail loss can be reduced effectively with data and analytics and there are numerous studies that prove this point. Many such cases will be explored throughout this book.

It is not just data that is exploding. The use of technology within loss prevention is growing rapidly as well. New tools and technology are flooding loss prevention personnel and every year there are more and more tools available to help them do their jobs. This growth is astonishing and includes an impressive list of tools to analyze data, warehouse and access video footage, track customers through a store, monitor aberrant employees, and so on. Over the last 10 to 15 years, there has been a shift from a very manual process where closed circuit television cameras (CCTVs) were watched by store loss prevention personnel to apprehend, interview, and possibly arrest potential shoplifters, toward a digital age drenched in data, where a room full of analysts watch the movements and digital signatures of employees, customers, suppliers, stores, products, and any other item that can be tracked and monitored. At the center of the technology is an increased focus on data and analytics. Close to 100% of loss prevention professionals today use data or analytics in some form or another to perform their day-to-day jobs.

Billions of automated decisions from analytical systems are being made daily to prevent and detect crime:

1. Exception reporting tools are used to analyze point of sale data and catch employees (or customers) who are stealing from retailers.
2. Real-time credit card fraud detection systems are monitoring all of the transactions at the point of sale or online to look for stolen credit cards or fraudulent transactions.
3. Real-time predictive models monitor returned merchandise to look for fraudulent returns.
4. Crime indices are compiled using data from multiple crime reporting systems to create an index that can be used to allocate loss prevention resource.
5. Facial recognition systems are monitoring patrons at the store to detect when persons of interest enter a store.
6. Experimental design methods are implemented to scientifically measure the impact of loss prevention programs.
7. And there are many more examples.

All of the solutions listed require data and analytics to make them function. Therefore, organizations such as the Loss Prevention Research Council at the

University of Florida have formed to encourage the application of good scientific processes and analytics to loss prevention.

Data does not analyze itself. Combining trained investigators and experienced loss prevention staff with analytical personnel is necessary to integrate more analytics into loss prevention. The ability to assess patterns in data and make decisions in real time is fundamental in solving complex issues related to customers, employees, sales, and loss. As potential offenders become more sophisticated, they seek targets that increase reward and minimize risk. They target areas of weakness in vulnerable retailers (i.e., those lacking an aggressive analytical strategy for detection and prevention of loss). Adopting strategies requires the right knowledge and expertise within loss prevention departments.

In the past few decades, with improvements in computer processing, data collection, and storage, analytics has increasingly played a more central role in loss prevention. However, the use of analytics in loss prevention is much earlier in its development than several other business verticals. In other sectors, like insurance, finance, telecommunications, and even retail marketing, analytics has been used since the 1960s and 1970s. In loss prevention, analytics has slowly evolved over the last 10 to 20 years, with much of the growth in the past 10 years. In this period, however, there are countless examples to show how data and analytics have been used by loss prevention teams to save their companies money and catch nefarious employees or customers. Most retail loss prevention teams are already evolving toward a more analytical infrastructure and recognize that data and advanced statistical methods will lie at the heart of loss prevention in the future. In particular, data and analytics are critical in:

1. Making decisions regarding store operations and resource allocation;
2. Testing the effectiveness of loss prevention tools and programs;
3. Identifying fraudulent transactions, checks, or credit cards;
4. Identifying shoplifters;
5. Making decisions regarding the best use of loss prevention tools;
6. Correctly estimating costs and benefits for multiple loss prevention programs;
7. Determining policies that reduce loss.

Various analytic techniques can be used to assess these topics. Techniques include basic trend and frequency analysis, A/B testing (test-and-learn), graphical methods to visualize data, correlations, outlier detection, and predictive modeling. Correct use of analytics can aid loss prevention in detecting which employees are stealing, identifying which customers are exploiting coupon loopholes, determining which stores need more security, identifying and linking organized retail crime groups, analyzing video analytics, and investigating numerous other loss prevention issues.

Why is Analytics Important in Loss Prevention?

The popularity of analytics and the reason for using it within any line of business is simple; money. When thousands upon thousands of decisions are made each day, or analysis of a large number of items is required, any change in procedure that improves efficiency or effectiveness will save the retailer money. Analytics helps you insert intelligence into a procedure; the savings come from applying that change over and over to the many decisions or items.

To apply analytics effectively, the practitioner must begin by carefully defining an objective. Identifying what problems you are trying to solve or what you are trying to improve leads to the method of attack. For example, you may want to identify whether shrink will increase or decrease next year for a store. Once you have established your objective, you need to decide whether the model is used for inference or prediction. Inference models generally answer questions regarding the relationship between variables, whereas predictive models predict an outcome. For example: is employee morale related to shrink? Is the presence of cameras related to shrink? An inferential model can answer these. Other examples: what is the shrink likely to be the next time I measure the inventory? What are the expected number of robberies in a geographic area next quarter? A predictive model is the right approach here. In either case, predictive or inferential, once you have defined your model and objective, you can intuitively create a list of predictor variables (e.g., missed shipments, lost inventory, or manager turnover) and begin the data extraction process.

What Problems Can Be Addressed with Analytics in Loss Prevention?

In today's typical loss prevention team, the methods shown in Figure 1.1 are used by many (if not all) loss prevention teams. The reason each method has been employed is that it generates value for the retailer.

A limited number of loss prevention teams and vendors are pushing the envelope and are using more advanced methods (Figure 1.2). As the methods become better defined, and the value proposition can be well articulated to a retailer's management, it is likely that these methods will become more commonplace.

We will explore many of these methods in this book, as well as the underlying methodology used to execute them.

Overview of This Book

This book contains material essential for anyone in crime or loss prevention, anyone interested in data and analytics and how to apply them to real-world issues, and anyone

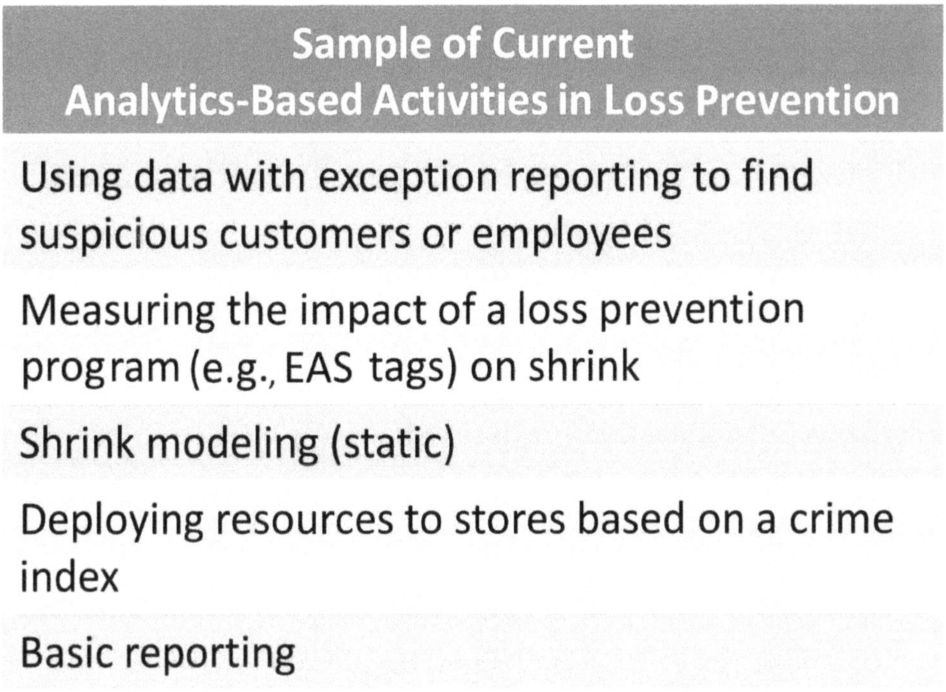

Sample of Current Analytics-Based Activities in Loss Prevention

Using data with exception reporting to find suspicious customers or employees

Measuring the impact of a loss prevention program (e.g., EAS tags) on shrink

Shrink modeling (static)

Deploying resources to stores based on a crime index

Basic reporting

Figure 1.1: Common Loss Prevention Analytics-Based Activities

interested in research and statistics. The motivation for this book is the lack of practical fact-based analytical handbooks in retail loss prevention. We are passionate about this particular subject matter and have applied other industries' best practices and statistical knowhow to retail loss prevention. We have analyzed, modeled, and deterred fraud and risk in the insurance, healthcare, telecommunication, direct marketing, and banking industries prior to our work in retail. We have also spent several years interviewing active and apprehended shoplifters (i.e., the target audience of loss prevention programs) to better understand their strategies and reactions to loss prevention techniques. Furthermore, regardless of the industry, one must apply similar analytical techniques to study trends and spot data abnormalities. Our combined 40+ years of experience in analyzing data for over 100 companies has taught us a valuable lesson: crime is crime and data is data. In other words, once you start thinking like a data analyst or a data scientist you will start to assess the risk more accurately, regardless of industry or work sector.

Loss prevention is rooted in finding and stopping criminal activity. For that purpose, we included a chapter on popular criminology theories. Understanding why a person is targeting your store is half the battle. Using data and analytics, along with

A Sample of New & Future Analytics-Based Activities in Loss Prevention

Video analytics used to screen activities in real time across all stores

Using predictive models to find organized retail crime

Video stored and analyzable centrally

Predictive models used for identifying employee fraud

Predicting crime trends using social media

Predictive models that forecast shrink by store next year

Association-based linking: linking individuals that share significant shopping characteristics

Figure 1.2: New and Future Loss Prevention Analytics-Based Activities

criminology-based knowledge, will help loss prevention professionals direct their analysis and more accurately interpret results.

This book will cover the application of analytics used to identify loss prevention problems, address them, and improve your loss prevention strategies. We will help you develop loss prevention objectives as they relate to analytics and help you determine which analytical tools would be appropriate to analyze your data. For example, you may want to identify: (1) whether shrink will increase or decrease next year for a given store; (2) whether employee turnover is related to shrink; or (3) whether the presence of enhanced public view monitors or security guards is related to shrink.

In this book, you will learn how to prepare, clean, and transform data. Additionally, you will learn how to assess relationships, build models, and report results. For this, we will provide many examples related to loss prevention. The book is organized around real-world examples, together with the necessary formulas, as well as applicable statistical software examples (i.e., SPSS and SAS). We will cover the importance of variable transformations for optimal use in modeling. We will make it clear what we mean by fitting a model, which will be presented to you, with statistical software examples and formulas.

Analytics can also be applied to build a business case for loss prevention procedures and tools (e.g., assessing return on investment and impact on key metrics). In this book, we will provide examples of how to write up the results of your analysis in a comprehensible way. With this in mind, you will learn how to interpret results and, ultimately, apply them to real-world situations. Moreover, you will be more confident in your decision making and garner the support of other teams.

Access to data is critical for analytics and building predictive models. There may be many sources of data from various systems within an organization. Data sources may include point of sale data, an employee database, shipment and stock data, or surveys to determine employee or manager performance. With that said, integrating the right technologies to assess and analyze the data, and acquiring the expertise that most loss prevention teams currently do not possess, can take time. We encourage loss prevention leaders to begin preparations, internally and externally, now in order to create an analytical infrastructure that can bring significant value through the use of data and analytical methods.

The use of big data and predictive modeling is a critical component in the future of loss prevention. Therefore, in this book, we will devote a chapter to the importance of integrating analytics in your loss prevention function. This chapter will: (1) provide answers to the questions we regularly receive on the new advances of big data; (2) explain its conjunction with predictive analytics techniques; and (3) offer loss prevention leaders best practices learned from working with more than 35 national retailers on how to take advantage of this technology directly or with knowledgeable vendors as your partners. We will outline how you can create a big data infrastructure within your loss prevention organization and how to acquire the right people. This chapter will also outline the data management software (e.g., Oracle, SQL Server, and Netezza), analytics hardware (e.g., Hadoop, Hive, and Teradata) and analytics software (e.g., SAS, SPSS, and R) required to build a big data infrastructure.

This book will also cover new and future trends in loss prevention analytics; for example, predicting crime trends using social media, associations based linking, building score-based models, and using predictive models to find organized retail crime.

Thus, this book is intended to help you be more proactive in your loss prevention strategies.

In summary, statistics is playing a growing role in how retailers approach loss prevention issues and solutions. Data and analytics are important in any economic climate; but in a mixed economy where profit margins are uncertain, it is imperative for retailers to have a clear-cut picture of their business that is rooted in solid data analytics.

In this book, we will teach you how to better harness the data you already have, analyze it, and use fact-based proactive decisions to improve loss prevention. Our goal, through data and analytics, is to contribute to the understanding of the different types of loss, how to better detect loss, how to predict it, and, ultimately, how to prevent it.

The material in this book is intended to be a how-to handbook for business and loss prevention analytics. This book may also be used by anyone interested in better understanding data and analytics. The danger is to present too much complex material and have the reader be overwhelmed. Therefore, our intention is to provide illustrations, examples of code, examples from statistical software, step-by-step instructions for assessing and analyzing data, and, for more advanced practitioners, some formulas representing the analysis.

By the time you finish reading this book, you should be more comfortable with the notion of assessing data for assumptions, assessing the strength of variable relationships, assessing the fit of data models, predictive modeling, new analytics trends, and big data infrastructure. You should be more confident in using data to make proactive business decisions. Finally, you should be convinced (we hope) that data and analytics are shaping the future of loss prevention.

Chapter Two
Criminology Theory and Crime Prevention

To have once been a criminal is no disgrace.
To remain a criminal is the disgrace.

—Malcolm X

Introduction

At the foundation of retail loss prevention is general criminological theory. In this chapter, we will explore several theories and show how they relate to retail situations and where analytics may be applicable. Criminological theories play important roles in crime prevention and crime analytics. Criminology theory provides us with a framework to assess loss prevention situations and solve problems in a structured way. Therefore, this chapter is designed to provide a theoretical context for understanding the psychological and social forces that drive people to become criminals, and how criminogenic opportunities can be reduced, as well as where analytics fits into the theoretical aspects of criminology. To understand crime and loss prevention, the chapter will begin with a short review of crime analytics and place-based crime. We will then discuss the interaction between an individual and the environment and will cover the criminological theories and concepts presented in Figure 2.1.

Each of the theories and concepts discussed provides insight into the ability of an offender to respond to crime opportunities and deterrence. As each of these theories is explored, the role of analytics in each component of the theory is discussed.

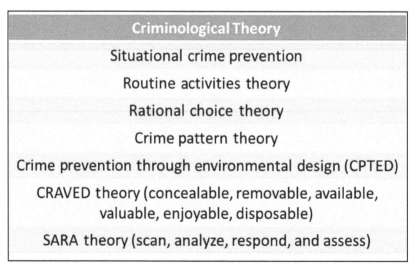

Criminological Theory

Situational crime prevention

Routine activities theory

Rational choice theory

Crime pattern theory

Crime prevention through environmental design (CPTED)

CRAVED theory (concealable, removable, available, valuable, enjoyable, disposable)

SARA theory (scan, analyze, respond, and assess)

Figure 2.1: Criminal Theories

Being grounded in a theoretical understanding of crime, we can better examine and apply strategic prevention and deterrence methods. This chapter elucidates why crime takes place in certain situations and how to prevent loss using various criminology theories. It provides a foundation for future chapters, which will use these theoretical frameworks to illustrate how to assess the efficacy of various crime prevention techniques. Using theory and analytics, we will expound on how to analyze crime and data scientifically to support the implementation of effective loss prevention techniques.

The Intersection of Criminological Theory and Analytics: Crime Analytics

Crime analytics is the methodical study of crime and loss that includes environmental and spatial factors to develop methods to detect risk and improve deterrence. Crime analytics involves the rigorous study of crime theory and its application to crime prevention; it is not anecdotal. Rather, it is composed of theory, scientific data collection, analytical methods, and statistical modeling.

Research supports crime analytics as a central loss prevention strategy (Hayes & Downs, 2011; Hayes *et al.*, 2012). The first step of crime analytics is to understand, via crime theory, why and how crime happens. Once we better understand the causes of criminality and crime events, we can change crime opportunities and the decisions offenders make. The next step is to select loss prevention strategies to implement (e.g., exception reporting, behavioral tracking, signage, security guards, locked cabinets, electronic tagging, or public view monitors). Once implemented, the next step is to monitor the loss prevention strategies and collect data. The final step is to evaluate their efficacy using science-based analytics. Figure 2.2 summarizes this process.

There are two steps in the process where analytics is utilized directly, assuming a crime opportunity is already known. The first step is within the loss prevention strat-

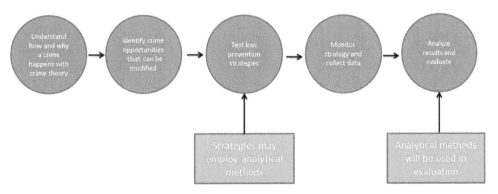

Figure 2.2: Analytics and Crime Prevention Strategy

11

egies themselves. Predictive models, exception reporting systems, facial recognition technology, and the like, will often be part of the solution set of loss prevention strategies. The second place where analytics comes into play is experimental design and analysis of the new strategy. In later chapters, a variety of methods for each of these steps will be discussed.

Beyond analytical-based approaches, there are many nonanalytical loss prevention strategies such as physical security (locked cabinets and security guards) and electronic article surveillance, which may be used to modify criminal activity. Crime prevention strategies vary in their effectiveness and length of deterrence, depending on the type of crime. Understanding the underlying theories of why some environments are more criminogenic than others will help explain why some crime prevention strategies are more effective than others.

Place-Based Crime

Why does crime occur more in some places than others? The design of physical space is important in understanding criminal events. Larceny, like other types of crime, arises from an interaction between an individual, with a propensity for offending, and the environmental context, which provides criminogenic opportunities. Research has posited that the choice of theft targets is highly reliant on an assessment of the immediate context of the target (Brantingham & Brantingham, 1995; Felson, 2002; Cornish & Clarke, 2003). This, in turn, has led to an increasing focus on the role of environmental context in shaping theft outcomes. Essentially, this research obviates dispositional explanations for crime and supports the incorporation of elements of social context in understanding crime. Situational crime prevention provides a pragmatic approach to loss prevention, since crime opportunities are concentrated in time and space.

Example: Applying Analytics to Place-Based Crime Theory

One example of combining analytics and criminological theory involves the layout of the store or the location of the store in the city or in a mall. A loss prevention professional may suspect that the layout of a store, or its location within a mall, is related to increases in shoplifting and shrink. For example, let's explore the first suspicion. It is suspected that stores with a return counter in the back of the store have higher theft rates than stores with return counters in the front. There are a few ways to build evidence to support this hypothesis using experimental methods and basic statistics. The first method, which will not involve any actual store design changes, is simply to compare shrink rates and other shoplifting related metrics between various store formats. Suppose the retailer has 50 stores and 25 have the return counter in the front and 25 have the return counter in the back. Table 2.1 represents the shrink data from 2016 separated by store and divided into two groups. The first group has the return counter in the front of the store and the second group has the return counter in the back of the store.

The initial data and overall store average suggest that the shrink rate is higher in stores with a return counter at the back of the store. But are the results significant? What other factors should be considered? Based on the information provided in later chapters, a loss prevention professional will be able to conduct statistical tests on the data and draw some conclusions about the statistical significance of the relationship between the return counter's location and shrink. However, we will also explore other questions, which need to be asked as well:

- Is the difference that is observed due to other factors? For example, the higher risk stores may have placed their return counters in the front because, originally, it was suspected this might reduce shrink. In that case, the conclusions would be completely circular. Loss prevention person A placed the counters in the front in high shrink stores in an attempt to reduce shrink. Even if shrink was lowered, it may still be higher than

Table 2.1: Sales and Shrink by Return Counter Location

Store Number	Location of Return Counter	Sales for 2016	Shrink Dollars 2016	Shrink
1	Back	$ 124,141.5	$ 733.0	0.6%
2	Back	$ 1,697,938.1	$ 35,828.5	2.1%
3	Back	$ 427,281.7	$ 3,390.3	0.8%
4	Back	$ 959,795.8	$ 10,322.7	1.1%
5	Back	$ 585,075.1	$ 5,817.3	1.0%
6	Back	$ 399,571.5	$ 3,517.7	0.9%
7	Back	$ 348,342.0	$ 2,514.4	0.7%
8	Back	$ 144,335.0	$ 901.2	0.6%
9	Back	$ 1,661,991.5	$ 31,954.5	1.9%
10	Back	$ 562,632.0	$ 5,366.9	1.0%
11	Back	$ 281,772.2	$ 2,068.4	0.7%
12	Back	$ 466,574.4	$ 3,644.6	0.8%

(Continued)

Table 2.1 (Continued)

Store Number	Location of Return Counter	Sales for 2016	Shrink Dollars 2016	Shrink
13	Back	$ 226,187.8	$ 1,580.3	0.7%
14	Back	$ 1,685,101.2	$ 32,787.8	1.9%
15	Back	$ 1,071,197.2	$ 11,566.0	1.1%
16	Back	$ 354,798.7	$ 2,496.0	0.7%
17	Back	$ 531,897.9	$ 4,252.1	0.8%
18	Back	$ 241,699.3	$ 1,799.5	0.7%
19	Back	$ 150,695.5	$ 913.4	0.6%
20	Back	$ 217,452.6	$ 1,446.2	0.7%
21	Back	$ 3,101,264.3	$ 72,582.0	2.3%
22	Back	$ 764,509.5	$ 8,754.3	1.1%
23	Back	$ 405,689.8	$ 3,265.1	0.8%
24	Back	$ 302,946.0	$ 2,387.2	0.8%
25	Back	$ 7,560,596.8	$ 533,048.6	7.1%
Total	**Back**	**$ 24,273,487.0**	**$ 782,938.2**	**3.2%**

Store Number	Location of Return Counter	Sales for 2016	Shrink Dollars 2016	Shrink
26	Front	$ 2,854,708.0	$ 96,511.6	3.4%
27	Front	$ 405,693.9	$ 3,132.3	0.8%
28	Front	$ 430,755.5	$ 3,888.9	0.9%
29	Front	$ 549,388.5	$ 4,443.5	0.8%
30	Front	$ 1,122,250.3	$ 15,702.1	1.4%
31	Front	$ 425,211.7	$ 3,570.0	0.8%
32	Front	$ 1,414,909.1	$ 21,136.1	1.5%
33	Front	$ 276,759.5	$ 1,917.3	0.7%
34	Front	$ 499,384.4	$ 3,837.4	0.8%
35	Front	$ 787,082.8	$ 9,015.2	1.1%
36	Front	$ 2,153,311.3	$ 45,945.4	2.1%
37	Front	$ 969,149.1	$ 12,138.3	1.3%

(Continued)

Table 2.1 (Continued)

Store Number	Location of Return Counter	Sales for 2016	Shrink Dollars 2016	Shrink
38	Front	$ 1,634,717.7	$ 30,850.3	1.9%
39	Front	$ 2,075,209.8	$ 42,708.5	2.1%
40	Front	$ 841,867.2	$ 8,760.1	1.0%
41	Front	$ 570,481.9	$ 5,038.1	0.9%
42	Front	$ 2,713,503.1	$ 61,583.4	2.3%
43	Front	$ 857,588.7	$ 11,371.0	1.3%
44	Front	$ 76,937.4	$ 422.1	0.5%
45	Front	$ 374,670.4	$ 3,226.3	0.9%
46	Front	$ 96,758.6	$ 550.1	0.6%
47	Front	$ 216,748.0	$ 1,543.7	0.7%
48	Front	$ 250,095.1	$ 1,827.4	0.7%
49	Front	$ 1,310,974.0	$ 23,965.6	1.8%
50	Front	$ 259,676.0	$ 1,792.0	0.7%
Total	**Front**	**$ 23,167,832.0**	**$ 414,876.8**	**1.8%**

the original low shrink stores. Now loss prevention person B (perhaps many years after loss prevention person A has left the company) sees that the shrink in the stores with the counter in the back is higher than the stores with the counter in the front.

- How can the practitioner improve the analytical approach to account for the issues raised by other possible factors? How is it possible to untangle the two effects of (1) the return counter's location and (2) whatever factors made those stores have higher shrink in the first place?
- Is there a more scientific way to measure the effects? A more scientific approach to the analysis is for the practitioner to build evidence for the hypothesis that the return counter location affects shrink, by conducting an experiment. The procedure for the experiment will be to switch some of the stores' return counters from the front to the back and vice versa and measure the change in shrink.

Situational Crime Prevention

Individual factors are highly influential in explaining crime but, in the view of situational crime prevention, so is the opportunity to commit crime. Situational crime prevention is grounded in the rational choice perspective in that it intends to alter the environment to change criminogenic opportunities and, in turn, manipulate the decision making of potential offenders. Situational crime prevention techniques are based on the understanding that people are situated decision makers and changing the situational context influences their decisions.

Situational crime prevention is a pre-emptive approach that consists of techniques, derived from several crime theories, used to impede the commission of crimes by making the crime more difficult and less profitable. Situational crime prevention is predicated on the routine activity theory and contends that three key elements are needed for a crime to take place: the convergence of (1) a likely offender and (2) a suitable target, and (3) the absence of a capable guardian (Felson, 2002). The three elements of crime are illustrated in Figure 2.3. As noted by the red arrows, for crime to be committed, there needs to be a likely offender with an unguarded desired target.

Situational crime prevention requires the immediate environment to be designed in a way to hinder opportunities for crime by increasing the efforts (e.g., target hardening

Figure 2.3: Situational Prevention Theory—The Three Elements of Crime

and access control), reducing the rewards (i.e., decreasing the benefit) and increasing the risks (e.g., extend guardianship or surveillance) of committing a crime, as perceived by offenders (Clarke, 1997; Sutton *et al.*, 2008). Situational crime prevention eschews dispositional theories of crime because it argues that opportunity plays a more important role. That is, individuals without pre-existing dispositions for crime may be drawn into crime if opportunities present themselves. Thus, reducing crime opportunities, overall, will reduce crime (Smith & Clarke, 2012).

To prevent crime, stakeholders must analyze opportunity structures for specific types of crime. Once opportunity structures are uncovered, Cornish and Clarke's (2003) 5 situational crime prevention strategies and 25 techniques can be applied and tested (see Table 2.2). Situational crime prevention employs measures that are directed at specific crime types (e.g., retail theft) and succeeds by means of manipulation of the immediate environment to: (1) increase the perceived effort of committing the crime; (2) increase the risks of committing the crime; (3) reduce the rewards from committing the crime; (4) reduce the opportunities for crime; and (5) remove excuses for committing the crime. Situational crime prevention should be both interdisciplinary and multifaceted. That is, in order to build a successful crime prevention framework, crime analytics and techniques of situational crime prevention should be combined.

Table 2.2: Clarke's 25 Techniques of Situational Crime Prevention

Increase the Effort	*Increase the Risks*	*Reduce the Rewards*	*Reduce Provocation*	*Remove Excuses*
Target harden	Extend guardianship	Conceal targets	Reduce frustration and stress	Set rules
Control access to facilities	Assist natural surveillance	Remove targets	Avoid disputes	Post instructions
Screen exists	Reduce anonymity	Identify property	Reduce emotional arousal	Alert conscience
Deflect offenders	Utilize place managers	Disrupt markets	Neutralize peer pressure	Assist compliance
Control tools, weapons	Strengthen formal surveillance	Deny benefits	Discourage imitation	Control drugs and alcohol

Source: Adapted from Clarke (1997); Cornish & Clarke (2003).

For example, let's assume that a loss prevention team at an electronics retailer is facing high employee theft, noted by high shrink. Employing Cornish and Clarke's (2003) five situational crime prevention strategies, the loss prevention team can do the following:

Increase the effort	Limit the number of employees with access to high shrink items (only allow managers to have the key to the cages or to unlock keepers).
Increase the risk	Increase the number of CCTVs that are monitoring employees.
Reduce the rewards	Ensure that high shrink items can only be used with an access code that is provided during the purchase.
Reduce provocations	Invest in team building and organizational structures that reinforce ethical behavior that benefits the employees and the company.
Remove excuses	Invest in employee training and ensure that employees know all the rules and consequences.

Situational crime prevention is based on classic research methodology: (1) collect data regarding the nature and dimensions of a specific type of crime; (2) analyze the situational conditions that facilitate this crime; (3) study possible methods to block opportunities for this crime; (4) implement the most effective, feasible, and economic measures; and (5) monitor the results and then propagate the knowledge.

Example: Applying Analytics to Situational Crime Theory

Suppose an electronics retailer has a problem with shrink for a small handheld tablet that is sold in its stores. The device is currently on a shelf accessible by the customers, and the loss prevention team would like to determine the effects of placing the device behind a locked glass display case, while at the same time leaving a single device on display. The team designs an experiment to test the effects of the change on both shrink and sales. Later in the book, we will discuss the key elements of the experimental design: randomization, sample size determination, store selection, and the methods used to analyze the resulting data.

Rational Choice Theory

Situational crime prevention is also informed and guided by rational choice theory; it is derived from the notion that people make choices rationally and include both contextual factors and a cost–benefit analysis (Cornish & Clarke, 2003;

Farrington *et al.*, 1993). Rational choice theory is more individualistic, compared with situational crime prevention, and assesses the decision making processes that may lead to an offender choosing to become involved in a specific type of crime (Clarke, 2005). Its main supposition is that offending is a purposive behavior, intended to benefit the offender. That is, offender behavior is guided by hedonistic values; potential offenders seek pleasure and avoid pain, which is important in employing crime prevention techniques.

According to Cornish and Clarke (1986), rational choice theory views criminality as a result of decisions made by an offender, where crime is committed if the offender weighs the rewards of committing a crime higher than the risk. Rational choice theory suggests that potential offenders choose to commit a crime if the net expected benefits of crime outweigh the net expected benefits of an alternative behavior. Figure 2.4 illustrates the inverse relationship between the perceived risk of committing a crime and the perceived reward.

According to rational choice theory, an offender's decision to commit a crime is based on the available opportunity and choice, which is influenced by costs and benefits (Akers, 2000; Nagin & Paternoster, 1993). Situational crime prevention depends on the idea that an offender is rational and will gauge the environmental risks involved in committing a crime (Clarke, 1997). Hence, according to situational crime preven-

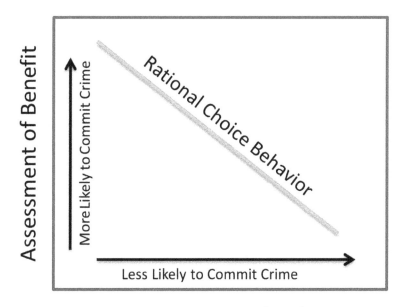

Figure 2.4: Rational Choice Decision

tion, crime can be prevented by increasing an offender's subjective probability of being caught (i.e., increasing the subjective costs of being caught). According to Cullen, Agnew, and Wilcox (2014), in a situation where the risk of detection is high, motivated offenders may not want to subject themselves to the efforts of committing a crime. Thus, an offender's behavior can be manipulated by altering environmental cues. With this knowledge in place, crime will be prevented if the costs are made higher than the benefits of committing a crime (e.g., enhancing protection, target hardening, and surveillance).

Example: Where Rational Choice Theory Meets Individual-level Analytics

The previous examples in this chapter were concerned with general changes to a shopping environment that were not focused on an individual. Since it is difficult to redesign your store as each new person walks in or approaches the electronics department, some loss prevention decisions cannot be tailored to the individual. Since individual perceptions of the risks and benefits of committing a crime may vary, the best loss prevention tactics will be measures that target each individual. For example:

1. Suppose a known shoplifter enters your store; you may instruct a store associate to approach the shoplifter to offer help. The analytics approach there may be to employ facial recognition software, which compares the faces of all people entering a store against a known database of shoplifters.
2. An extension of the first example is a hybrid model, which combines facial recognition with a predictive model to determine different ways to approach people, based on their criminal history.
3. Suspected fraudulent purchases of gift cards may be limited based on the person's history of activity, the value of the card being purchased, or other factors available at the time of purchase. This denial of a transaction may cause the individual to avoid that criminal activity in fear of being caught.
4. For e-commerce shoppers, the return policy may be changed dynamically based on each shopper's return history and likelihood of fraud or abuse. The tighter return policies may prevent fraudulent purchases where the shopper perceives that it may not be possible to return the merchandise.
5. A person returning merchandise to the store may be warned that future returns will not be accepted if fraud or abuse is suspected. This warning will deter these shoppers from making future fraudulent or abusive returns.

Routine Activity Theory

Physical and social environments provide and influence criminal opportunities (Clarke, 1983; Gottfredson & Hirschi, 1990). There is a plethora of literature devoted to conceptualizing the relationship between criminal opportunity and theft. One of the dominant theoretical frameworks shaping this line of inquiry is the routine activity theory (Cohen & Felson, 1979), which assumes that crime represents a convergence in time and space of motivated offenders, suitable targets, and a lack of effective guardianship. Thus, a crime is possible when a motivated offender and a suitable target or victim converge in space and time, in the absence of a capable guardian (Clarke, 1997; Cohen & Felson, 1979; Felson, 2006). Opportunity that is engendered by the lack of a capable guardian cannot be underestimated. Guardianship is vital in a proactive prevention strategy and can be achieved by various methods, such as implementing audiovisual devices (e.g., enhanced public view monitors or CCTVs), increasing lighting, and improving security.

Figure 2.5 illustrates the routine activity theory and the convergence of the offender, target, space, and guardianship. The triangle shows that when an offender and a target converge in space, a crime will take place. The external forces represent guardianship for all three levels; a guardian to protect the target or person, a handler to prevent the offender from committing crime, and a manager to protect the space.

The routine activity theory assumes that criminal events do not occur via a random distribution within society; rather, crime is a function of the convergence of lifestyle and opportunity (Felson & Cohen, 1980). Furthermore, daily activities and routines cultivate opportunity structures by exposing motivated offenders to the proximity of targets. Since offenders exercise rational decisions in their selection of a particular target, within a socio-spatial context, an offender's choice will be contingent on the subjective value of the target.

The routine activity theory is imperative in understanding how crimes occur and how to prevent them; it states that crime is highly likely when offenders converge with targets in the absence of an effective controller (Felson, 2002). Implementing guardianship is therefore a necessary condition to deter loss and crime. In conducting numerous offender interviews during our field research, offenders often stated that having attentive employees who acknowledged their presence in the store was one of the most effective methods of deterring them from committing crime.

Data analytics is an integral part of crime prevention techniques. If, according to the routine activity theory, guardianship or controllers are necessary to reduce the

Figure 2.5: Problem Analysis Triangle (Adapted from Cohen & Felson, 1979)

opportunity associated with crime, which techniques are effective? For how long are they effective? What is the cost–benefit relationship for these techniques? Data analytics help loss prevention teams answer these important questions via multiple methods, such as A/B testing (i.e., test-and-learn), inference models, predictive modeling, outlier detection, and correlation.

Example: Using EAS Tagging as a Guardianship and Testing its Effects on Shrink

One of the earliest forms of loss prevention was the EAS (electronic article surveillance) tag. EAS tags are attached to merchandise and work in tandem with scanning towers placed near the doors of the store.

If an item from the store is taken through the scanners without the EAS tags removed, alarms will be sounded. EAS demonstrates the notion of guardianship in the routine activity theory. It sends a message to perpetrators of a crime that they may be apprehended if they attempt to steal an item. The analytical question to be answered is:

"What are the effects of EAS tags on shrink?" In measuring the effects of EAS tags on inventory shrink, a few things need to be considered. While inherently the EAS tags are a piece of equipment in the store, they requires interaction by store personnel. A few key facts must be considered in the execution of an EAS program:

1. When the alarm sounds, someone needs to react to it.
2. Associates must remove the tags when merchandise is purchased.
3. False positives may occur when the alarm sounds and no merchandise is actually leaving the store. Associates need to help to minimize these occurrences and investigate that they are actually false positive events.

When monitoring the program, it is important to investigate the execution of the EAS program within the store with regard to items like those listed.

Taking into consideration the execution of the program, measurement of its effectiveness involves several steps. The details of such an endeavor will be covered later in this book, but it will involve an experimental procedure to test the EAS program and choosing outcomes to measure (e.g., shrink and sales), as well as the statistical methodology used to measure the differences in these metrics between stores.

CRAVED Model

Research has shown that the utility or perceived reward of a particular target can be explained by numerous elements (Clarke & Cornish, 1985). Cohen and Felson (1979) fashioned the *VIVA* model (value, inertia, visibility, and accessibility) for explaining suitable targets. In 1999, Clarke posited the *CRAVED* model, which was aimed at the theft of *hot* products. According to Petrossian and Clarke (2014), the acronym CRAVED is heuristic and enables us to understand what makes targets especially attractive to potential offenders. CRAVED incorporates six key properties:

Concealable Items that can be hidden in pockets or bags are more vulnerable to shoplifters.
Removable Items that are easy to remove and carry, such as beauty aids, medicine, cigarettes, and alcohol.
Available Items that are accessible and easy to attain. High availability of a hot product, like cell phones, can result in theft waves.
Valuable Offenders will generally choose the more valuable items, particularly when they are stealing to resell. Value is not simply defined in terms

of resale value, but also personal value, in which an item is weighed by how much it confers status.

Enjoyable Hot products have a proclivity to be enjoyable, for example: liquor, tobacco, and games.

Disposable Offenders have a propensity to select items that are easy to resell; this explains why batteries and disposable razors are among the most frequently stolen items.

CRAVED helps us understand the various forms of theft and why some items become hot products. However, it's important to note that these elements are not necessarily static as they can change throughout the course of a product's lifespan. Depending on the stage in an item's lifecycle and rate of adoption, the specific elements of CRAVED may fluctuate in relevance and importance.

Examples of Analytical Methods Applied to Loss Prevention Aimed at Hot Products

There has been a lack of research conducted using randomized control trials to assess the effect of situational crime prevention on hot products. However, a recent study using a randomized control trial indicated that protective keeper boxes significantly reduced shrink levels of a hot product (in the study, razor blade cartridges) in test stores compared with control stores (Hayes *et al.*, 2011). In a similar study, Hayes and Downs (2011) conducted a randomized controlled trial of three situational crime prevention tools, in-aisle CCTV public view monitors, in-aisle CCTV domes, and protective keepers, to assess their effectiveness in deterring theft of a hot product. The tested treatments were designed to reflect the situational crime prevention framework, as they were each designed to prevent crime events by making theft more difficult or risky for offenders.

Hayes and Downs (2011) assessed the effectiveness of the aforementioned loss prevention tools, which act as cues designed to increase an offender's perception of detection and increase the effort required to shoplift the targeted hot product (in the study, razor blade cartridges). The study consisted of a 47-store test with a 6 week pre-test period, a 1 week period for treatment installation and a 6 week post-test period. The stores were randomly selected from 400 stores and were randomly assigned to one of three treatment conditions or control. Sales and loss levels were studied in the test and control stores to assess the efficacy of each solution. The study found that, based on a statistical analysis, all three prevention measures significantly decreased shrink in the test stores compared with the control stores.

Crime Pattern Theory

The crime pattern theory intersects the rational choice theory, the routine activity theory, space, and time to provide an explanation for crime. Understanding one's routine activity and rational decision making are important elements for understanding patterns of crime. Activities are structured in time and space; regulated by offenders, targets, and the environment (Brantingham & Brantingham, 2008). To date, there has been limited research on the relationship between temporal aspects of crime and crime levels.

Crime pattern theory explains how crimes emerge from spatio-temporal routines. To understand this, crime should be studied in both space and time. Crime pattern theory seeks to explain how offenders may come across opportunities for crime in the course of their everyday lives (Clarke, 2005). More specifically, crime pattern theory proposes that crime fits particular patterns when viewed in terms of where and when it occurs (Brantingham & Brantingham, 1995).

One key element to understanding crime patterns involves using socio-crime templates in the environmental context. While these dimensions are not static, it's possible to discern certain patterns. In essence, offenders create cognitive maps (i.e., through the process of recognition, prediction, evaluation, and action) or templates of what will happen at certain times and in certain situations (Smith & Patterson, 1980). This, in turn, allows offenders to make more calculated decisions. Research has found that different microscale spatio-temporal crime patterns were apparent for different types of crime. Crimes, such as drugs, robbery, burglary, and auto theft, all had their own distinctive spatio-temporal crime patterns (Shiode *et al.*, 2015).

Analysis of the temporal dimension is vital to understanding crime patterns and will result in the development of a more proactive prevention strategy. For example, time of day, day of week, and time of year are all extremely important to the theory. Furthermore, the criminogenic nature of places is influenced by time; therefore, responses should be rapid and consistent once a discernible pattern is discovered. Guardians could be employed during certain times or days to deter crimes and disrupt crime patterns. For example, additional employees can be present and alert during known high crime times. Personnel or security can also be placed near entrances and exits as a way to extend guardianship.

Example: Studying the Role of Time in Shoplifting Rates

The data shown in Table 2.3 reflects a hypothetical recording of the incidences of shoplifting by hour of day over a 4 month window for a retailer.

Table 2.3: Hypothetical Shoplifting Incidences

Time of Day	Number of Shoplifting Apprehensions (last 4 months)	Average Number of Shoppers	Rate
9:00 AM	10	1,000	1.00%
10:00 AM	15	3,000	0.50%
11:00 AM	22	4,000	0.55%
12:00 PM	34	6,000	0.57%
1:00 PM	37	5,000	0.74%
2:00 PM	16	4,000	0.40%
3:00 PM	18	3,500	0.51%
4:00 PM	12	3,000	0.40%
5:00 PM	10	2,500	0.40%
6:00 PM	11	2,000	0.55%
7:00 PM	14	1,200	1.17%
8:00 PM	17	500	3.40%

There are several ways to illustrate the data above. One way is to look at the number of shoplifting incidences in their raw form (Figure 2.6).

Based on Figure 2.6, it looks like most of the shoplifting happens in the middle of the day. However, the number of shoppers is also very high at that time of day. One way to adjust for the increase in shoppers is to look at the ratio of shoplifters to shoppers.

Unlike Figure 2.6, Figure 2.7 shows that the highest rate of shoplifting, per customer in the store, occurs later in the day.

SARA Model

It is during the *SARA* process that the routine activity theory can be applied for loss prevention. Furthermore, loss prevention can be implemented using the SARA process—scanning, analysis, response, and assessment (see Figure 2.8). Once crime patterns are scanned, identified, and narrowly defined (e.g., theft of handbags), the loss prevention team can analyze the issue to understand both its characteristics and causes. Based on this analysis, the loss prevention team can develop responses to prevent future theft (e.g., new technology, benefit denial, or surveillance). These responses may go beyond typical loss prevention strategies to disrupt the causes of the problem. Finally, loss

Figure 2.6: Number of Shoplifting Incidences

prevention teams will assess, scientifically, the overall impact of the response and modify the strategy accordingly, contingent on the results.

Crime is not randomly distributed in time and space. Targets are CRAVED, people are repeatedly victimized, and places are criminogenic (e.g., Eck *et al.*, 2007). The routine activity theory and the SARA model show what procedures should be taken to prevent crimes stemming from the same problems. Thus, using the routine activity theory during the SARA process may reveal the absence or ineffectiveness of a controller, who needs to be empowered or held accountable. Moreover, the SARA model might reveal the activity patterns that systematically produce the opportunity for crime and suggest points of intervention.

Let's build on the previous example of handbag theft using the SARA process. For example, through the first method of SARA, we *scan* and identify a pattern of handbag theft. Based on the *analysis*, the second method in the SARA process, it is revealed that the area where the handbags are displayed has blind spots, as well as a lack of suitable protection or controllers. As a *response*, the third method in the SARA process, the loss prevention team could randomly select and assign test and control stores in order to

Figure 2.7: Ratio of Shoplifters to Shoppers

test the effectiveness of multiple loss prevention strategies. Based on randomization, each set of test stores could receive one of three loss prevention tools for testing (e.g., an ink tag, enhanced public view monitors, or benefit denial). In the final method of the SARA process, the *assessment*, a return on investment calculation and analyses can be done to assess the best use of resources based on the value and effectiveness of the different loss prevention tools that were tested, while considering the effects on sales activity (see Chapter 8 for in-store experiments).

Crime Prevention Through Environmental Design

Crime Prevention through Environmental Design (CPTED) and situational crime prevention can and should be used in conjunction, since they complement each other. CPTED has become universally accepted because its core principle is the effective use of defensible space; aiming at reducing crime by manipulating the design of the built environment (Cozens, 2008; Crowe, 2000; Reynald, 2011). The main purpose of CPTED is to harden the targets for a potential offender. CPTED is a multidisciplinary

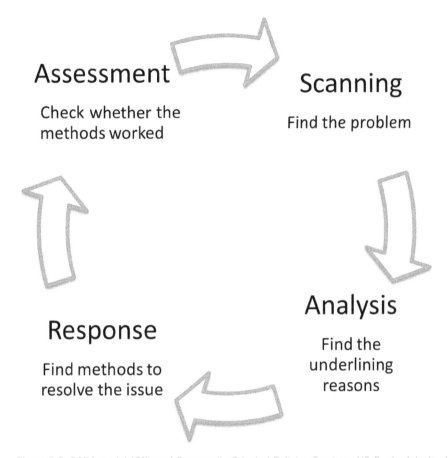

Figure 2.8: SARA model (Office of Community Oriented Policing Services, US Dept. of Justice)

approach that draws on both sociology and behavioral psychology in order to manipulate the environment to deter and control crime opportunity.

CPTED is demonstrated by designing spaces that include five facets:

Access control	for example, reduce the number of points of entry;
Surveillance	for example, CCTV;
Territoriality	for example, displaying security signage;
Maintenance and image improvement	for example, criminality flourishes in neglected and poorly maintained environments;
Activity support	for example, maintaining a well-kept environment.

CPTED asserts that the proper design and effective use of the built environment can both lead to a reduction in fear and dissuade offenders from committing crimes (Crowe, 2000). The focus of CPTED is on creating areas that have good lighting and that prevent places for potential offenders to hide. The evidence in support of CPTED is burgeoning, although unlike other crime prevention strategies, CPTED has not been thoroughly evaluated. Research suggests that there is some evidence that CPTED is a promising approach, since there is a strong relationship between certain characteristics of the built environment and crime levels (Cozens *et al.*, 2005). While further research into the effectiveness of CPTED is warranted, there is suitable evidence to support the application of its principles, as well as the assessment of time and space more broadly, as a key consideration in the development of crime prevention in the built environment.

A recent study assessed two in-store situational crime prevention measures: (a) a protective display fixture and (b) special CRAVED product handling, in order to assess CPTED using a randomized control trial (Hayes *et al.*, 2012). The results indicated that the tested treatments helped to deter chronic theft in the test stores compared with the control stores. A rational choice perspective could help explain these results. That is, potential offenders were deterred owing to the treatments producing increased effort, more risk, and less reward (Cornish & Clarke, 2003). Additionally, the results provided support for using the SARA problem solving process to apply situational crime prevention and CPTED measures (Hayes *et al.*, 2012). CPTED's utility in loss prevention lies in applying a thorough evaluation of the environment. Key to this evaluation is an assessment for vulnerabilities, such as multiple unprotected ingress, egress, and regress, unprotected CRAVED products, a disheveled environment, and the absence of suitable controllers.

Ten Principles for Crime and Loss Prevention

Given our experience as criminologists, fraud analysts, and researchers, we have developed a set of principles to assist in crime and loss prevention. These principles are the culmination of a study of the components of crime detection and fraud prevention, testing a multitude of loss prevention tools, conducting rigorous loss prevention randomized controlled trials, assessing loss prevention data for crime trends, consulting loss prevention teams from around the country to build customized models, and listening to the concerns that plague the directors of loss prevention. Since this book is a crime and loss prevention book focusing on using data and analytics in retail, our principles advocate a science-based data-driven approach to crime prevention. The principles are built on three key elements: prevent, respond, and solve. These are not all-inclusive, but will be valuable for any team's efforts to prevent crime and loss.

Ten Principles—Prevent, Respond, and Solve

1. Build an analytical crime prevention team—join forces—**prevent**.
2. Develop a crime prevention plan—**prevent**.
3. Educate and train employees—**prevent**.
4. Know and protect theft targets—**respond**.
5. Change the environment—don't be vulnerable—decrease opportunity—**respond**.
6. Collect good intelligence and use reliable data—garbage in, garbage out—**solve**.
7. Embrace technology—facial identification, target profiling, nanotechnology—**solve**.
8. Predictive analytics—examine patterns—**solve**.
9. Analyze techniques—evaluate return on investment—**solve**.
10. Adapt, iterate, and improve—**prevent, respond, and solve**.

Conclusions

The field of criminology has evolved from its early primitive forms, now involving more science-based methods for modifying the situational context to prevent crime. Situational crime prevention has emerged as a vital control and crime prevention strategy, by focusing on reducing opportunities that are provided to offenders motivated to commit crimes. Proactive crime prevention is a dynamic process and is far preferred, compared with a traditional reactive approach by which crime controllers make gut instinct decisions. Based on the theories covered in this chapter, we can conclude that:

1. Opportunities play a role in causing crime.
2. Crime opportunities are highly specific.
3. Crime opportunities are concentrated in time and space.
4. Crime opportunities depend on everyday movements.
5. Some products offer more tempting crime opportunities.
6. Crime depends on rational decision making.

7. Crime prevention relies on increasing subjective risk.
8. Opportunities for crime can be reduced.
9. Data and analytics are a vital piece to the loss prevention puzzle.

Exercises

1. Next time you walk through a store, identify some places or areas that may benefit from situational crime prevention.
2. What are some of your "hot" products? Do they align with the CRAVED framework?
3. How does time and space play a role in loss prevention in your industry?
4. Provide an example of the SARA model in your line of work. Make sure to define how the problem was discovered and analyzed, how you or your team responded to the problem, and how the method's results were assessed.

Chapter Three

Retail Theft and Security

The rain it raineth on the just
And also on the unjust fella;
But chiefly on the just, because
The unjust hath the just's umbrella.

—Bowen

Introduction

The previous chapter dealt with general criminological theory. While the theories apply well to retail, the theories presented in the last chapter can also apply to many areas outside retail. In this chapter, we focus on crimes specific to retailers and how analytics may serve a role. After reading this chapter, you will understand key terms in shoplifting, the different categories of shoplifters, and the main sources of retail theft. Furthermore, this chapter is designed to equip you and your team with the tools to develop strategies to address and mitigate retail theft in your stores. The following chapters will build on the concepts and examples in this chapter.

Larceny

In the United States, larceny is a common law crime involving theft and generally refers to a nonviolent offense. Under the common law, larceny is the trespassory taking and carrying away (i.e., asportation and removal) of the tangible personal property of another with the intent to deprive him or her of its possession permanently. Shoplifting is a type of larceny and is considered one of the most widespread crimes in the United States. According to the 2016 National Retail Security Survey (Moraca *et al.*, 2016), US businesses lost around $45.2 billion in 2015 to retail theft, more than 1.38% of overall sales, making retail theft one of the leading issues facing retailers today. However, since many of the incidents are undetected or not reported to the police, the true extent of the problem is far greater. To better understand the significance, according to the National Association of Shoplifting Prevention (2006), more than 9% of consumers are shoplifters and they are apprehended on average only once in every 48 times they shoplift.

States usually separate larceny into different classes based on the values of the stolen items. Grand larceny applies to higher-value items; petty larceny applies to stolen items of a lesser value. Each state legislature selects the amount that separates a grand larceny from a petty larceny. For example, one state could designate grand larceny to larcenies above $3000, whereas another state could decide that grand larceny only occurs when the value of the stolen property exceeds $2000. Anything below those amounts would constitute petty larceny. In addition, some states treat some larcenies as felonies, and others as misdemeanors. Again, states have the power to set their own guidelines for what divides a felony larceny from a misdemeanor.

Professional and Amateur Shoplifters

Who shoplifts? Knowing the answer to this question would certainly help in creating an effective loss prevention solution. However, there is no typical profile of a shoplifter; therefore, anyone who enters a store could be a potential offender. According to the National Association for Shoplifting Prevention (2006), there are 27 million shoplifters in the USA; that is, 1 in 11 Americans is a shoplifter, and shoplifters come in all shapes and sizes. Offenders vary in terms of sex, ethnicity, social status, and age. Based on our experience of interviewing offenders, shoplifters can be male or female, any race, as young as five or well over their seventies. Offenders also vary in their level of experience, motivation, and method of shoplifting.

The majority of shoplifters can be categorized as either amateurs (opportunistic) or professionals (highly skilled). Amateurs are typically driven by personal use or desire for a product (e.g., food, clothing, or status) and shoplift when they perceive little or no risk. The amateur is usually cautious and apprehensive. A significant percentage of all retail theft is conducted by professionals, often working in pairs or as part of a larger network or retail crime ring. The professional, often called a booster, is much more ingenious than the amateur. The professional is skillful and blends in so as not to attract any attention. The professional may have a "hit list" of very specific small high-valued items for which there is a high demand on the black market. Generally, the professional is vigilant and steals for a living.

Although a majority of research adheres to the two categories of shoplifters (i.e., amateur and professional), interestingly a study (Nelson & Perrone, 2000) was conducted that divided shoplifters into five categories and assessed frequency of theft, motivations, and shoplifters' responses when apprehended (see Table 3.1).

A growing number of professional shoplifters are part of sophisticated organized retail theft rings, stealing for a living, and shoplifting items with high resale value. E-fencing is a growing trend, in which organized retail crime rings resell high-valued stolen products through online sites. According to the National Retail Federation Organized Retail Crime Study (Cantrell & Moraca, 2015), retailers have identified stolen gift cards and merchandise from a number of different physical and e-fence localities. Participants to the survey were asked if they had identified or recovered merchandise or gift cards in the previous 12 months from the different localities within both physical fences and e-fences. Almost 64% responded that they had identified

Table 3.1: Types of Shoplifter

Category of Thief	Frequency	Motivation	Response when Apprehended	Percentage
Impulse	Often only once or twice	Not planned	Exhibited shock, shame and guilt	15.4
Occasional	3 to 10 times in last year	Enjoyed the challenge	Admitted guilt but downplayed the seriousness of the act	15.0
Episodic	Periodic episodes	Exhibited emotional psychological problems	Compliant; usually requires treatment to alter behavior	1.7
Amateur	Regular (often weekly)	Economically rewarding	Admitted guilt but usually downplayed previous acts	56.4
Semi-professional	Frequently (at least once a week)	Took more expensive items; only type who did so for resale purposes	Likely to have a "prepared story"; and to claim unfair treatment if the story is rejected	11.7

merchandise from a physical fence, such as a pawn shop, while almost 69% identified merchandise from an e-fence, such as an online auction site.

From our experience in conducting offender interviews, professionals work in teams and use elaborate distractions, such as shields and diversions. Shields involve multiple shoplifters; one or more of these will shield the thief from the view of employees or cameras. Once the shield is in place, the thief will then pocket or conceal the products. In the diversion tactic, a team of shoplifters creates a diversion to divert store employees from the thief, such as sending an employee to the stock room to look for a product, knocking over merchandise, faking a medical emergency, or starting a fight to draw the attention of store employees away from the offender committing the crime.

Example: Applying Analytics to Organized Retail Crime

Although we do not have the ability to profile a shoplifter, data is available that can improve our loss prevention tactics. Risk analysis can be used to allocate resources effectively, since knowing how much to spend and on what to spend is pivotal when facing limited capital. For example, using and analyzing transaction and inventory data can allow us to understand shoplifting patterns, shoplifted products, high-loss stores or regions, and effective tools and, ultimately, to predict future shrink in stores. Data can also aid in the identification of organized retail crime rings via fraud ring analysis.

People tend to group together based on similarities, and this is particularly true among criminals. This behavior is particularly useful for detecting organized retail

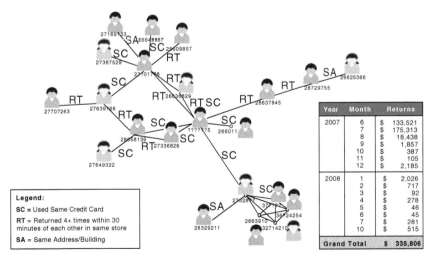

Figure 3.1: Organized Fraud Ring Linking Analysis

crime rings. Fraud ring analysis is a method of identifying organized retail crime rings by first identifying high-risk consumers, and then mapping out clusters of similar consumers (or aliases) and analyzing their transaction behavior (see Figure 3.1). Using sophisticated linking algorithms, loss prevention analysts can connect known fraud-sters to other dubious consumers. Often uncovering clusters of associated identities that constitute either crime networks or aliases of the same criminal, provides a more complete view of the types of fraud affecting shrink. This method will be discussed in more detail in future chapters. Figure 3.1 illustrates an example where individuals were linked together based on their transactional histories, by using the same credit cards, returning merchandise within a short period of time of each other and having the same address or living in the same vicinity of each other.

Sources of Retail Loss

In 2015, retail loss was 1.38% of retail sales. The overall rate of retail loss or shrink of 1.38% translates into more than $120 million being stolen from retailers every day (Moraca *et al.*, 2016). According to the 2016 Annual Retail Theft Survey (Jack L. Hayes International, Inc., 2016), shoplifting and employee theft has increased by 2% from the previous year. In 2015, there were a total of 1,246,003 employee and shoplifter appre-hensions combined.

There are many different types of retail theft, which can originate from customers, employees, and other sources. Retail loss or shrink can be measured by calculating the loss from employee theft, shoplifting or organized retail crime, administrative errors, vendor fraud, and return fraud (see Figure 3.2).

Employee Theft

Employee theft pervades the retail industry. It was the second leading cause of shrink in 2015, accounting for one third of all retail loss and equating to $16.2 billion annually. According to the National Retail Security Survey (Moraca *et al.*, 2016), the average loss from dishonest employees was $1234. According to Hayes' 2016 Annual Retail Theft Survey (Jack L. Hayes International, Inc., 2016), 1 in 38 employees is appre-hended for theft. On a per-case average, employee theft, in 2015, was more than three times the amount stolen by shoplifters.

Although the profile of a typical shoplifter is unclear, a recent study examined the characteristics of internal theft (Baxter, 2014). The study found that internal theft was highest in stores with the most managers (i.e., indicating theft is higher in larger stores) and stores in wealthier suburbs (Baxter, 2014). Additionally, the study revealed

Figure 3.2: Sources of Retail Loss (Moraca *et al.*, 2016)

that most of the employees apprehended were male, between 18 and 25, and short-term employees. The study also examined apprehended case reports and conducted interviews with loss prevention personnel. The case reports and the interviews both revealed a similar trend, in that one of the leading causes of internal theft was that the employees alleged that they were not being compensated fairly (Baxter, 2014).

Additional research has shown that the more dissatisfied the employees, the more likely they are to engage in offender behavior (Hollinger & Clarke, 1983). Furthermore, Chen and Sandino (2012) found that higher wages promoted social norms. Employees who felt they were not paid sufficiently were more likely to steal; higher wages may discourage workers from conspiring to shoplift.

To better prevent, or respond to, employee theft, it is imperative to understand the different ways that it occurs. Here are specific forms of employee fraud and trends to be aware of:

- An employee may void transactions and pocket the cash.
- A cashier can ring up a reduced price on a product to hide theft from the till.
- A cashier may overcharge a customer and pocket the difference.
- An employee may hide stock in trash bins, and collect it later.
- An employee may save customer receipts and use them to return stolen products.

- An employee may process a fake return, steal the money, or credit his or her own credit card with money allegedly paid back to a fake customer.
- An employee may process a return for a larger amount than the amount of the product and pocket the difference.
- An employee may forge inventory logs.
- An employee may falsely use employee discounts.
- An employee may assist friends or family members in theft (i.e., sweethearting).

Internal theft does not occur in isolation—internal theft is a combination of opportunity and motive. The opportunity and the lack of guardianship feature of the routine activity theory can also be purported as a key motivation for internal theft. In many cases of internal theft, a proper control is not in place. That said, there are a number of steps that can be taken to prevent and catch employee theft. Criminological theory reminds us that we should have some controls in place to prevent internal theft; loss prevention should be designed to eliminate the opportunity for employee theft. Security cameras, management oversight, vigilant controls over the cash drawers, and encouragement of anonymous tips are pivotal first steps.

The ability to isolate and quantify the various kinds of internal theft with data and translate it into proactive strategies that will prevent loss is critical. Initially, leveraging company-wide data and conducting a rigorous analysis, down to the store and employee level, can help identify concealed fraud and limitations in the control environment. Next are two processes that can be used to assess internal fraud with data-driven techniques.

One method for analyzing employee fraud is through outlier detection. An outlier is simply an observation (in this case, a transaction) that is far outside the norm. When using outlier detection, it is the goal of the analysis to identify employees, products, and stores that are not behaving like their peers. For example, one method of perpetrating sweethearting internal fraud is to use line voids to "give" the customer (who is a friend or family member) merchandise without paying for it. To the retailer, the transaction looks legitimate, but when inventory is counted, the item is short. When conducting outlier detection, the analyst must first determine (through modeling) the expected value for the metric in question. So, following the example above, what is the normal rate of line voids in a particular store? To determine the expected rate, the analyst will want to compare the employee to like employees (so, a manager to other managers), stores to like stores, and account for seasonality and product type. Once the expected value is determined, outlier analysis reveals which records are far enough from the norm to arouse suspicion. Again, if the normal or expected line void rate for a particular store is 5% and the employee in question has a 20% line void rate, it is likely that the employee is either lacking in training or committing internal fraud.

Taking this scenario one step further, the outlier detection models can be combined with a set of risk variables and each of the outlier models and the risk variables can be correlated to known outcomes, such as terminations relating from successful investigations in the past. By determining the relationship between risk variables and known outcomes, retailers can develop specific predictive models that predict which employees should be investigated to maximize success in investigations (Speights & Hanks, 2014).

Another technique is to implement real-time alerts. Real-time monitoring alerts can be sent to managers that are triggered by unusual employee transactions and trends. For example, some stores do not accept nonreceipted returns, or a return with a receipt that was purchased in the distant past; a real-time alert can notify the store manager if an employee is attempting either scenario. Some trends to look for may be an increase in returns or voided return transactions, particularly with regard to one employee or in one department, returns for large amounts, repeated returns for even amounts or the same amounts, and repeated returns to the same credit card. By using data to monitor employee risky behavior in real time, a manager's time can be better allocated to other areas of concern and employee fraud management can be more proactive, rather than reactive.

Organized Retail Crime and Shoplifting

Historically, as a global threat, external theft has typically always been the leading cause of loss. In 2015, shoplifting accounted for 39.3% of retail inventory loss, with an average of $377 per shoplifting incident, according to the National Retail Security Survey (Moraca *et al.*, 2015). That is up 7% from their 2010 survey.

Some amateur shoplifting occurs simply due to opportunity, while other shoplifting events are detailed crimes that are well organized, thus harder to prevent. Shoplifting losses have been increasing and mostly occur as a result of the growing problem with organized retail crime rings (Hollinger & Adams, 2007). These are networks of well-trained individuals who function as organized gangs to boost products that have high resale value from retailers all across the country, using sophisticated methods and tools (Hollinger & Langton, 2005).

According to the 2015 Organized Retail Crime Survey (Cantrell & Moraca, 2015), 97% of retailers surveyed noted that they had been a victim of organized retail crime activity in the previous 12 months. Moreover, in that year, organized retail crime activity increased for more than four out of five retailers surveyed. The financial impact of organized retail crime is considerable. Although the exact shrink from organized retail crime is unclear, estimates range from $15 billion to $37 billion annually (Finklea, 2012).

Organized retail crime rings generally include a network of individuals that serve as: (1) boosters—individuals who act as professional shoplifters who work either alone or in groups to steal the goods; (2) handlers—individuals who sell the goods to fences; and (3) fences—individuals who purchase the stolen goods at a reduced price. Generally, a booster is provided with a fence sheet, a list of hot products to be shoplifted, and the number of items requested.

Boosters often use tinfoil-lined bags to defeat EAS tags; they carry special tools to remove security tags or to open protective boxes, and they often use cell phones to communicate with other individuals in the network while shoplifting. Boosters may change bar codes so that merchandise is rung up at much lower prices (i.e., ticket switching). Boosters may also purchase goods with stolen credit cards and then use the receipts to return stolen goods to the store for cash or store credit.

Boosted goods may be held in rented storage units before being taken to the organized retail crime home base. Fences generally pay boosters about 10% to 25% of the ticket value of a product and will then resell the products to their consumers or other

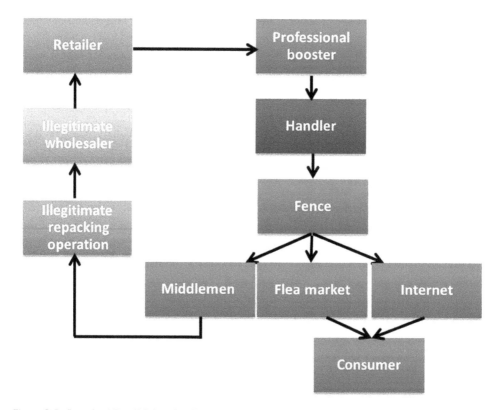

Figure 3.3: Organized Retail Crime Syndicate Flow Chart

businesses (Miller, 2005). Fences will prepare the boosted products for resale by clean-ing and repackaging them to look like new. Fences may also resell the boosted products to wholesale diverters, who might combine them with legitimate products for sale back to the retailers. Figure 3.3 shows an organized retail crime syndicate flowchart.

Organized retail crime rings have engaged in many different schemes to deceive retailers and attain merchandise or cash. In another form of receipt fraud, for example, boosters steal merchandise, create fake receipts for the stolen goods, return the stolen goods to the retailers using the fake receipts, and obtain the money from the fraudulent returns. This type of fraud removes the need for a fence altogether, potentially netting a higher amount for the organized retail crime network.

Target Products

Organized retail crime is more pervasive than most people realize. According to the National Retail Federation (Cantrell & Moraca, 2015), organized retail crime costs retailers more than $82 million a day. Understanding specific targeted products of organized retail crime groups can help in shaping a loss prevention response and becoming proactive in implementing the most effective tools. Interviews of shoplifters and members of organized retail crime rings have revealed a wide variety of merchan-dise targeted to be stolen and resold on the black market. Not surprisingly, many of the products fit the CRAVED model (i.e., products that are concealable, removable, available, valuable, enjoyable, and disposable). These items are more often targets on a booster's shopping list because of the effortlessness with which they can be shoplifted from stores and converted into cash. More specifically, some hot products that organ-ized retail crime rings target include:

Grocery items	Infant formula, laundry detergent, cigarettes, teeth whitening strips, energy drinks, and high-end liquor;
Over-the-counter medications	Allergy medicines, pseudoephedrine-based cold medicines, weight loss pills, diabetic testing strips, and pain relievers;
Health and beauty items	Pregnancy tests, high-end lotions and creams, razor blades, and electronic toothbrushes;
Electronics	Cell phones, digital cameras, printer cartridges, GPS devices, lithium batteries, laptops, tablets, video games, and televisions;
Clothing	Designer brands, handbags, and denim;
Home goods	High-end vacuums, mixers, blenders.

Coordinated organized retail crime syndicates are pilfering massive volumes of high-value products to ship overseas, often using their profits to support and fund terrorism. Correspondingly, agencies such as Immigration and Customs Enforcement, the Federal Bureau of Investigation, and the Department of Homeland Security have all tracked organized retail crime activity and have traced their money trail back to global terrorist groups. The profits made from organized retail crime activity have been found to supply weapons, fake passports, and paramilitary equipment (Prabhakar, 2012). Coincidently, on September 11, 2001, a Texas trooper pulled over a rental truck filled with infant formula (Clayton, 2005). The driver of the truck, a Middle Eastern man, was later identified as a member of a terrorist organization recognized by the FBI. This was the first of many stops Texas troopers would make of Middle Eastern men transporting large amounts of infant formula in rental trucks (Clayton, 2005). When questioned by the state troopers, the suspects would claim that they were genuine wholesalers of the infant formula. However, they could seldom provide any evidence to validate where they had acquired the infant formula (Clayton, 2005). That said, there are broader implications to thwarting organized retail crime activity.

Administrative Errors

By focusing only on external and internal theft-related sources, retailers are ignoring areas of poor policies and processes as well as errors in which retail loss propagates. Another source of loss for retailers, that is often overlooked, is administrative error. This internal error typically includes errors with computer systems, paperwork, and human error. Administrative errors are the third largest source of loss for retailers. According to the 2016 National Retail Security Survey (Moraca *et al.*, 2016), administrative errors accounted for 16.8% of shrink, which is responsible for more than $7.5 billion annually.

Administrative errors may involve inventory pricing mistakes, such as incorrectly marking items up or down, misdirected shipments, careless paperwork on the loading dock, failure to record inventory transfers, unrecorded returns, employees illegally discounting merchandise, and paperwork error (Hollinger & Adams, 2007). Loss due to administrative error has trended up at approximately 15% annually.

Data analytics can help reconcile administrative errors by allowing a retailer to understand inventory losses down to the stock keeping unit level, not just the category. Access to quality data can allow retailers to flag anomalies in both their operations and inventory loss. Systematic alerts can be designed around parameters to inform retailers to take corrective actions. In addition, data analytics can be used to monitor trends in inventory by utilizing radio frequency identification sensor devices; these use a small microchip that allows retailers to track products through the supply chain from production to the point of sale in real time.

Vendor Fraud

Although vendor fraud contributes the smallest amount to retail shrink, it still costs retailers $2.1 billion annually. Generally, vendor fraud consists of a vendor stealing some of the products they are supposed to be delivering or stocking in the store (Hollinger & Adams, 2007). Vendor fraud is generally the least damaging source of loss for any organization.

An example of vendor fraud is when one of the vendor's employees shorts the order and takes the merchandise for themselves. To minimize vendor fraud, only allow trained employees to take receipt of deliveries, and carefully schedule vendor deliver shipments so as not to overlap deliveries. Data can provide insights into anomalies and trends in vendor fraud. Using data analytics can be helpful in reconciling delivery merchandise and inventory.

Return Fraud

Return fraud is a type of crime that occurs when a customer defrauds a retailer via the return process. According to the 2015 Organized Retail Crime Survey (Cantrell & Moraca, 2015), 66% of retailers surveyed have experienced the theft of merchandise which is then returned for store credit in the form of gift cards that are sold to secondary market buyers and sellers for cash. According to the National Retail Federation's Return Fraud Survey of 62 retail companies in the retail industry, the total that all US retailers lost was estimated at between $9 and $17 billion in return fraud in 2015. Almost all of the companies that participated (92%) said they had experienced the return of stolen merchandise in 2015.

Although return fraud is not typically included in shrink estimates, studies have shown a correlation between shrink and return rates; also, return fraud could have a substantial effect on shrink rates (Speights *et al.*, 2012). Speights *et al.* (2012) conducted an in-depth study of seven major retailers and more than 7400 stores and results indicated that as return rate increased, shrink also increased (see Figure 3.4).

There are many fraudulent and abusive return procedures; some schemes are more common than others. Understanding these schemes, despite their ever-evolving nature, is the first step toward choosing the best defense and preventing future loss.

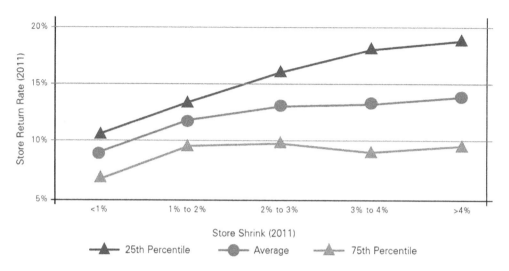

Figure 3.4: Return Rate by Shrink

Renting or Wardrobing

According to the National Retail Federation's 2015 Return Fraud Survey, 73% of the retailers said that the return of used, nondefective items, known as *wardrobing*, is a growing issue. Renting or wardrobing begins with a legitimate purchase. The product is then used temporarily and returned as if it were new. The classic example is the purchase of an expensive dress for a wedding, reunion, or other special event. The consumer simply conceals the tags into the dress in an inconspicuous manner, impresses partygoers with her attire, and returns the dress for a full refund the following day, in essence having rented it for free. This technique has also spread to other valuable merchandise. When consumers buy durable goods, such as a digital camera to video record a graduation, a big screen television to watch sports games, or a trendy watch to accessorize a job interview suit, and then return the items after using them once or twice, they are violating a retailer's traditional return policy.

Consumers committing this type of retail fraud have an established pattern of use; therefore, data and analytics can be used to detect them among the numerous legitimate returns. Specifically, renting or wardrobing consumers typically return all (or almost all) of their purchases, resulting in high return rates (near 100%). They will buy and return items within a small time window, repeating the type of stock keeping unit they are renting, and shop and return in high frequency.

Receipt Fraud

Sales receipts can be used to defraud a retailer, and criminals have devised numerous schemes for obtaining receipts. Some thieves create fake receipts, using computers and color printers. Sophisticated specialists may actually obtain the retailer's paper stock from store contacts or paper suppliers to enhance the appearance of the counterfeit receipt. Others simply find receipts in store trash receptacles, shopping carts, the parking lot, or discarded shopping bags. Internet-savvy individuals may visit questionable web sites that purchase or recreate legitimate receipts and sell them to criminals who need a receipt for a particular item.

Regardless of how the receipt is acquired, it can be used for a novel type of fraud called *shoplisting* because it works much like a shopping list. The individual enters a store with the receipt in hand and proceeds with one of two scenarios: (1) picks up the items listed on the receipt and heads to the returns counter; or (2) shoplifts the items and comes back at another time to conduct a fraudulent return. Shoplisting enables the booster to eliminate a fence (i.e., someone who will buy the stolen merchandise). Instead, the offender is essentially selling the product back to its owner, the retail store. This method has become the province of the less criminally inclined because it has shed its dark alley aura through some quick computer work and a daylight trip to the store.

Price Arbitrage

Criminals with working capital—called *go money*—can engage in several types of price arbitrage. One example occurs when an offender purchases two similar items with different retail prices. By repackaging the cheaper item in the expensive item's box and returning it for a full refund, the fraudulent returner has basically stolen the more expensive item. This is particularly effective with electronics because cheap items often resemble expensive ones. Selling the more expensive item online, even at a discount, adds money to the criminal's pocket.

Other forms of price arbitrage include switching boxes in the store to purchase a higher-priced item for less or purchasing an item at a discount and returning it for a full price refund. Regardless of the fraudulent returner's approach, the retailer pays the difference. A specific example of a price arbitrage scheme was committed by one group at a large retailer. It cost the retailer a total of $1.5 million across 19 states. The group switched the bar codes from low-priced items to high-priced items before the purchase. Then the group removed the phony bar code and returned the item to obtain the full price as store credit, cash, or a gift card (Speights & Hilinski, 2005).

Analytics can help stop price arbitrage by targeting and stopping the individuals who perpetrate the fraud. Using complex linking algorithms, data scientists can link together an organized retail crime group or single individuals using multiple forms of identification or aliases. Then, the data scientists can find individuals or organized retail crime groups who commit price arbitrage in various ways:

1. A model can be built to detect when an individual has made too many returns—compared with the general population—where the amount returned exceeded the amount purchased (outlier behavior).
2. If price arbitrage is committed with a receipt, the prices paid are easily traceable and comparable with the price at the time of the refund.

Check Fraud

Fraudsters who engage in theft for a living are typically drawn to the world of bank accounts, preferably false ones. They scheme retailers by purchasing merchandise with an illegitimate check or with one backed by insufficient funds and then return the merchandise before the check clears the bank. One retailer reported that investigations uncovered an organized fraud ring that wrote a suspected $100,000 in bad checks to that retailer and more than $450,000 to other retailers (Speights & Hilinski, 2005). This problem may be isolated to the USA and is diminishing, owing to the rapid decrease in the usage of checks.

Returning Stolen Merchandise

Profiting from stolen merchandise, one of the many ways to defraud retailers, has many faces. Offenders may steal merchandise themselves or buy it directly from another thief. They then return it to the store for a full cash refund (plus the sales tax), either with a forged, found, or purchased receipt or without a receipt at all, depending on the store's return policy. More complex forms of this scheme entail stealing entire truckloads of merchandise and distributing them to a network of organized criminals, who will return the items to different stores in a large geographic area. As aforementioned, the store is buying the merchandise twice, first from the manufacturer and secondly from the thief.

A *Washington Post* article detailed a scheme in which shoplifters returned merchandise without a receipt, obtained store credit, and then sold the store credit online for 76 cents on the dollar (Speights & Hilinski, 2005). A similar scam, posted in *USA Today* in 2015, described a scam in which an organized syndicate would shoplift from a major retailer and enlist several different offenders to return the merchandise, to several different stores, without a receipt. The retailer would, in turn, give the offenders a store credit and they would sell the store credits at a discounted price. The scam cost the retailer between $600,000 and $800,000 (Brasier, 2015).

Like other forms of fraud, those returning stolen merchandise follow shopping and returning patterns that can be identified through data analytics and modeling. Trends to look for are: a high percentage of returns made without a receipt; a high percentage of returns given cash back; multiple store credits associated with an individual or group; visiting many stores to avoid recognition.

Although return fraud may drive a retailer to adopt harsher return policies, research has shown that stricter return policies significantly harm net sales (Speights, Downs, & Raz, 2016). In a recent study, Speights et al. (2016) found that stores that adopted a strict return policy (like "no receipt—no return") in comparison to stores with a friendly return policy, showed almost a 9% reduction in net sales. In addition, using predictive analytics to prevent return fraud resulted in similar return rate reduction as did using strict return policies (Speights et al., 2016).

Employee Fraud

According to the National Retail Federation's 2015 Return Fraud Survey, 77% of the retailers report that they experience employee return fraud or collusion with external sources. Employees have the necessary insider information to conduct a vast amount of retail fraud. Acting alone or in collusion, they are uniquely positioned to cause significant financial damage in a relatively short period. For example, some employees act as facilitators, provide sales receipt paper stock to friends and family, and some actually execute a fraudulent return transaction for their co-conspirators. The insidious nature of employee fraud can be debilitating if left unchecked. Fortunately, analytics has the ability to catch many of the aforementioned types of fraud.

Data and Analytics

Retailers collect data from many sources, including store sales transactions, store video, traffic counters, alarms, merchandise movement, loyalty programs, and e-commerce click paths. A large retailer collects millions of transactions and hundreds of millions of line items per day, as well as 30 to 60 GB of video per store, per day. For a 1000-store retailer, this could total 22 petabytes per year (the equivalent of 23,068,672 gigabytes) (Speights, 2014). But having data is not enough. Companies need to harness the power of the data with analytics and modeling. Companies can process the data from all the transactions in the chain and identify suspicious behavior indicative of any form of fraud or abuse, including renting or wardrobing, returning stolen merchandise, receipt fraud, price arbitrage, price switching, double dipping, organized retail crime, check fraud, and tender fraud. For example, when an individual attempts to make a return, models can perform calculations in a fraction of a second that predict the likelihood of the return being fraudulent.

Complex queries can be used to identify organized retail crime rings and fraudulent returners by linking seemingly independent events. Linking multiple identifiers provides a more complete view of all of a consumer's interactions (i.e., purchases, returns, and exchanges). In addition, linking also connects associated individuals—providing an even more complete view of criminal networks. Figure 3.5 shows a cluster of suspicious purchase and return events that includes 8 loyalty cards, 39 credit cards, 37 store credits, and 5 in-house charge cards.

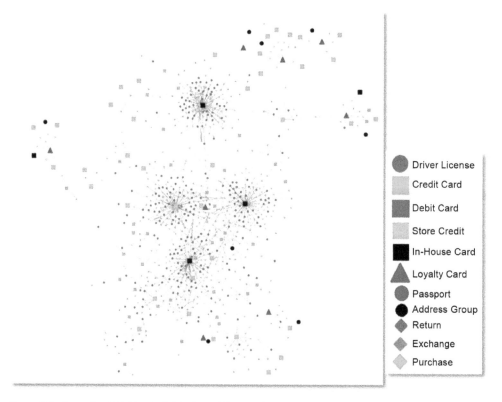

Figure 3.5: Example of Linking Individuals and Transactions to Illustrate Fraud

Predictive Model Lifecycle

Gather Data	Model Development	Integration	Monitor Models
Data Collection and Cleaning	Develop models, test in production, and demonstrate the value	Integrate models into production processes	Monitor performance and make improvements

Figure 3.6: Predictive Model for Fraud

The data and information captured are the key to a model's analytical power. The objective is to combine as much information as possible—on the individual shopper, the items they are returning, the original and return transactions, the location, the time, tender used—and run it through a predictive model to create a fraud risk index score that predicts the likelihood of fraud or abuse for a specific person. Figure 3.6 depicts the steps to create a predictive model. This will be discussed in more detail in later chapters.

General Loss Prevention Strategies

Before implementing any loss prevention strategy or solution, retailers should understand both the costs and associated benefits of using a specific technique. Controlled tests, followed by statistical analyses, aid this understanding. Using experimental and control groups of stores—and tracking key metrics, such as shrink, sales, employee turnover, return rates, and other important outcomes, in before–during–after analyses—loss prevention professionals can accurately calculate a given strategy's return on investment. Controlled trials also let analysts manipulate elements that make up an overall strategy by correlating changes in strategy with changes in the return on investment, to optimize loss prevention policies.

Interviews conducted with boosters reveal much about how to deter them from causing losses. First and foremost, shoplifters recommend that you view your merchandise as a thief would. Also, many shoplifters report that they are influenced by rational or utilitarian considerations, suggesting that rational choice theory and situational prevention are applicable to shoplifting prevention (Farrington *et al.*, 1993).

It is imperative to establish an environment in the store and among your employees that is vigilant; make sure staff are alert and well trained. A good way to encourage this is to reward employees for spotting shoplifting. According to shoplifter interviews, employee presence and awareness remains one of the leading shoplifting deterrents. This is true both for amateur and professional shoplifters; the cost of offending out-weighs the benefit when you are being served well and watched. During shoplifter interviews, offenders have admitted that they actively look for stores with poor service. This holds true for a store's physical appearance as well; maintain the property. A run-down business will attract shoplifters, so make sure that the environment is clean and well maintained. Also, remove old or damaged displays and keep aisles orderly. A messy environment also makes it harder to tell if anything has been shoplifted.

Store layout is also critical to deterring theft; maximize visibility and make sure that your store has enough open space to allow your employees to see all areas of the store. Blind spots can be eliminated by placing mirrors in the corners. Using electronic article surveillance systems as well as cameras to monitor your store and merchandise are other ways to deter theft. Another option is to post signage, such as, "Shoplifters Will Be Prosecuted." Visible electronic public view monitors and security systems also dissuade some shoplifters. Make sure that all points of ingress and regress to the business are under constant visual surveillance. Many thieves like to use emergency exits or garden centers to make their escape. Keep expensive hot products in locked cases, and limit the number of items that employees can remove at any given time for a customer. Limit the number of items taken into a fitting room and carefully monitor restrooms for shoplifting behavior.

Conclusion

In summary, shrink has a number of underlying causes and continues to plague many retailers. Employees cannot be everywhere all the time and many of the loss preven-tion strategies that previously worked are no longer adequate to solve the myriad of retail fraud schemes. To assemble a better picture of shrink, it is essential for retailers to harness data from across the business chain. It is also imperative for loss prevention to shift the focus from traditional reactive strategies, to predictive analytics.

Fortunately, the retail industry has been historically one of the most data rich busi-ness verticals. Unfortunately, this data richness often lives in siloed data structures, and retail has been generally slow on the ability to access data and unable to utilize it prop-erly, owing to limited resources. The lack of adequate tools to mine and analyze huge amounts of data continues to undermine the effectiveness of loss prevention programs.

Retailers have the capability with data analytics to gain a better understanding of shoplifting behavior patterns and develop proactive loss prevention strategies. By exam-ining millions of data points, data analytics can determine relationships that would otherwise be indiscernible. The result is that today's retailers have a set of novel loss pre-vention techniques that were unavailable only a few years ago. Once you begin the data analytical process to discover where your loss is occurring and determine the best loss prevention solutions, you will be well on your way to reducing and preventing retail loss.

Exercises

1. Who are shoplifters? What is a common way to classify shoplifters?
2. What is organized retail crime? What is a critical element needed to identify these crime rings?
3. Describe the roles of a booster, a handler, and a fence.
4. What are the sources of retail loss? What is the leading source of retail loss?
5. What are some of the ways employees commit theft? How might you mitigate some of these methods?
6. Name some of the return fraud types. How are they committed?

Chapter Four

Basic Statistical Analysis

Statistics ... is the most important science in the whole world,
for upon it depends the practical application of every other (science)
and of every art.

—*Florence Nightingale*

Introduction

The prior chapters have focused on the theory of criminology and retail security. This chapter's focus will be to present an introduction to statistical concepts. On completion of this chapter, you should be able to do the following:

1. Understand the different types of variables.
2. Prepare and clean your data.
3. Find and interpret measures of central tendency and dispersion.
4. Determine the measure of central tendency that best represents a set of data.
5. Calculate a confidence interval.
6. Use SAS or SPSS software to compute measures of central tendency and dispersion.

Variables

Understanding variables is essential to understanding statistical analysis. The type of analysis to be performed is almost always dictated by the types of variable being analyzed. This section discusses the basic types of variables, and gives several examples of each type. There are two basic categories for variables, numeric and category. Dates require special treatment and will be discussed separately from numeric and category variables.

Numeric or Continuous Variables

A numeric (also known as a continuous) variable is a variable that can take values on the real number line. The real number line contains the positive and negative numbers and is illustrated in Figure 4.1.

Variables such as return amount, shoplifter's age, and number of burglaries are considered numeric variables. The difference between two dates is also a numeric variable.

There are two different types of a numeric variable, continuous and discrete. A discrete numeric value is such that the possible values of the variable can be counted (possibly to infinity). Examples of discrete variables are the number of days between shipments, the number of stolen products, and the number of managers in a store. A continuous numeric variable can theoretically take on an infinitely fine measurement. For example, the age of a shoplifter can be expressed as a discrete measure, 1, 2, 3, etc., or it can be expressed as the number of minutes or seconds from birth. Traditionally, age is considered continuous; however, all continuous variables can be expressed as discrete variables. The reverse is not true; inherently discrete variables cannot be expressed as continuous variables. Let's say that you flip a coin ten times and want to count the number of times it lands on heads. We could not, for example, get 5.5 heads. Thus, the number of heads counted must be a discrete variable.

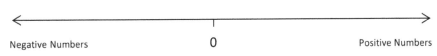

Negative Numbers   0   Positive Numbers

Figure 4.1: The Real Number Line

Category Variables

A category (also known as a discrete) variable is a variable that takes on the value of a characteristic. An example of a category variable is theft type. The variable "theft type" can take on the values of "internal" or "external." Sometimes, category variables can take on seemingly numeric values, which are just numeric codes for the category. For example, property type may have the following coding scheme:

1. Big box;
2. Small box;
3. Discount store;
4. Warehouse store;
5. Other.

The values of property type are 1, 2, 3, 4, and 5, which are discrete numeric values. However, they represent a characteristic and not a measure of any kind. Property type could have just as easily been coded as:

21. Big box;
72. Small box;
93. Discount stores;
104. Warehouse store;
115. Other.

While there has been no actual change of information, treating this variable as numeric would be incorrect and misleading.

There are two types of a category variable, ordered (or ordinal) and unordered. An ordered category variable is such that there is a natural order for the categories presented that does not rely on other information. An example of an ordered categorical variable is risk grade for a store. Risk grade can take on values "A, A−, B+, B, B−," etc. and falls into a natural order. We can say that a grade of "A" implies that a store's risk is less than a store with a risk grade of "B." Property type is an example of an unordered category variable because there is no way to order the categories naturally without including other information.

Dates

Dates do not clearly fall into the numeric or the categorical grouping of variables. However, if dates are represented as the number of days since an event, then they clearly are discrete numeric values. However, they cannot be manipulated like traditional numeric values. When dates are categorized into years, they are analogous to discrete numeric variables. When dates are categorized into months and the months are numbered, the months are discrete numeric values. However, each month is not equal in length and this violates a basic idea behind the number line that would stipulate that one month always means the same thing. Dates can be both categorical (e.g., days of the week or months of the year) and quantitative (date of an incident or date of a payment).

Describing Data

Accessing and collecting data these days can be easy. However, it can be difficult to describe the data to other people in meaningful ways. That is when statistics plays a key role. Statistics are descriptive measures derived from a sample of data. In this section, we will cover a variety of common statistics used in describing data.

Measures of Central Tendency

Measures of central tendency focus on key features of a distribution and describe a distribution of data in terms of its most frequent, middle, and average data value. The descriptive statistics most often used for this purpose are the mean (the average), the mode (the most frequently occurring value), and the median (the middle value in a distribution).

The mean, or average, is probably the most commonly used measure of central tendency. To compute the mean, one must add all the values and divide by the number of observations. For example, the mean or average ($\bar{x}$) number of apprehensions per store in a retail district is determined by summing all the apprehensions in the retail district and dividing by the number of stores in the district.

$$\bar{x} = \frac{\text{sum of the observations}}{N}$$

4.1

A common way to express a sum is with the Greek capital letter sigma (Σ). Using the common formula for the mean, Equation 4.1 is written as

$$\bar{x} = \frac{\sum_{i=1}^{N} x_i}{N}$$

4.2

Let's break down the symbols used in this equation.

- N represents the total number of observations in the data.
- x_i represents the ith observation in the data.
- The subscript ($i = 1$) and superscript (N) on the Σ represent that the observations should be summed from ($i = 1$), which is the first observation, to $i = N$, which is the last observation.
- $\bar{x}$ represents the sample mean.

Consider the dataset shown in Table 4.1; it lists the number of apprehensions in eight stores. The mean equals the sum of apprehensions in the eight stores (151) divided by the number of observations (8). The mean (average) number of apprehensions per store is $151/8 = 18.875$.

The median is the middle number when the numbers are first sorted in order. If the distribution has an even number of values, then the median is the average of the two middle numbers. A common way to compute the median is to list all scores in numerical order, and then locate the score in the center of the sample. For example, if there are 1000 values in the list, the average of the 500th and the 501st records would be the median. If we order the eight stores of Table 4.1 by number of apprehensions, we would get:

10, 10, 10, 19, 20, 21, 27, 34

Since N is even, the median is the average of the two middle numbers, 19 and 20. The median is therefore, $(20 + 19)/2 = 39/2 = 19.5$.

Table 4.1: Apprehensions by Stores

Store Number	Number of Apprehensions
1	10
2	19
3	20
4	21
5	34
6	10
7	27
8	10

The mode of the distribution is the number that occurs most frequently. If two values tie for most frequent occurrence, the distribution has two modes and is called bimodal. In our example distribution, ten apprehensions occur in three different stores; ten is the mode.

Which of the three measures of central tendency should be used to represent the distribution? The answer is not straightforward. It is contingent on the distribution of the data, the way in which you want to represent the data, and the meaningfulness of the data. In our example, the mean value is probably the most telling and interesting information about our data.

To assess central tendency in SAS, you need to first import your data into SAS using proc import or with a data step using the infile statement. Once your data is in SAS, you can compute the aforementioned statistics using a procedure called univariate. The SAS code is as follows:

```
Proc means data = store_apprehensions N range sum mean median mode;
                 var apprehensions;
run;
```

In this SAS code, the first line identifies the procedure we wish to use (proc means), the data we are using for the calculation (store_apprehensions) and the statistics we want SAS to produce. We included some additional statistics to further examine the data. If you were interested, you could include the variance and the standard deviation. The second row identifies the variable of interest (apprehensions). The third row says "run," which tells SAS to execute the procedure.

Figure 4.2 shows an output that SAS produces that includes the statistics of interest. As you can see in the output, the means procedure conducted statistics on the variable

The SAS System

The MEANS Procedure

Analysis Variable : apprehensions

N	Range	Sum	Mean	Median	Mode
8	24.0000000	151.0000000	18.8750000	19.5000000	10.0000000

Figure 4.2: SAS Output

apprehensions and produced: (1) N, the sample size; (2) the range; (3) the sum; (4) the mean; (5) the median or the 50th percentile; and (6) the mode or the 50th percentile.

SPSS Example

As with our SAS example, we will assume that the dataset is in MS Excel and needs to be imported into SPSS. In SPSS, there are two easy methods to move the data from an external source into SPSS. You can copy and paste the data or you can open the saved Excel file in SPSS.

Using the first method, copy your data from Excel (ctrl-C). Then with SPSS open, go to "File" → "New" → "Data." This is illustrated in the top section of Figure 4.3.

Figure 4.3: Cut and Paste Data into SPSS

Then paste the data (ctrl-V) directly in the cells, resulting in the dataset illustrated in the middle section of Figure 4.3. When you are looking at the data you just pasted in, you are in the "Data View" tab of SPSS. You may choose to rename VAR00001 and VAR00002 by double clicking on VAR00001 and VAR00002; another tab opens automatically, the "Variables View" tab, where you can directly type the names where it says "Name" (bottom section of Figure 4.3).

Another method of bringing data into SPSS is by saving the file in Excel first. In this example, I will save the file as "StoreApprehensions.xls." Then in SPSS, go to "File" → "Open" → "Data," illustrated in the top section of Figure 4.4. Then navigate to the location in which the file is saved in the "Look in" window, and make sure to select *Excel* in the "Files of type." Highlight your file and click on "Open" (middle section of Figure 4.4). A window will open that will allow you to ensure that the range of data selected is

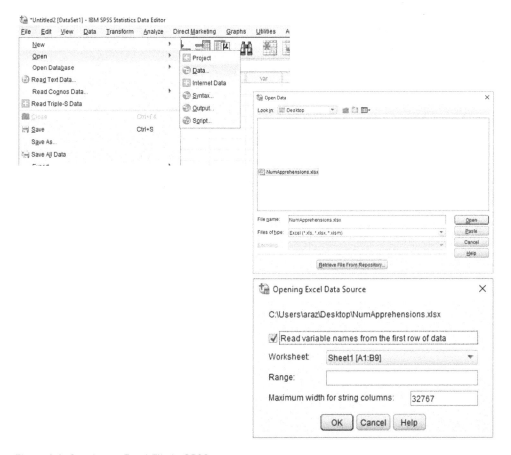

correct and the names of columns in Excel will automatically populate as column names in SPSS (bottom section of Figure 4.4).

Now that that data is in SPSS, we can run an easy descriptive analysis by going to "Analyze" → "Descriptive Statistics" → "Frequencies," illustrated in the top section of Figure 4.5. A box will appear and you should move the variable of interest (in our case, NumApprehensions) from the box on the left to the box on the right, using the arrow between the boxes, illustrated in the lower left section of Figure 4.5. Click on the box called "Statistics" and select mean, median, mode, and range (illustrated in the lower right section of Figure 4.5).

The output is displayed in Figure 4.6. It illustrates the number of observations (*N*), which is 8, and notes that we have no missing observations. That is always something to pay attention to when conducting analyses. The resulting mean, median, mode, and range are the same as those presented in SAS, just rounded to two decimal places.

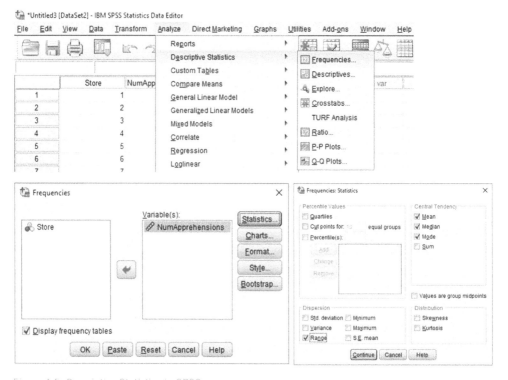

Figure 4.5: Descriptive Statistics in SPSS

➡ **Frequencies**

Statistics

NumApprehensions

N	Valid	8
	Missing	0
Mean		18.88
Median		19.50
Mode		10
Range		24

Figure 4.6: Descriptive Statistics Output in SPSS

Percentiles

Percentiles are the values at which a certain percentage of the observations fall below that value. For example, if we say that the 75th percentile of a shoplifter's age is 45, then this means that 75% of all shoplifters are younger than 45. If we say that the 30th percentile of shoplifter's age is 32, this implies that 30% of all shoplifters are younger than 32. The median is a special case of the percentiles and is also known as the 50th percentile. It is the value where 50% of the data falls below that value. The interquartile range is calculated by assessing the range between Q_3 (the 75th percentile) and Q_1 (the 25th percentile).

Measures of Dispersion

Measures of dispersion are used to indicate how spread out the values are in a distribution or how different they are from the mean. A few measures of dispersion are the range, interquartile range (described already), variance, and standard deviation.

Range

The range is calculated by first ordering your values from least to greatest and then taking the difference. For example, consider the dataset in Table 4.2, recording the number of CCTVs in eight stores.

Store Number	Number of CCTVs
1	3
2	4
3	6
4	7
5	9
6	10
7	12
8	16

Table 4.2: Number of CCTVs by Store

range = highest value − lowest value   4.3
range = 16 − 3 = 13   4.4

The range is a simple statistic, but can also be misleading owing to outliers. For example, if the highest value in the previous example was 260, the range would be 257, but most of the values are around 7. That is why the standard deviation may be a better way of describing data dispersion.

Standard Deviation and Variance

The standard deviation is a measure of how spread out the values are in a distribution or how much a number in the distribution differs from the mean. Standard deviation is used to measure dispersion around the mean; it measures variability. It can be considered the "mean of the data away from the mean"—so, on average, how far the scores or values in a distribution are from the mean. When comparing datasets with approximately the same mean, the greater the spread, the greater the standard deviation.

Example of Standard Deviation: Height

Suppose we have a sample of 10,000 individuals from a population and we measure their heights to the nearest inch. Suppose the average height in the population is 69 inches (5′9″). Figures 4.7, 4.8, and 4.9 show how that sample may look for various values of standard deviation (2 inches, 3 inches, and 5 inches).

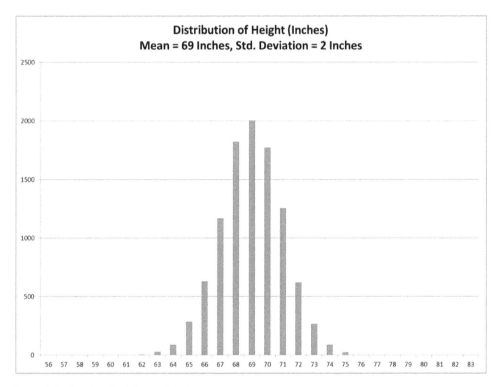

Figure 4.7: Standard Deviation = 2 inches

You should note that as the standard deviation increases, the data is more spread out and fewer observations accumulate near 69 inches. As the standard deviation decreases, there are more observations near 69 inches and the data is less spread out.

Example Calculations

Take, for example, the following three sets of data:

- Dataset #1 has the values 5, 5, 5, 5 → mean =5, standard deviation = 0.
- Dataset #2 has the values 4, 4, 6, 6 → mean =5, standard deviation = 1.
- Dataset #3 has the values 3, 3, 7, 7 → mean =5, standard deviation = 2.

The mean is 5 for all three sets of data, but the standard deviations are 0, 1, and 2, respectively. So, the larger the standard deviation the more the values in the set vary from the mean.

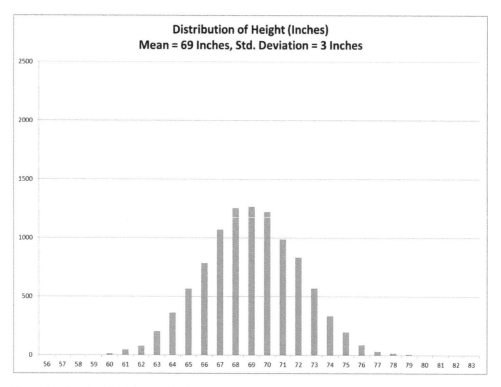

The standard deviation is represented by the Greek lower case letter sigma (σ) and the formula is the square root of the variance. The variance (σ^2) is the average of the squared differences from the mean. To calculate the variance, one must: (1) determine the mean of the distribution; (2) for each number, subtract it from the mean and square it (i.e., the squared difference assures that the standard deviation is never negative); and (3) determine the average of the squared differences. For example, you have just measured the number of stolen products in five stores, represented in Table 4.3.

The first step is to calculate the mean:

$$\bar{x} = \frac{700 + 570 + 270 + 330 + 400}{5} = 454$$

4.5

So, the mean number of stolen products is 454. Now we calculate each store's difference from the mean. The second step is to take each value's difference, square it, and then take the average of the squares.

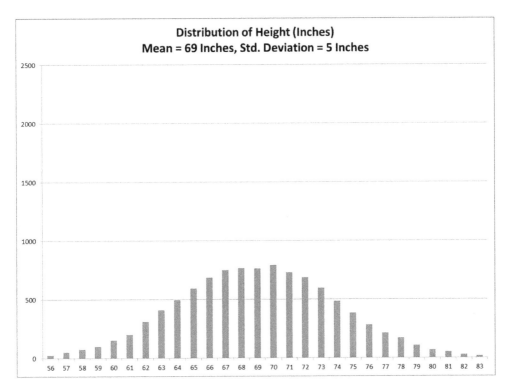

Figure 4.9: Standard Deviation = 5 inches

Table 4.3: Stolen Products by Store

Store Number	*# of Stolen Products*
1	700
2	570
3	270
4	330
5	400

$$\text{variance}: \sigma^2 = \frac{\left\{ \left(700 - 454\right)^2 + \left(570 - 454\right)^2 + \left(270 - 454\right)^2 + \left(330 - 454\right)^2 + \left(400 - 454\right)^2 \right\}}{5}$$

$$= \frac{\left\{ \left(246\right)^2 + \left(116\right)^2 + \left(-184\right)^2 + \left(-124\right)^2 + \left(-54\right)^2 \right\}}{5}$$

$$= \frac{\{60,516 + 13,456 + 33,856 + 15,376 + 2916\}}{5}$$

$$= \frac{126,120}{5} = 25,224 \tag{4.6}$$

The variance is 25,224 and the standard deviation is the square root of the variance, so

$$\text{standard deviation} = \sigma = \sqrt{25,224} = 158.821 \tag{4.7}$$

Knowing the standard deviation has utility. Now we can determine which stores are within one standard deviation of the mean for stolen items. To determine "one standard deviation from the mean," we take the mean and subtract one standard deviation to get a lower bound (454 − 158.821 = 295.179), and we take the mean plus one standard deviation to get an upper bound (454 + 158.821 = 612.821). Using this approach, we have a standard way of knowing what is close to normal and what is considered high or low. Once we determine stores that are considered high, we can better allocate resources to riskier stores.

There is a minor change to the formula when calculating the standard deviation for a sample. In the previous example, we divided by N, to get the population standard deviation. This approach assumes that we know the mean in advance (which is not common). When calculating the standard deviation for a sample, you divide by $N - 1$ for the variance to adjust for the fact that the mean is estimated. It turns out that, if you do not divide by $N - 1$, the estimate will, on average, be slightly lower than the true population value. So, if the above data was from a sample, the standard deviation would be 177.567.

$$\text{population standard deviation:} \sigma = \sqrt{\frac{1}{N} \sum_{i=1}^{N} (x_i - \mu)^2} \tag{4.8}$$

$$\text{sample standard deviation:} s = \sqrt{\frac{1}{N-1} \sum_{i=1}^{N} (x_i - \bar{x})^2} \tag{4.9}$$

In Equation 4.9, the formula for the sample standard deviation (s), the symbols denote:

- N = the size of the sample;
- Σ = sum;
- x = a data value;
- $\bar{x}$ = the average.

SAS Example #2

The example is calculated based on the data of Table 4.3 being drawn from a sample. We can use the following SAS procedure:

```
proc univariate data = shoplift;
    var stolen_hp;
run;
```

In this SAS code, the first line identifies the procedure we wish to use (proc univariate) and the dataset we are using for the calculation (shoplift); the second row specifies the variable to analyze (stolen_hp); and the third row (run) tells SAS to execute the procedure.

SPSS Example #2

We can calculate percentiles in SPSS in a very similar manner to how we generated the mean, median, and mode. With the data in SPSS, go to "Analyze" → "Descriptive Statistics" → "Frequencies." Again, move the variables of interest (StolenProducts) to the box on the right and click on "Statistics." Then choose the percentiles, as illustrated in Figure 4.11. We decided to choose the "Quartiles" option (25th, 50th, and 75th percentiles), but you can choose whichever number suits your analysis. We also added two percentile points of interest, the 1st and 100th percentiles. You can type them into the white box by the word "Percentile(s)" and click on "Add."

The output is presented in Figure 4.12.

Correlation

A common measure of the association of two variables is known as correlation (or more accurately, Pearson's correlation). Correlation measures the association between two numeric variables and takes on values between "−1.0" and "1.0." A value of "1" represents perfect positive correlation and a value of "−1" represents perfect negative correlation. A value of "0" indicates that there is no relationship between the two

```
                          The SAS System

                      The UNIVARIATE Procedure
                      Variable:   stolen_hp

                              Moments

N                              5    Sum Weights                 5
Mean                         454    Sum Observations         2270
Std Deviation         177.566889    Variance                31530
Skewness               0.6068569    Kurtosis           -1.4184337



                     Basic Statistical Measures

           Location                       Variability

        Mean      454.0000     Std Deviation          177.56689
        Median    400.0000     Variance                   31530
        Mode            .      Range                430.00000
                               Interquartile Range  240.00000




                     Quantiles (Definition 5)

                     Level            Quantile

                     100% Max             700
                     99%                  700
                     95%                  700
                     90%                  700
                     75% Q3               570
                     50% Median           400
                     25% Q1               330
                     10%                  270
                     5%                   270
                     1%                   270
                     0% Min               270
```

Figure 4.10: SAS Output

numeric variables. The following formula shows how to calculate the correlation coefficient (r):

$$r = \frac{\sum_{i=1}^{n}\left(X_i - \bar{X}\right)\left(Y_i - \bar{Y}\right)}{\sqrt{\sum_{i=1}^{n}\left(X_i - \bar{X}\right)^2}\sqrt{\sum_{i=1}^{n}\left(Y_i - \bar{Y}\right)^2}}$$

4.10

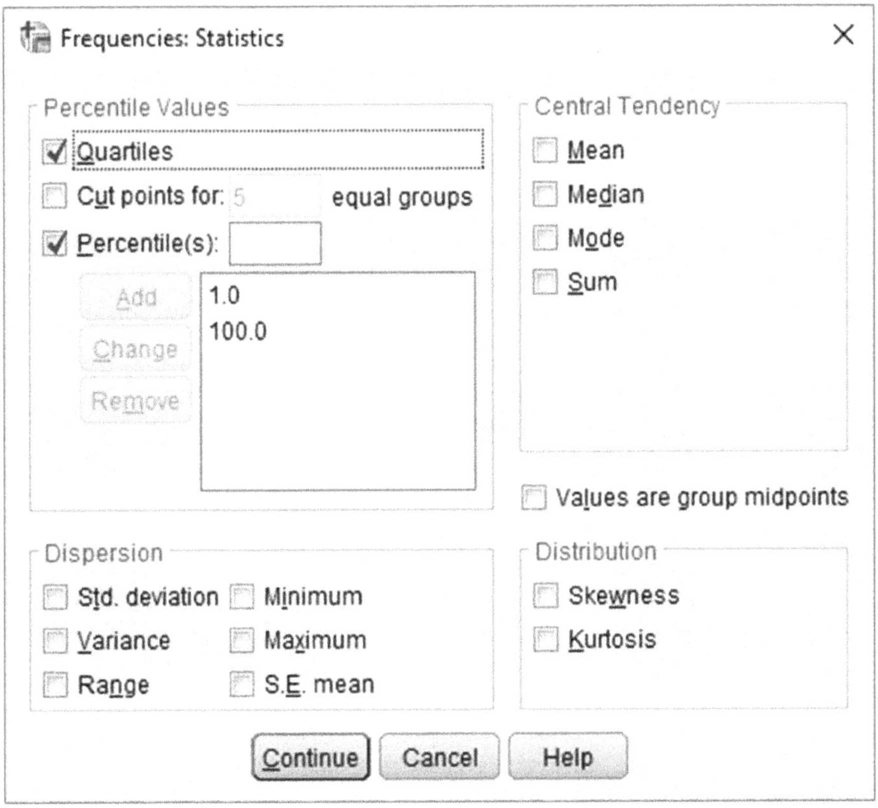

Figure 4.11: Percentiles in SPSS

➡ Frequencies

Statistics

StolenProducts

N	Valid	5
	Missing	0
Percentiles	1	270.0000
	25	300.0000
	50	400.0000
	75	635.0000
	100	700.0000

Figure 4.12: Percentiles Output in SPSS

Probably the best way to begin understanding correlation is to see scatter plots of correlated information at different levels of correlation. See Figure 4.13 for various scatter plots and different levels of correlation. You should note that as the correlation increases, the data begins to look more like a line. This shows that as two variables become more correlated, knowing one will help you determine the value for the other variable. A positive correlation means that as one variable increases in value, the other variable will also increase in value. Likewise, a negative correlation means that as one variable increases in value, the other variable will decrease in value. In Figure 4.13, the first four scatter plots illustrate a positive correlation while the last one shows a negative correlation.

One common misconception with correlation is that a strong correlation means that one variable *causes* the other one to increase. This misconception is commonly

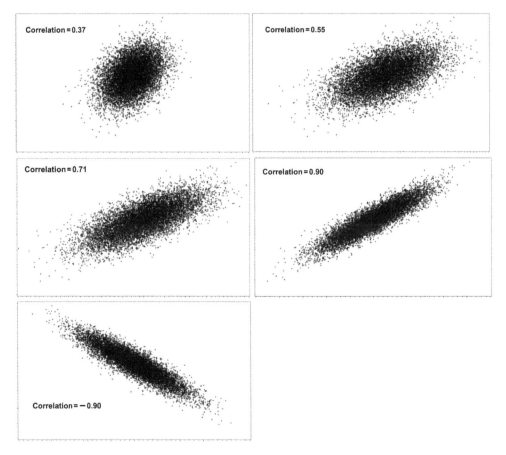

Figure 4.13: Scatter Plots Illustrating Correlation Values

referred to as "Correlation does not imply causation." An example of this in retail is the store's square footage compared with annual sales in that store. These two quantities are likely to be correlated, but the large square footage does not necessarily cause more sales. It is very likely that the large square footage was acquired in response to a densely populated area and the densely populated area is more the causal factor for the increased sales.

Probability

At the foundation of statistics is probability. Probability is the likelihood of a given outcome given a set of possible outcomes. A probability will always take on a value between zero and one and can include the values of "0" and "1" as well. If the probability of an outcome is "1," it is certain to happen. If the probability of an outcome is "0," it will never happen. We will cover a few key topics in probability in this chapter.

Probability Distributions and Calculating Probabilities

There are two types of outcome for which one may wish to compute the probability: discrete outcomes and continuous outcomes. Discrete outcomes can be enumerated; each outcome will have a specific probability assigned to it such that if you sum up all the probability values for all possible outcomes, the total will equal one. Adding up to one simply means that something will happen. To calculate the probability for some discrete events, like flipping quarters or rolling dice, you can compute the number of ways that an outcome can occur, divided by the number of possible outcomes that may occur. At the foundation of many probability calculations is the concept of combinations and permutations, which are covered in the next two sections.

When an outcome is a continuous numerical value, the number of possible outcomes is infinite and the probability distribution will be defined by a curve. Just as all the probabilities in a discrete distribution had to add to one, the area under a continuous distribution curve must equal one as well.

Combinations

Combinations are the number of ways that objects can be grouped, not considering the order of the grouping. One example would be: in a group of five people, how many sub-groups of three can be made? Let's label these people P1, P2, P3, P4, and P5. The following is an exhaustive list of the groups of three that can be formed:

1. P1, P2, P3;
2. P1, P2, P4;
3. P1, P2, P5;
4. P1, P3, P4;
5. P1, P3, P5;
6. P1, P4, P5;
7. P2, P3, P4;
8. P2, P3, P5;
9. P2, P4, P5;
10. P3, P4, P5.

So there are ten possible groups of three that can be selected from a group of five, assuming order is not important. There is a very nice formula for computing the number of combinations:

$$\binom{n}{k} = \frac{n!}{(n-k)!k!}$$

4.11

The symbol $\binom{n}{k}$ represents the number of ways "k" things can be chosen from "n" things. The symbol $n!$ represents multiplying "n" by all numbers less than "n." For example, $5! = 5 \times 4 \times 3 \times 2 \times 1 = 120$. For our example,

$$\binom{5}{3} = \frac{5!}{(5-3)!3!} = \frac{120}{2 \times 6} = 10$$

4.12

The way to interpret the equation is as follows. If I would like to choose three items from the group of five, the first choice can be one of five items, the second choice can be one of the remaining four items, and the last choice can be one of the remaining three items. Combining the three choices together yields $5 \times 4 \times 3 = 60$ possibilities. Another way to write $5 \times 4 \times 3 = (5 \times 4 \times 3 \times 2 \times 1)/(2 \times 1) = 5!/2! = 5!/(5 - 3!) = 60$. However, within the 60 possibilities, (P1, P2, P3) is there along with (P3, P2, P1) and (P2, P1, P3). In order to remove all of the duplicate groupings, we note that for any group of three things, there are $3 \times 2 \times 1 = 6$ ways to order them. Dividing $60/6 = 10$. This can also be written as $5!/((5 - 3!)3!)$, which is our formula.

Permutations

Permutations are similar to combinations, but the order is important. Using the example from above, we may augment the request to ask how many ways can three out of five people sit on a bench together. In this case, the order of the people on the bench is important. The formula for determining the answer to this question is very similar to the formula for the number of combinations:

$$P_k^n = \frac{n!}{(n-k)!}$$

4.13

Using Equation 4.13 to answer the questions about how many ways can three out of five people sit on a bench together results in $(5 \times 4 \times 3 \times 2 \times 1)/(2 \times 1) = 5 \times 4 \times 3 = 60$. There are five people who can sit on the left part of the bench, four more for the center part of the bench, and then three remain for the right portion of the bench (see Figure 4.14).

Why are Combinations and Permutations Important in Probability?

Combinations and permutations play an important role in computing the probability of certain events. In this section, we present two examples that illustrate the role of these concepts in computing probabilities.

Example 1: The California Lottery

Suppose we would like to know the probability of winning the Fantasy 5 in the California lottery. There are 39 numbers to choose from and the person playing the lottery must choose 5 numbers from the 39 (but no number can be chosen more than once and the order does not matter). Once we pick our numbers, there is a process where five balls are chosen from a basket containing the 39 balls (each with the corresponding numbers from 1 to 39). To win the jackpot, we must match all five numbers.

$$P(\text{winning}) = \frac{\text{number of ways to win}}{\text{number of possible ways to select 5 numbers from 39}}$$

4.14

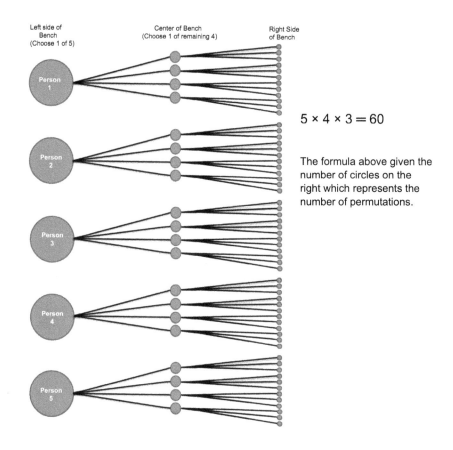

Figure 4.14: Permutations, Bench Example

There is only one way to win. All five numbers must be selected. The denominator of this fraction is the number of combinations when choosing 5 things from 39.

$$\binom{39}{5} = \frac{39!}{(39-5)!5!} = \frac{39 \times 38 \times 37 \times 36 \times 35}{5 \times 4 \times 3 \times 2 \times 1} = 575,757$$

4.15

So the probability of winning is $1/(575,757) = 0.0000017368$, which is a very low probability.

The following screen capture (Figure 4.15) from Excel illustrates how combinations can be computed with Excel. In Excel, the "COMBIN" function is used to compute combinations.

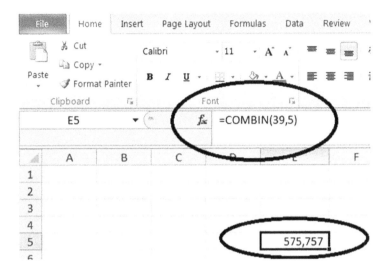

Figure 4.15: COMBIN Function in Excel

Example 2: Store Employees

Suppose that there are four employees working in a store and the manager will allocate two of them to work registers 1 and 2 and the other two will work in other parts of the store. What is the probability that employee #4 is working on register #1 (assuming all employees are equally likely to work in any job in the store)?

$$P\left(\text{employee #4 working on register #1}\right) = \frac{\text{number of options with employee #4 on register #1}}{\text{number of ways to allocate employees to registers or other parts of store}} \quad 4.16$$

The numerator of this equation requires that employee #4 is on register #1. There are three remaining employees that can work at register #2 (this value is the number of permutations for selecting one employee from a group of three). The denominator of this equation is the number of permutations of two employees out of four. So the answer to this question is:

$$P\left(\text{employee #4 working on register #1}\right) = \frac{P_1^3}{P_2^4} = \frac{3!/\left(3-1\right)!}{4!/\left(4-2\right)!} = \frac{3}{12} = 25\%$$

$$4.17$$

Common Statistical Distributions and Properties

In statistics, a variable is described by its distribution. A distribution tells you the likelihood that a variable will take on certain values. In general, each variable may follow its own unique distribution, but there are many well-defined distributions that will serve as approximations for a variable's distribution. There are many key elements of a distribution and several common distributions, which we will discuss in this chapter.

Skewness

If the distribution of data is exactly normal or symmetric, then the mode, mean, and median are exactly equal. Sometimes extreme values, particularly on one side of the distribution, but not the other, or outliers in a distribution can create a skewed distribution (see Figure 4.16). However, the median is not generally affected by a small number of outliers, so it may be a better representation of the distribution if your data has outliers.

Discrete Distribution Functions

There are many well-known discrete distribution functions. In this chapter, we will cover the binomial distribution. Some other discrete distribution functions that you may encounter are the multinomial distribution, the hypergeometric distribution, the Poisson distribution, and the negative binomial distribution.

Binomial Distribution

The binomial distribution represents the number of successes from a sequence of independent experiments where there are only two possible outcomes. A simple example

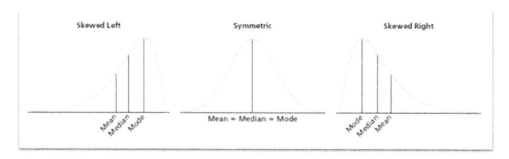

Figure 4.16: Histograms and Central Tendency-Determining Skewness

of a binomial experiment is a series of coin flips. If we flip a quarter 10 times, the number of heads will have a binomial distribution. The formula for this distribution is

$$\text{Prob}\left(x = k \mid n, p\right) = \binom{n}{k} p^k \left(1 - p\right)^{n-k}$$

4.18

- "n" represents the number of trials (e.g., the number of coin flips).
- "k" represents the number of successes (e.g., the number of heads).
- "p" represents the probability of a head.

Using Excel, we can compute the binomial distribution for various values of "n," "k," and "p." For example, the distribution of the number of heads from flipping a quarter 10 times is shown in Figure 4.17 Excel. The Excel function "BINOMDIST(k,n,p,false)" will return the probability for a specific value in the binomial distribution.

Continuous Distribution Functions

There are many well-known continuous distribution functions. In this chapter, we will cover the normal distribution. Some other common continuous distribution functions, which we will not cover but that you may encounter, are the log–normal distribution, the t distribution, the chi-square distribution, and the beta distribution.

Normal Curve

The properties of the normal curve are: (1) a specific normal curve is completely described by giving its mean and its standard deviation; (2) the mean determines the center of the distribution and is located at the center of the curve's symmetry; and (3) the standard deviation determines the shape of the curve; it is the distance from the mean to the values on either side. The normal curve, or Gaussian curve, is defined by the formula

$$f\left(x \mid \mu, \sigma^2\right) = \frac{1}{\sqrt{2\sigma^2 \pi}} e^{-\frac{(x-\mu)^2}{2\sigma^2}}$$

4.19

We now know that the distance from the mean is measured in terms of the number of standard deviations. The normal distribution is symmetric and is also known as the

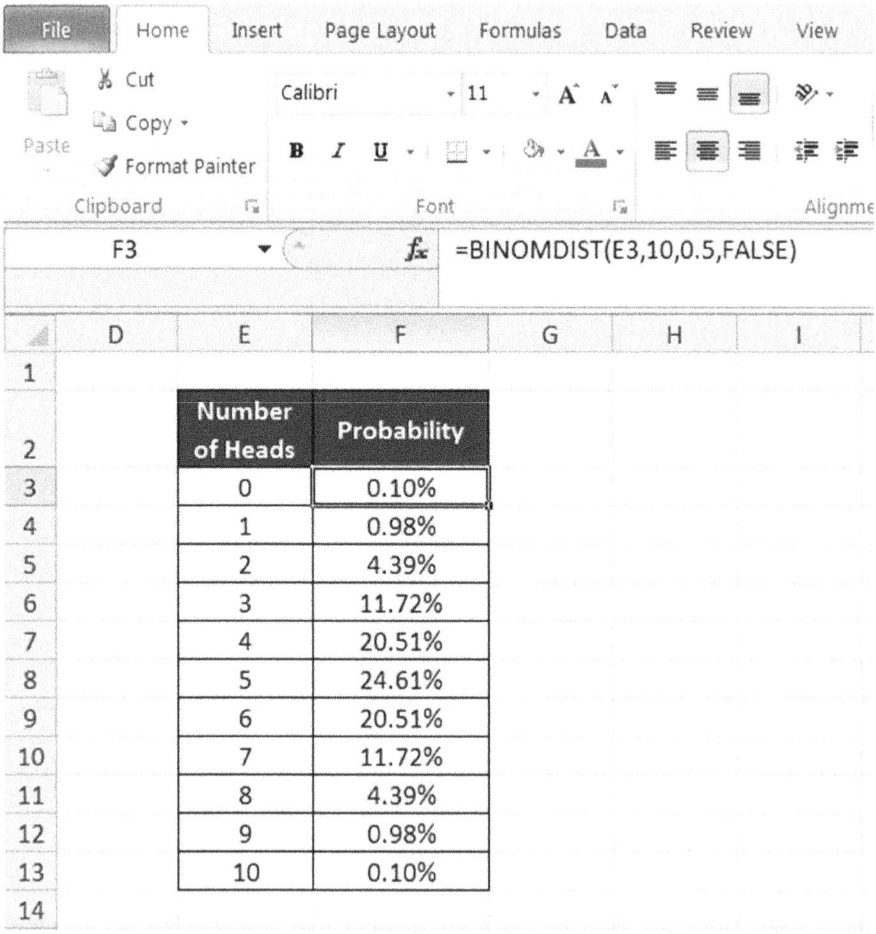

Number of Heads	Probability
0	0.10%
1	0.98%
2	4.39%
3	11.72%
4	20.51%
5	24.61%
6	20.51%
7	11.72%
8	4.39%
9	0.98%
10	0.10%

Figure 4.17: Excel Binomial Distribution

bell-shaped curve. The normal or Gaussian distribution was named after Karl Gauss (1777–1855).

The empirical rule states that almost all of the data falls within three standard deviations of the mean. Therefore, outliers are defined as observations that lie beyond the mean ± 3 standard deviations (see Figure 4.18). If a dataset has an approximately bell-shaped (normal) distribution, then

1. Approximately 68% of the observations lie within one standard deviation of the mean, that is, in the range $\overline{x} \pm 1s$ for samples, and for populations $\mu \pm 1\sigma$.

2. Approximately 95% of the observations lie within two standard deviations of the mean, that is, in the range $\overline{x} \pm 2s$ for samples, and for populations $\mu \pm 2\sigma$.
3. Approximately 99.7% of the observations lie within three standard deviations of the mean, that is, in the range $\overline{x} \pm 3s$ for samples, and for populations $\mu \pm 3\sigma$.

Let us assume for a moment that we have a normal distribution of apprehensions for 1000 stores. Let us also assume that the mean number of apprehensions of these stores is $\mu = 100$ and that the standard deviation σ is 15. How does this help you? First, the average number of apprehensions of all the stores is 100. Second, if the standard deviation is 15, then about 68% of the stores had between 85 and 115 apprehensions, since $100 - 15 = 85$ and $100 + 15 = 115$. In other words, about 680 of the 1000 stores have apprehensions between 85 and 115. The apprehensions that are two standard deviations from the mean range from 70 to 130, since $100 - 2(15) = 70$ and $100 + 2(15) = 130$. From the empirical rule, we know that about 95% of all stores' apprehensions will fall within this range. Thus, about 950 of the 1000 stores fall in this range. This means that out of 1000 stores, we would expect only 50 stores to have apprehensions that are either less than 70 or greater than 130. For example, finding a store with 140 apprehensions would be highly unlikely. Therefore, stores that have more than 130 apprehensions may warrant some investigation and possibly more resources.

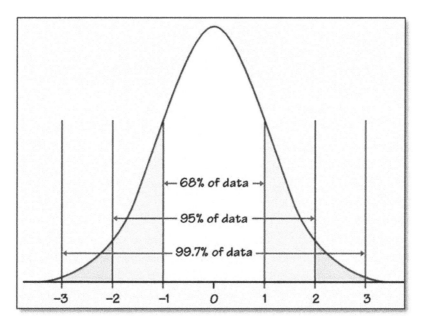

Figure 4.18: The Empirical Rule

Standardized Data

Sometimes, we may want to look at one specific store in regards to risk of theft rather than summarizing all stores. We may want to tell leadership that a specific store is above the average in risk. We may also want to compare stores across data distributions or where a store lies compared with the rest of the data, above or below the mean. This is where standardizing your data is helpful. The z score for a store indicates how far, and in what direction, that store deviates from its distribution's mean, expressed in units of its distribution's standard deviation. In other words, a standardized variable (z) redefines each observation, in a distribution, in terms of the number of standard deviations from the mean. This is helpful because standardizing data puts your variables on one scale so comparisons are easy to make.

Standardization formula for a population: $$z_i = \frac{x_i - \mu}{\sigma}$$ 4.20

Standardization formula for a sample: $$z_i = \frac{x_i - \overline{x}}{s}$$ 4.21

In Equation 4.21 for the sample z score, the symbols denote:

- x = a data value;
- $\overline{x}$ = the average;
- s = the sample standard deviation.

Data that is two standard deviations below the mean will have a z score of -2, and data that is two standard deviations above the mean will have a z score of $+2$. Data beyond two standard deviations away from the mean will have z scores beyond -2 or 2.

So, why should we use a z score or standardize our data? z scores allow you to place equal weighting between distributions; they allow you to equally measure stores across many distributions or variables. For example, you can examine one store's risk, compared with all other stores, based on several different risk variables. If a particular store's risk has a z score of 2, this tells you that 97.72% (based on a z table) of the other stores' risks lie below that particular store and 2.28% (100% − 97.72%) of the stores lie above that store. This means you may want to focus your loss prevention efforts on this store.

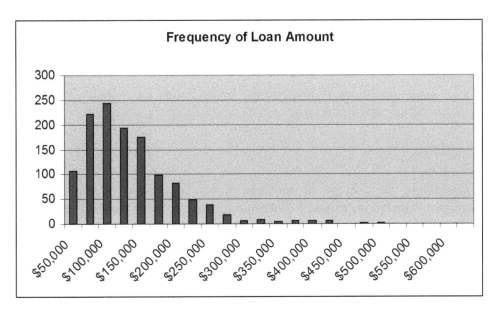

Figure 4.19: Right Skewed Shrink Amount

Transforming Numeric Variables

There are various forms of variable transformations. The primary goal of transformation is to change a variable with a skewed distribution into a distribution that is symmetric, or nearly symmetric, about its mean. Many analytical methods will have more favorable properties if the data elements are symmetric versus skewed. Some transformations include:

- Log transformation → Log(variable);
- Inverse transformation → (1/variable);
- Power transformation → (variable)^p;
- Exponential transformation → exp(variable).

Many numeric variables encountered in retail will need to be viewed on the log scale. A basic rule of thumb is that if the variable has a long right tail, then transformation to the log scale is needed. Assess the distribution of a variable by plotting a histogram. A long right tail means that the values on the right hand side of the scale are unbounded and can have a few outliers.

Annual shrink amount is a good example of a variable that would be best viewed on the log scale. For example, for a certain retailer, annual shrink falls in the $50,000 to $500,000 range, but there are enough stores in the $1,000,000+ or $2,000,000+ range to mislead our results. The transformation makes the distribution of amounts more symmetric and easier to interpret and analyze. Figures 4.19 and 4.20 illustrate this point.

The shrink amount in Figure 4.19 has a heavy right tail. Figure 4.20, however, demonstrates the effects of viewing shrink amount on the log scale.

Conclusion

Understanding the concepts in this chapter, such as measures of central tendency, measures of dispersion, statistical distributions, and displaying data, is a fundamental foundation for data analysis. These techniques will allow you to better understand the distribution of data, detect outliers, and assess key metrics.

Exercises

1. Imagine you are given the task of assessing the magnitude of employee theft at your company. You have 500 stores, so you take a random sample to generalize the results. You take a random sample of 30 stores and obtain the number of employee apprehensions:

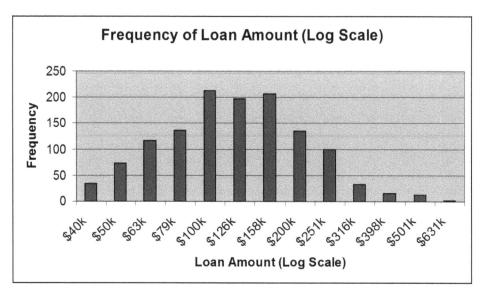

Figure 4.20: Shrink Amount Logged

5,7,8,14,10,12,16,21,13,15,24,23,31,28,4,3,2,7,8,22,24,26,27,31,16,14,13,12,19,16

For your data, calculate the:

- Mean, median, and mode;
- Standard deviation and range.

2. If 80 employees take an exam, how many will score within two standard deviations of the mean? How many employees will score more than two standard deviations from the mean?
3. When should you consider reporting the median instead of the mean?
4. Why is data standardization important? How is it useful?
5. What are some methods of transforming numeric variables? Why might you choose to transform a numeric variable?

Graphical Representation

If I can't picture it, I can't understand it.

—Albert Einstein

Introduction

The prior chapter focused on the calculation of general statistics, such as mean, median, mode, range, and percentiles. This chapter's focus will be to present an overview of graphical options used to visually represent some of the statistics discussed in Chapter 4. The graphical options are almost endless but in this chapter we will focus on the basics: frequency charts, bar charts, line charts, scatter plots, and box-and-whiskers plots. We will illustrate how to create these charts in Excel and SPSS. Many of these can be produced in SAS as well, but the results are visually more appealing (and require far less work) if executed in Excel.

Data—Graphical Presentations

In this chapter, we will use the fictional data presented in Table 5.1. It includes five variables:

Store number	We have stores 1, 2, 3, and 4.
Sales	Monthly gross sales.
Month	1 represents January, 2 represents February, and so forth.
District loss prevention manager	Stores 1 and 3 are managed by A.R. Stores 2 and 4 are managed by D.S.
Stolen products	Monthly count of missing inventory (attributed to stolen goods).

Table 5.1: Fictional Data of Sales and Stolen Products at Four Stores

Store	Sales	Month	LP Manager	Stolen Products
1	$ 25,000	1	A.R	25
1	$ 27,654	2	A.R	15
1	$ 30,170	3	A.R	21
1	$ 39,115	4	A.R	26
1	$ 30,568	5	A.R	35
1	$ 29,603	6	A.R	39
1	$ 33,165	7	A.R	31
1	$ 32,211	8	A.R	26
1	$ 31,886	9	A.R	18
1	$ 32,540	10	A.R	21
1	$ 33,525	11	A.R	25
1	$ 40,067	12	A.R	16
2	$ 30,000	1	D.S	20
2	$ 32,654	2	D.S	10
2	$ 34,810	3	D.S	16
2	$ 43,755	4	D.S	21

(Continued)

Table 5.1 (Continued)

Store	Sales	Month	LP Manager	Stolen Products
2	$ 35,208	5	D.S	31
2	$ 34,243	6	D.S	35
2	$ 37,805	7	D.S	31
2	$ 36,851	8	D.S	26
2	$ 36,426	9	D.S	21
2	$ 37,080	10	D.S	24
2	$ 38,065	11	D.S	28
2	$ 44,607	12	D.S	20
3	$ 50,000	1	A.R	40
3	$ 52,354	2	A.R	28
3	$ 52,610	3	A.R	34
3	$ 61,355	4	A.R	39
3	$ 52,808	5	A.R	48
3	$ 43,123	6	A.R	54
3	$ 46,685	7	A.R	50
3	$ 45,731	8	A.R	45
3	$ 45,406	9	A.R	40
3	$ 46,060	10	A.R	45
3	$ 55,345	11	A.R	49
3	$ 61,887	12	A.R	41
4	$ 35,000	1	D.S	45
4	$ 37,854	2	D.S	35
4	$ 38,110	3	D.S	43
4	$ 46,855	4	D.S	48
4	$ 38,308	5	D.S	57
4	$ 37,343	6	D.S	63
4	$ 40,905	7	D.S	59
4	$ 31,391	8	D.S	54
4	$ 31,066	9	D.S	47
4	$ 31,720	10	D.S	50
4	$ 32,705	11	D.S	54
4	$ 39,247	12	D.S	46

Bar Charts and Frequency Charts

Variable Type for Which This Is Appropriate: Category Variable

Bar tables and charts present a summary of some value for each level of the category variable. Frequency tables and charts represent the count (i.e., frequency) of an item or a number of occurrences. In our example, we will calculate the total sales associated with each store. In Excel, you would first have to sum the sales for each of the four stores. That can be easily accomplished with a pivot table (see Figure 5.1).

The resulting table is presented in Table 5.2.

You can create the bar chart by highlighting your data, then going to "Insert" → "Column" → "2-D Column" (see Figure 5.2). The resulting bar chart is illustrated in Figure 5.3.

The summarization of the values and the creation of the chart are done in the same step with SPSS. Once the data is in SPSS, to create the bar chart you should go to "Graphs" → "Legacy Dialogs" → "Bar," as illustrated in Figure 5.4.

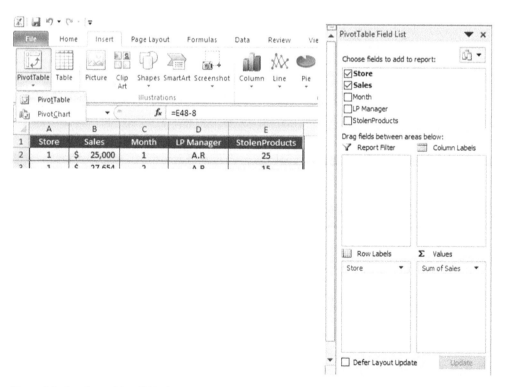

Figure 5.1: Creating a Pivot Table in Excel

Table 5.2: Total Sales by Store

Store	Total Sales
1	$ 385,504
2	$ 441,504
3	$ 613,364
4	$ 440,504

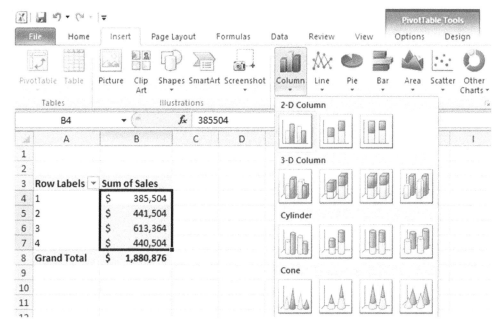

Figure 5.2: Creating a Bar Chart in Excel

In the dialog box that opens, select the variable in the left box for the category axis (the *x*-axis) by highlighting the variable and using the small arrow in the "Bars Represent" section to choose that variable. The variable chosen in Figure 5.5 is the sum of stolen goods, labeled "StolenProducts." Choose "Other statistic (e.g. mean)," and click on the "Change Statistic" button; then select "Sum of Values." Click on "Continue" and "OK." See Figure 5.5.

The resulting bar chart is illustrated in Figure 5.6.

The results in SPSS and Excel can be formatted to change the color of the bars, the titles of the axis, and the fonts and size of all titles, and to remove or add gridlines, background color, etc.

Total Sales by Store

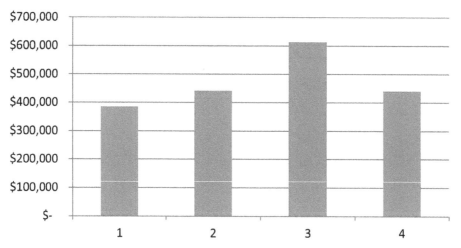

Figure 5.3: Resulting Bar Chart in Excel

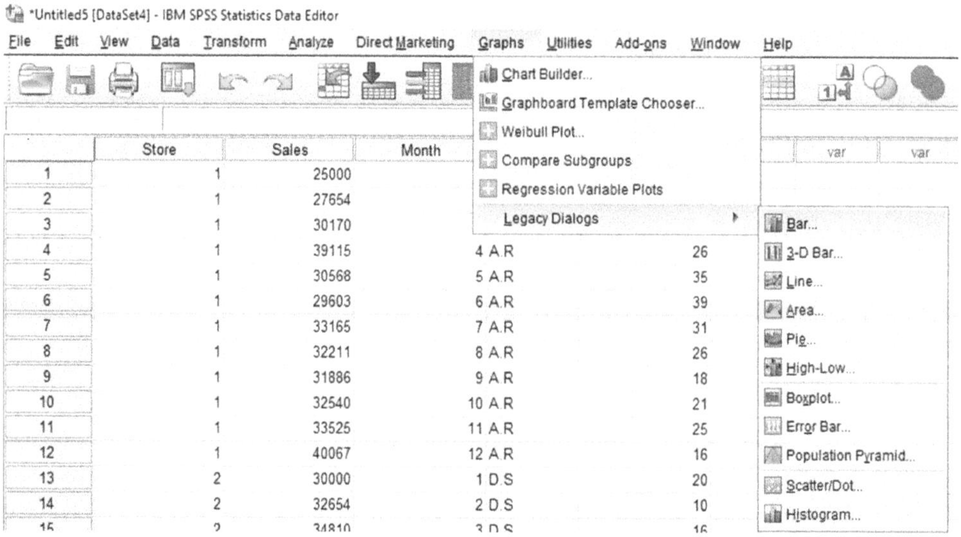

Figure 5.4: Creating a Frequency Bar Chart in SPSS

A frequency chart is similar to a bar chart but it is typically reserved to illustrate the percentage of the data represented by each of the values of the category variable. In our case, we can present the percentage of sales accounted for by each store. Using the pivot table that we calculated earlier, we will add a column that will show the

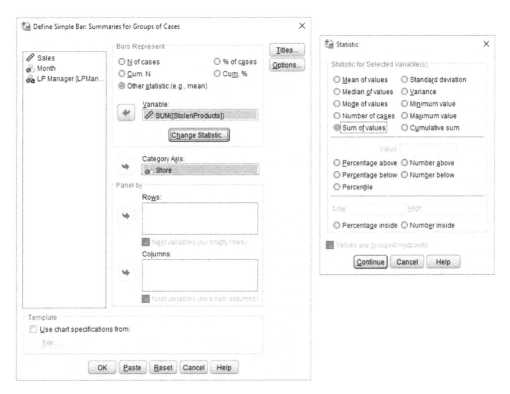

Figure 5.5: Creating a Bar Chart in SPSS

percentage of sales accounted by each store. The percentages should add up to 100%: see Table 5.3.

To create the chart in Excel, highlight the "Percentage of Sales" data and follow the same steps as previously mentioned: "Insert" → "Column" → "2-D Column." The results are illustrated in Figure 5.7.

Box-and-Whiskers Plots

Variable Type for Which This Is Appropriate: Numeric Variable

Box-and-whiskers plots are described in this section. They are a simple way to show the rough distribution of a variable by only using five points in the distribution; the minimum, the 25th percentile (also known as Q_1 or the 1st quartile), the 50th percentile (median), the 75th percentile (also known as Q_3 or the 3rd quartile), and the maximum. The box-and-whiskers plot is also another way to express central tendency and

➡ Graph

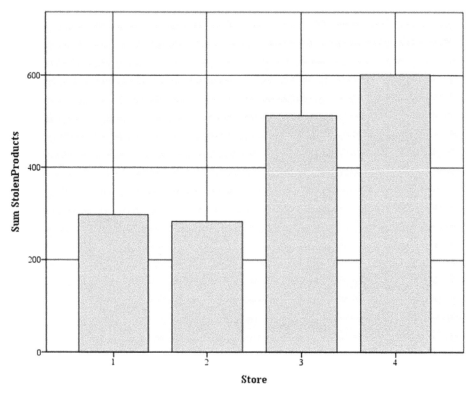

Table 5.3: Percentage of Sales by Store

Store	Total Sales	Percent of Sales
1	$ 385,504	20.50%
2	$ 441,504	23.47%
3	$ 613,364	32.61%
4	$ 440,504	23.42%

dispersion, as well as give a general representation of the overall distribution. Figure 5.8 shows a sample box-and-whiskers plot.

Creating a box-and-whiskers plot in Excel involves two steps; the creation of the five distribution points and then the creation of the plot itself. Creating the five distribution points is not complicated. One can use the min and max functions for the top and bottom

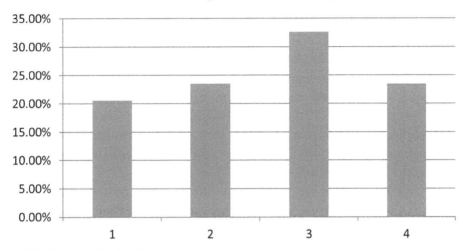

Figure 5.7: Frequency Chart in Excel

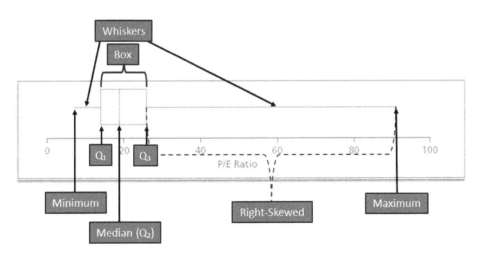

Figure 5.8: Box-and-Whiskers Plot

points, and the percentile function for the 25th, 50th, and 75th points. To create the plot we need to create another column of data that represents the difference between a value and the value that preceded it. For the minimum, the difference is the same as the minimum value. For the 25th percentile, the difference value is calculated as the 25th percentile value minus the minimum value. For the 50th percentile, the difference value is calculated as the 50th percentile value minus the 25th percentile value, and so forth (see Figure 5.9).

To create the plot, make sure the differences column is highlighted and go to "Insert" → "Column" → "2-D Column/Stacked Column." Then click on "Switch Row/Column." From that point, the rest is formatting. You can remove the fill for the lowest box, and add error bars (under layout) for the whiskers. The resulting plot for stores 1 and 2 is illustrated in Figure 5.10.

The summarization of the percentile values and the creation of the chart are done in the same step with SPSS. Once the data is in SPSS, to create the plot

	Store 1			Store 2		
		Difference			Difference	
Minimum	$ 25,000	$ 25,000		$ 30,000	$ 30,000	Formula: Min (range of values)
25th Percentile	$ 30,028	$ 5,028		$ 35,009	$ 5,009	Formula: Percentile (range of values,.25)
50th Percentile	$ 32,049	$ 2,021		$ 36,851	$ 1,842	Formula: Percentile (range of values,.5)
75th Percentile	$ 33,255	$ 1,206		$ 37,935	$ 1,084	Formula: Percentile (range of values,.75)
Maximum	$ 40,067	$ 6,812		$ 44,607	$ 6,672	Formula: Max (range of values)

Figure 5.9: Calculating Percentiles for Box-and-Whiskers Plot in Excel

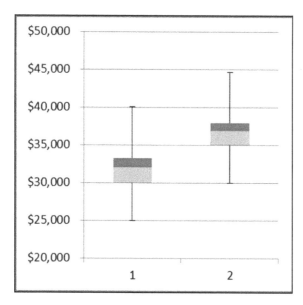

Figure 5.10: Box-and-Whiskers Plot in Excel

you should go to "Graphs" → "Legacy Dialogs" → "Boxplot," as illustrated in Figure 5.11.

Figure 5.12 shows the resulting plot. We removed the guidelines to improve the whiskers' visibility.

Histograms

Variable Type for Which This Is Appropriate: One Numeric Variable

A histogram is a chart produced to analyze the distribution of one numeric variable. To produce a histogram, a numeric variable is divided into sub-categories. In each sub-category, the frequency of observations is counted. The result is displayed in a chart that is identical to a frequency chart. Figure 5.13 illustrates a histogram of shrink amount. The values listed on the horizontal axis reflect the midpoint of the range where the frequency was obtained. For example, the category labeled 100,000 represents all shrink amounts between 75,000 and 125,000.

Using our fictitious sample data, we can create a histogram in SPSS rather easily. Again, go to "Graphs" → "Legacy Dialogs" → "Histogram." Then into the top box ("Variable"), move the variable of interest; in our case, sales. You can also choose to display the normal curve on top of your histogram to assess whether your distribution is normal (see Figure 5.14).

The resulting histogram is illustrated in Figure 5.15.

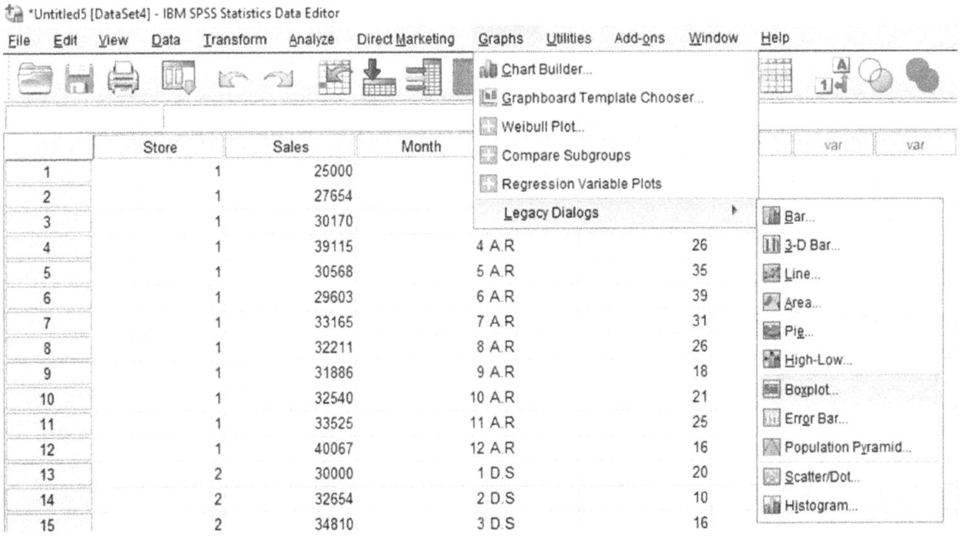

Figure 5.11: Creating a Box-and-Whiskers Plot in SPSS

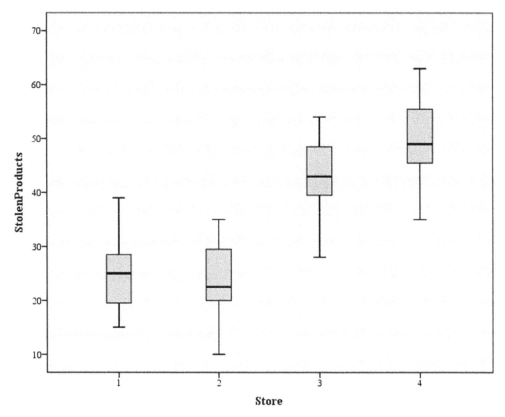

Scatter Diagrams

Variable Type for Which This Is Appropriate: Two Numeric Variables

Scatter diagrams are a way of illustrating the relationship between two numeric variables. For example, we may want to look at the relationship between employee theft and shrink amount (see Figure 5.16).

Using our fictitious data, we can create scatter plots in Excel and SPSS. Let's assume that we would like to investigate the relationship between monthly sales and the number of stolen products. In Excel, highlight both columns and then go to "Insert" → "Scatter" → "Only with Markers" (the first option). See Figure 5.17 for an illustration. The output is shown in Figure 5.18.

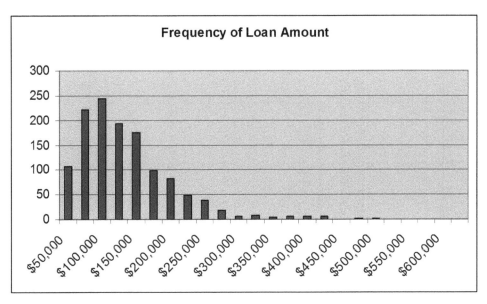

Figure 5.13: Histogram of Shrink

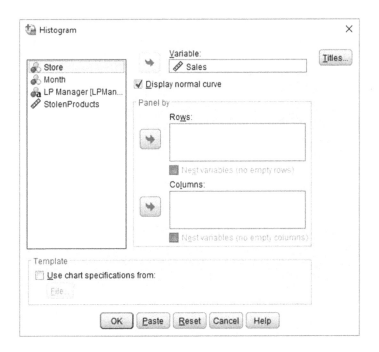

Figure 5.14: Histogram in SPSS

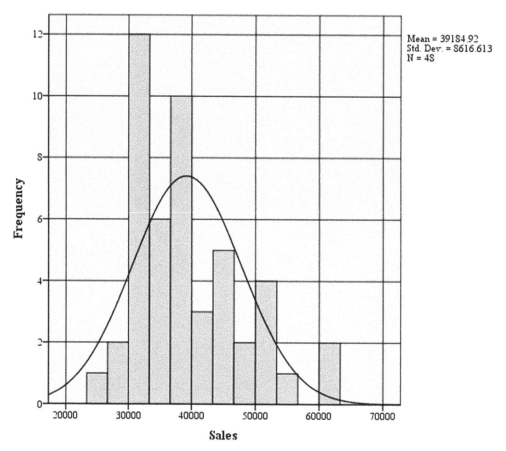

Mean = 39184.92
Std. Dev. = 8616.613
N = 48

Figure 5.15: Histogram Output in SPSS

To produce the same plot in SPSS, go to "Graphs" → "Legacy Dialogs" → "Scatter/ Dot" (Figure 5.19). Select "Simple Scatter," as shown in the left portion of Figure 5.20. In the next window, use the arrows to move one numeric variable to the y-axis ("StolenProducts") and one numeric variable to the x-axis ("Sales"). Then click on "OK."

The output is shown in Figure 5.21.

Line Charts

Variable Type for Which This Is Appropriate: One Numerical Variable

Line charts are a great way to illustrate trends in data. For example, which months have the highest number of stolen products? Has that increased when compared with

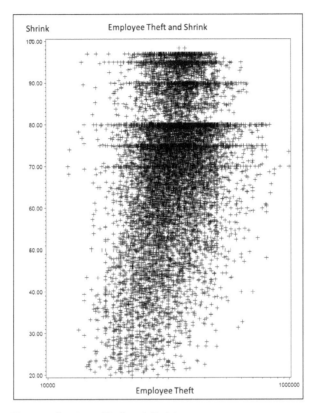

Figure 5.16: Scatter Diagram: Employee Theft and Shrink

Sales	Month	LP Manager	StolenProducts
25,000	1	A.R	25
27,654	2	A.R	15
30,170	3	A.R	21
39,115	4	A.R	26
30,568	5	A.R	35
29,603	6	A.R	39
33,165	7	A.R	31

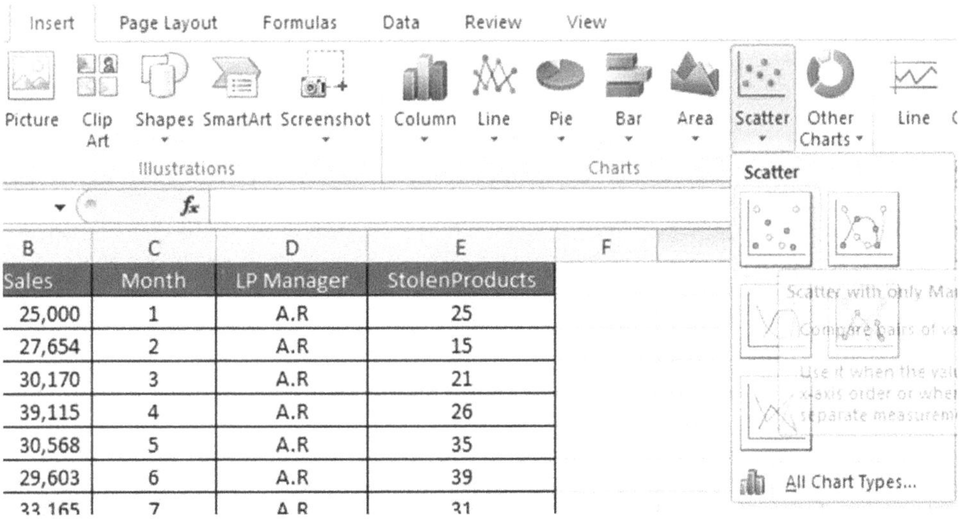

Figure 5.17: Creating a Scatter Plot in Excel

Monthly Sales and Stolen Products

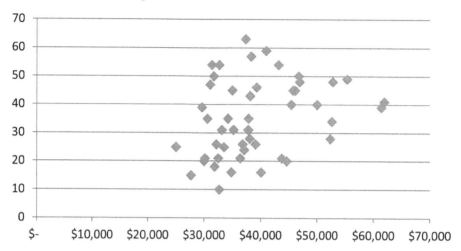

Figure 5.18: Scatter Plot Output in Excel

	Store	Sales	Month			var	var
1	1	25000					
2	1	27654					
3	1	30170					
4	1	39115	4 A R	26			
5	1	30568	5 A R	35			
6	1	29603	6 A R	39			
7	1	33165	7 A R	31			
8	1	32211	8 A R	26			
9	1	31886	9 A R	18			
10	1	32540	10 A R	21			
11	1	33525	11 A R	25			
12	1	40067	12 A R	16			
13	2	30000	1 D S	20			
14	2	32654	2 D S	10			
15	2	34810	3 D S	16			
16	2	43755	4 D S	21			

Figure 5.19: Creating a Scatter Plot in SPSS

the previous year? When comparing stolen product and sales, do they follow the same trend? How do the two loss prevention managers compare over time?

To answer these questions, we first need to summarize our data in Excel by using a pivot table. We will sum sales and stolen products by month and loss prevention man-

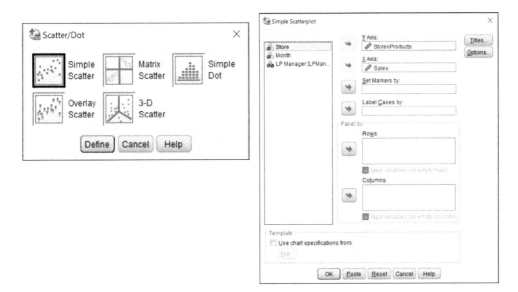

Figure 5.20: Creating a Scatter Plot in SPSS

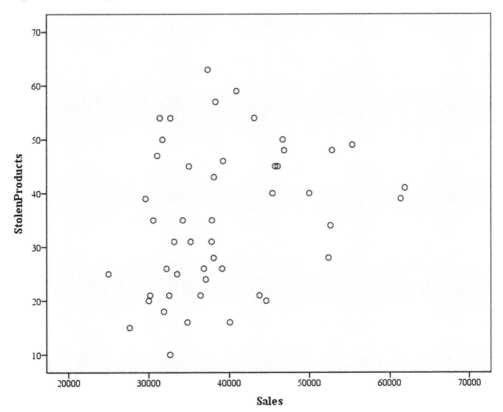

Figure 5.21: Scatter Plot Output in SPSS

ager (see Figure 5.22). We will then create a rate for stolen products as a percentage of sales (stolen products/sales). See Figure 5.23 for our pivot table and the final dataset.

Once the data has been summarized, we can start creating line charts to investigate the annual trends in sales and stolen products. Create the line charts by going to "Insert" → "Line" → "2-D Line."

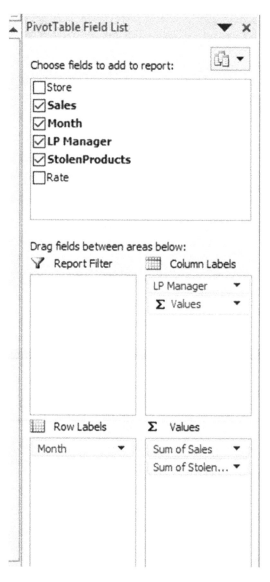

Figure 5.22: Creating a Pivot Table

Column Labels ⌄	A.R.		D.S.		Total Sum of Sales	Total Sum of StolenProducts
Row Labels ⌄	Sum of Sales	Sum of StolenProducts	Sum of Sales	Sum of StolenProducts		
1	75000	65	65000	65	140000	130
2	80008	43	70508	45	150516	88
3	82780	55	72920	59	155700	114
4	100470	65	90610	69	191080	134
5	83376	83	73516	88	156892	171
6	72726	93	71586	98	144312	191
7	79850	81	78710	90	158560	171
8	77942	71	68242	80	146184	151
9	77292	58	67492	68	144784	126
10	78600	66	68800	74	147400	140
11	88870	74	70770	82	159640	156
12	101954	57	83854	66	185808	123
Grand Total	998868	811	882008	884	1880876	1695

Month	A.R. LP Manager			D.S. LP Manager			Overall		
	Sales	Stolen Products	Stolen as a % of Sales	Sales	Stolen Products	Stolen as a % of Sales	Sales	Stolen Products	Stolen as a % of Sales
1	$ 75,000	65	0.09%	$ 65,000	65	0.10%	$ 140,000	130	0.09%
2	$ 80,008	43	0.05%	$ 70,508	45	0.06%	$ 150,516	88	0.06%
3	$ 82,780	55	0.07%	$ 72,920	59	0.08%	$ 155,700	114	0.07%
4	$ 100,470	65	0.06%	$ 90,610	69	0.08%	$ 191,080	134	0.07%
5	$ 83,376	83	0.10%	$ 73,516	88	0.12%	$ 156,892	171	0.11%
6	$ 72,726	93	0.13%	$ 71,586	98	0.14%	$ 144,312	191	0.13%
7	$ 79,850	81	0.10%	$ 78,710	90	0.11%	$ 158,560	171	0.11%
8	$ 77,942	71	0.09%	$ 68,242	80	0.12%	$ 146,184	151	0.10%
9	$ 77,292	58	0.08%	$ 67,492	68	0.10%	$ 144,784	126	0.09%
10	$ 78,600	66	0.08%	$ 68,800	74	0.11%	$ 147,400	140	0.09%
11	$ 88,870	74	0.08%	$ 70,770	82	0.12%	$ 159,640	156	0.10%
12	$ 101,954	57	0.06%	$ 83,854	66	0.08%	$ 185,808	123	0.07%

Figure 5.23: Resulting Pivot Table and Final Dataset

Figure 5.24 illustrates the monthly trend in sales and stolen products. You should note that the number of stolen products increases in April and May, peaks in June, and then decreases through the year. Sales, on the other hand, are relatively flat, with small increases in April and December.

It would be more interesting to examine the rate of stolen products as a percentage of sales (so: stolen products/sales). Figure 5.25 shows that rate; again, we see the increase in April and May and the peak in June.

Finally, we should examine whether the two loss prevention managers display similar behaviors. Is one loss prevention manager always outperforming the other? Do they both exhibit the similar seasonality trends we saw in Figures 5.24 and 5.25? Figure 5.26 illustrates the rate of stolen products as a percentage of sales for both loss prevention managers. It shows that both managers follow a similar trend, but A.R.'s rate is consistently lower than that of D.S. Also note that the distance between

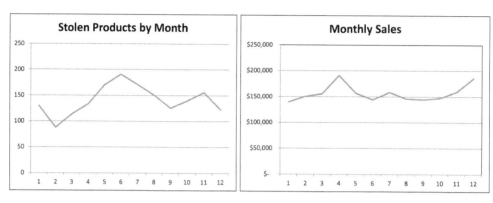

Figure 5.24: Trends in Sales and Stolen Products

Figure 5.25: Trend in Stolen Products as a Percentage of Sales

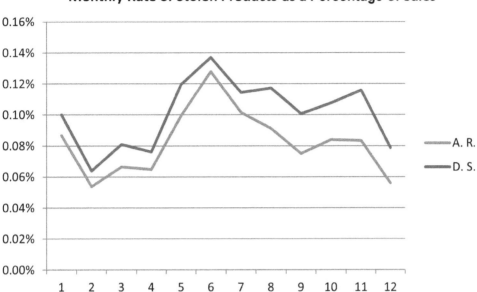

Monthly Rate of Stolen Products as a Percentage of Sales

Figure 5.26: Comparing Loss Prevention Managers

the lines has been increasing since July, so the performance differential is increasing. You should not assume the reason for this performance is due to the manager; it may be a geographical reason, products the stores carry, etc. Remember, correlation does not mean causation.

To create similar charts in SPSS, we will save the Excel pivot table information first, and open it in SPSS. Next, we need to create the "stolen products as a percentage of sales" variable for loss prevention managers A.R. and D.S. To do that, go to "Transform" → "Compute Variable," as illustrated in Figure 5.27. In the new window, under "Target Variable," enter the name of the new variable ("ARRatePerSales"). Then in the "Numeric Expression" box move the variables from the left using the arrow button. You can insert / and ★ using your keyboard or the buttons underneath the "Numeric Expression box": see Figure 5.28.

Now that we have all the data needed for the line chart, we can follow the same procedure as for the other charts: go to "Graphs" → "Legacy Dialogs" → "Line" → "Simple" and select the variables, as shown in Figure 5.29. Note that we changed the variable of interest by going into the "Change Statistic" button and selecting "Sum of values." The resulting line chart for D.S. is illustrated in Figure 5.30.

File	Edit	View	Data	Transform	Analyze	Direct Marketing	Graphs	Ut

Compute Variable...

Programmability Transformation...

Count Values within Cases...

Shift Values...

Recode into Same Variables...

Recode into Different Variables...

Automatic Recode...

Create Dummy Variables

Visual Binning...

Optimal Binning...

Anonymize Variables

Prepare Data for Modeling ▶

Rank Cases...

Date and Time Wizard...

Create Time Series...

Replace Missing Values...

Random Number Generators...

Run Pending Transforms   Ctrl+G

month   )SSa

| 1 |
| 2 |
| 3 |
| 4 |
| 5 |
| 6 |
| 7 |
| 8 |
| 9 |
| 10 |
| 11 |
| 12 |
| 13 |
| 14 |
| 15 |
| 16 |
| 17 |

Figure 5.27: Creating a Variable in SPSS

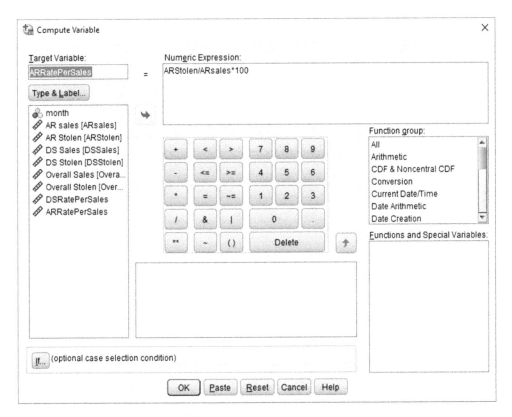

Figure 5.28: Creating a Variable in SPSS

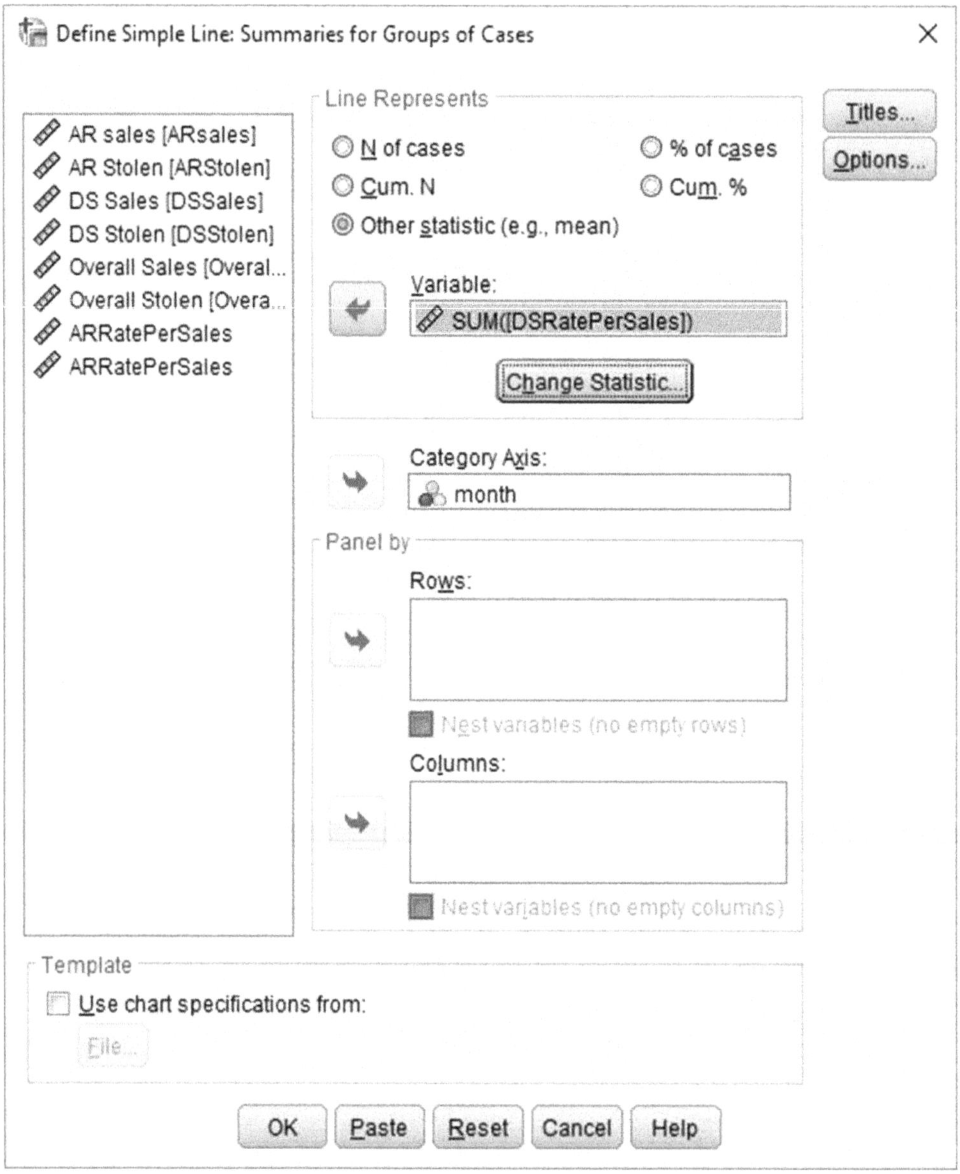

Define Simple Line: Summaries for Groups of Cases ✕

Line Represents

○ N of cases   ○ % of cases
○ Cum. N   ○ Cum. %
◉ Other statistic (e.g., mean)

Variable:
SUM([DSRatePerSales])

Change Statistic...

AR sales [ARsales]
AR Stolen [ARStolen]
DS Sales [DSSales]
DS Stolen [DSStolen]
Overall Sales [Overal...]
Overall Stolen [Overa...]
ARRatePerSales
ARRatePerSales

Titles...
Options...

Category Axis:
month

Panel by

Rows:

Nest variables (no empty rows)

Columns:

Nest variables (no empty columns)

Template
☐ Use chart specifications from:
File...

OK   Paste   Reset   Cancel   Help

Figure 5.29: Creating a Line Chart in SPSS

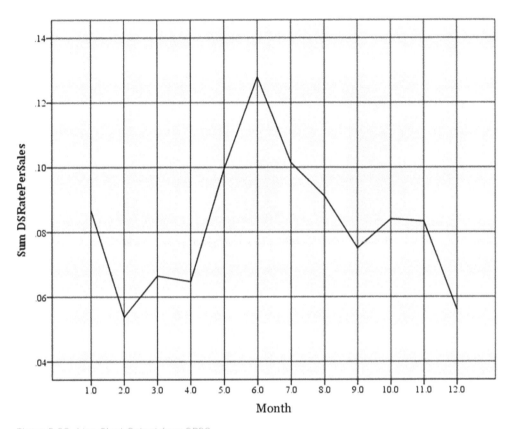

The Pareto chart is a combination chart that provides a typical frequency chart with a cumulative distribution chart. The cumulative distribution tells the percentage of the observations that are captured by looking at an increasing number of categories. The frequency chart is typically sorted in descending frequency order to demonstrate that the top few categories capture most of the data. Figure 5.31 demonstrates the chart using the distribution of product type.

The right hand vertical axis is used to display the cumulative percentage of product types from right to left. The cumulative distribution chart accumulates the percentages as we move from left to right along the category axis. Just considering health, we

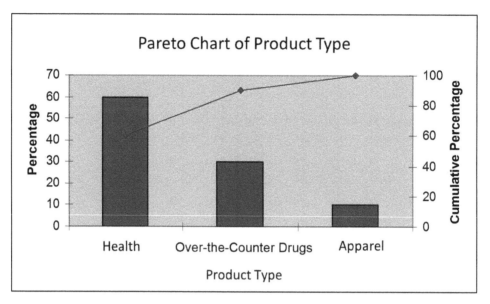

Figure 5.31: Pareto Chart of Product Type

capture 60% of the products; for health and over-the-counter drugs we capture 90% of the products; and including apparel we capture 100% of the products. The remainder of the graph is read just like the frequency charts.

A Few More Charting Options: Control Charts

A control chart is simply the plot of a numeric variable over time. The control chart can be used to identify when a process is becoming out of control. Figure 5.32 illustrates a plot of the number of burglaries each day.

The chart illustrates that the number of burglaries has escalated in recent days (days 17, 18, and 19). This indicates that additional staff may be needed to maintain security, as the number of burglaries is above normal fluctuations.

Conclusion

Understanding the concepts in this chapter, such as measures of central tendency and measures of dispersion, is a fundamental foundation for data analysis. Visualizing these concepts helps you explain data and trends in a way that is often obscured when just

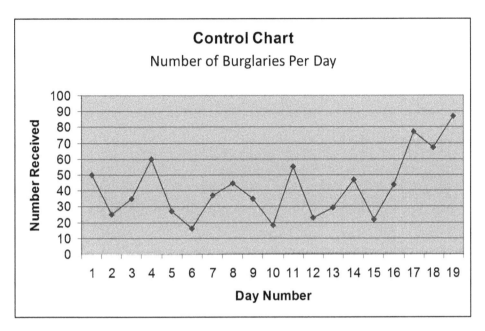

Figure 5.32: Control Chart of Burglary

looking at numbers. There are many visualization options in Excel and SPSS that can improve the understanding and presentation of your analysis.

Exercises

1. Use the sample data from Table 5.1 to create a bar chart that summarizes the number of stolen products by month. Create a bar chart that summarizes the number of stolen products by loss prevention manager. Create both bar charts in Excel and SPSS.
2. Use the sample data from Table 5.1 to create a frequency chart that illustrates the percentage of sales accounted for by month. Create the chart in Excel and SPSS.
3. Use the sample data from Table 5.1 to create a line chart showing the sum of stolen products by month for each of the stores.
4. When should you use a control chart?

Chapter Six

Inferential Statistics and Hypothesis Testing

> Statistics is the grammar of science.
>
> —*K. Pearson*

Introduction

This chapter presents an overview of inferential statistics and hypothesis testing. Many statistical techniques, along with examples of their use in analyzing retail data, are presented. While a few of the examples use some real anonymized data, most of the examples are fictional and will only be used to illustrate common situations encountered with retail data. Guidelines are provided to help understand which statistical technique is appropriate given certain circumstances. Inferential statistics takes analysis one step further by attempting to draw conclusions about the processes underlying the data. These concepts will be explored in more detail in the following sections.

What is Inferential Statistics?

When most people think about statistics, they think about data, graphs, charts, and the many other forms of data analysis you may conduct. These topics were all covered in previous chapters. While these things are an important part of statistics, the true nature of statistics is more about variation and the amount of variation you should expect in different situations. Variation is at the heart of the most fundamental concept in statistics, known as statistical inference. Statistical inference is the ability to infer things about the general population based on a sample of information.

To better understand the concept of statistical inference, consider the following example. Suppose you flip a quarter ten times in a row. How many times would you expect heads to come up? On average, assuming the quarter is fair, heads should come up about five times. However, at what point is it reasonable to question the quarter's fairness? If it landed on heads only three times, you might conclude that this is a reasonable outcome from time to time, based on random chance. However, how likely is that outcome? The true goal of statistics is to determine exactly those kinds of likelihoods, so that we can make educated guesses about what we cannot see (e.g., the true fairness of the coin). Using the binomial distribution, which was presented in previous

Table 6.1: Probability of a Coin Landing on Heads

Number of Heads	Probability
0	0.10%
1	0.98%
2	4.39%
3	11.72%
4	20.51%
5	24.61%
6	20.51%
7	11.72%
8	4.39%
9	0.98%
10	0.10%

chapters, we are able to calculate the probability that a certain number of heads will come up if the quarter is fair.

Table 6.1 shows the probability of flipping various numbers of heads with ten flips of the coin (assuming it is fair). The likelihood of flipping three heads out of ten is 11.72%. This means about one out of nine times, we should expect to get three heads. However, if we are really concerned with whether the coin is fair or not, we should be looking at the likelihood of an extreme throw. In that respect, 7 is equally as extreme as 3, and 0 through 2 and 8 through 10 are even more extreme. If we add up all of those percentages, we can make the following statement: there is a 34.38% chance of having three or fewer heads or seven or more heads.

A 34.38% chance seems pretty likely; therefore, with a toss of only three heads, it would not be reasonable to conclude that the quarter is not fair since an outcome like that is going to happen roughly one in three times. So, you should now ask yourself, what value is not likely? In general, for better or worse, the statistical community generally hones in on 1%, 5%, and 10% as thresholds for results extreme enough that we wish to question that fundamental assumption (in this case, the fairness of the coin). This is where the art in statistics emerges. There is no rule book for defining "not likely." In general, we assume that the quarter is fair, unless it can be proven not fair beyond a reasonable doubt. Here are some key numbers in our quarter flipping exercise and the likelihood of various outcomes:

- At 2 (or 8), there is a 10.94% chance of having a number of heads that extreme or more extreme.
- At 1 (or 9), there is a 2.16% chance of having a number of heads that extreme or more extreme.
- At 0 (or 10), there is a 0.2% chance of having a number of heads that extreme or more extreme.

The conclusion from this exercise is that we should begin to question the fairness of the quarter when we get 1 or 9 heads (which should occur about 2.15% of the time) or when we get 0 or 10 heads (which should happen about 0.2% of the time). Based on the key thresholds mentioned before of 1%, 5%, and 10%, these are the only values that cross the boundaries.

Populations and Samples

Expanding on the example in the previous section with the ten flips of the quarter, inferential statistics seeks to determine the variation of the statistics that were presented in the prior chapter (e.g., mean, median, variance) and many more. Specifically, one of the primary goals of the discipline of statistics is to determine the probability distribution of each of those statistics (i.e., how much fluctuation to expect in those statistics) so that a researcher can determine the significance of certain research results.

At the heart of inferential statistics is the concept of a sample and a population. A population is considered the universe of all possible outcomes. A sample is just a small representation of the population. One simple example of a population is the entire United States and of a sample is a selection of people from that population. If the sample is drawn completely at random, then statistical theory tells us what we may infer about the population only from information in the sample. If we measure the entire population and calculate a value, such as a mean or median, we do not refer to this as a statistic; rather, we would call it a parameter of the population (see Figure 6.1). When we take a sample and compute the mean, we would call it the mean of the sample; it is an estimate of the mean of the entire population.

We would prefer to measure the entire population, but it is typically infeasible because of associated cost and time constraints. Even in retail, where you can typically get all the data, even that is considered a sample, because we only see one representation of how the customers could act or shop in a certain time window. If we were able to randomly replay an entire year of a retailer's activity, we would probably see different customers, different sales, different returns, and different patterns of shoplifting. Therefore, samples of data only produce an estimate, along with some associated error,

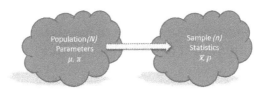

Figure 6.1: Sample Statistics and Population Parameters

for the population in which we are interested. Depending on the size of your sample, you can use the data and statistics calculated from the sample to make inferences or generalizations about the population at varying degrees of accuracy. For example, you could assess citizen's attitudes toward crime and crime rates using a random sample. In this case, it would be impossible to survey all US citizens to assess their attitudes toward crime.

Descriptive Statistics

Descriptive statistics are generally used to describe what the data shows. Descriptive statistics allow you to reduce your data to a few essential values, which express information about the aggregate of all observations. In other words, descriptive statistics allow you to represent some aspect of a distribution of a variable. Descriptive statistics can be split into two major categories: measures of central tendency and measures of dispersion or variability. Measures of central tendency and dispersion are called descriptive statistics because they provide a convenient way to describe and compare sets of data.

Descriptive statistics can also be used for statistical inference, which allows you to generalize from a limited number of observations in a sample to the entire population. Inferential statistics is used to reach conclusions or inferences about the population from which a sample was drawn. Inferential statistics may also be used to assess the probability that an observed difference between groups happened by chance. Inference is a major goal of scientific research.

Distribution of the Data vs. the Distribution of a Statistic

Statistical inference is typically interested in making conclusions about a statistic of a population but *not* each of the data elements in the population. For example, if we say that basketball players are on average taller than soccer players, we are not saying that every basketball player is taller than every soccer player. Similarly, if we conclude that stores with the return counters in the back of the store, on average, have higher shrink than stores with return counters in the front of the store, we are not concluding that every store with a return counter in the back of the store would have a higher shrink rate than every store with a return counter in the front of the store. Therefore, to make conclusions about the average shrink rate or height, we need to know the expected variability in the average, similar to how we needed to understand the variability in the flipping of a coin.

To illustrate the difference, consider the following simple example. Suppose we had a population of staff members at a retailer's store with the following ages: 27, 28, 29, 29, 29, 29, 29, 30, 30, 31, 31, 32, 32, 34, 34, 35, 35, 37, 38, 38, 38, 38, 39, 40, 40, 40, 41, 41, 41, 42, 43, 45, 47, 49. There are 34 ages with a mean age of 35.9. A histogram illustrating the distribution of the ages is shown in Figure 6.2.

You should note that the distribution does not look symmetric or bell-shaped and is slightly skewed to the right.

Now, suppose we did not know the ages of our employees and we were only able to use a sample of five of the employees to get an estimate of the average age. How

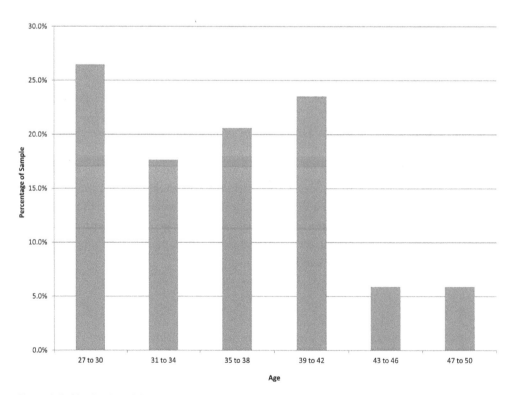

Figure 6.2: Distribution of Ages

close could we get to the 35.9 value that is the true average? To determine the answer to this question, we ran a computer simulation on the data and took 1000 random samples of size 5 from the data and computed the average of each of the 1000 samples. Figure 6.3 shows the distribution of the average.

The averages varied from about 30 to 42 with almost all of the simulation's averages within 6 years of the true average. You should note that while the population's distribution of ages in Figure 6.2 was not symmetric and was not bell-shaped, the distribution of the average of the ages shown in Figure 6.3 is bell-shaped and symmetric. The shift from Figure 6.2 to Figure 6.3 occurs because the first one is of the raw ages and the second one is of the mean of the ages. The mean's distribution will always approximate a normal distribution (this concept is known as the central limit theorem and will always hold, regardless of the underlying data's distribution). Based on the simulations, with a sample of size five, we know that the average obtained from the sample will probably be within 6 years of the true average (this is known as a margin of error and is related to a confidence interval, which will be covered in the next section).

As the sample size increases, we should expect our margin of error to decrease. Figure 6.4 represents the same type of simulation with sample sizes of 10, 15, and 20, compared with the sample size of 5.

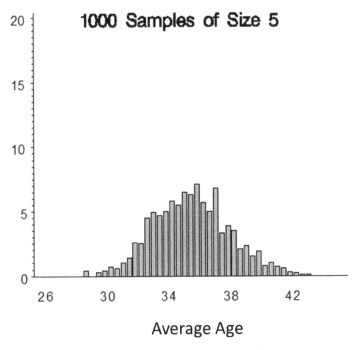

Figure 6.3: Distribution of Average Age of 1000 Random Samples of Five

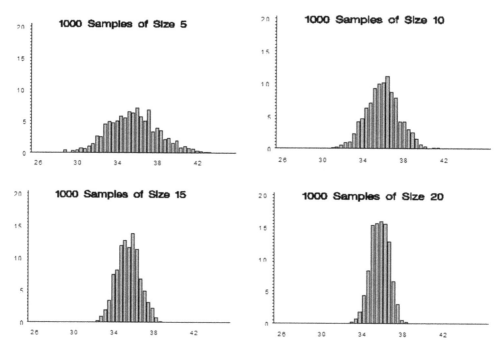

Figure 6.4: Distribution of Simulated Average Age Given Different Sample Sizes

You should note that, as the sample size increases, the variability in the histograms decreases. In addition, the decrease in variability represents a decrease in the margin of error in our estimates. For example, with a sample size of 20, almost all of the estimates from all 1000 simulated samples were within about 2 years of the true average age.

These simulations are provided for illustrative purposes only and you will not need to make such simulations to determine the statistical significance of a result. Based on statistical theory, the distributions above are known mathematically so that we can compute exactly the margin of error to expect with any sample size. Once we know the distribution for a statistic, we can determine its margin of error (and confidence interval) and also compare statistics between two groups (like our stores with the return counters in the front and in the back of the store).

Confidence Intervals and Margin of Error

By now, you know that we do not need to look at the whole population to find out key facts about the population; we only need to take a sample. However, when we take a sample, we lose some accuracy, as shown in the last section; the sample statistic is not equivalent to the population parameter and only provides an estimate. In statistics, the accuracy of an estimate is represented through a confidence interval. A confidence interval is a range that surrounds the statistic to represent its accuracy. The designated statistic plus or minus the margin of error is called the confidence interval. The margin of error is the range of values below and above the sample statistic in a confidence interval. Typically, it is written as 30 ± 2, which represents a confidence interval from 28 to 32. The value of "2," which is the distance from the statistic to the ends of the interval, is the margin of error of the statistic.

To interpret a confidence interval, remember that the sample information is random and that each sample gives us a different sample estimate and a different confidence interval. However, even though the results vary, statistical theory tells us how much variation is typical, which allows us to compute the confidence interval and margin of error and determine a likely range for the true population parameter.

The confidence interval is simply a measure of how accurate your sample statistic is (i.e., how close it is to the population parameter). The confidence interval is necessary because few organizations have the resources to survey the entire population and, in retail, the customer's behavior in a time window can be thought of as a sample of the behavior. Therefore, it is essential to know how accurately the results of the sample reflect the population. The confidence interval translates the variability in regards to your sample into a statement of how much confidence we can have in the results.

Confidence intervals are constructed at a confidence level. Confidence intervals are usually calculated so that the percentage of confidence is 95%. Why 95 times out of 100? A number like 95% is chosen so that we can be very sure, but not 100% certain. To be 100% certain, the confidence interval would be extremely wide. To be 95% sure (which some may say is beyond a reasonable doubt) provides for a reasonably wide confidence interval that captures almost all of the possible values for the parameter. If independent samples are taken repeatedly from the same population, and a confidence interval is calculated for each sample, then a certain percentage (95%) of the intervals will include the unknown population parameter or true mean. The width of the confidence interval gives us some indication of how certain we are about the unknown population parameter. Confidence limits are the lower and upper boundaries of a confidence interval (i.e., the values that define the range of a confidence interval). A confidence interval is a range of values, derived from sample statistics, that is likely to contain the value of an unknown population parameter.

Confidence Interval for a Mean

A 95% confidence interval for a mean is 1.96 (roughly 2) standard deviations from the statistic. The standard deviation is of the *mean* though and *not* the original observations.

The math behind a standard deviation of a mean is similar to the math behind the standard deviation of the underlying variable, but there is a factor in the equation that makes the standard deviation decrease as the number of observations increases. So, you can think of the margin of error at the 95% confidence interval as being equal to two standard deviations in your sample away from the statistic (see Figure 6.5).

The standard deviation of the mean (often referred to as a standard error) is the standard deviation of the observations divided by the square root of the sample size. The standard error is the standard deviation of the sampling distribution of the mean; it is the amount we expect the sample mean to vary for a given sample size due to random sampling error. It is important to note that the standard error is part of the margin of error and is used in the calculation of a confidence interval. The formula for the standard error of the sample mean is

$$SE_{\bar{x}} = \frac{S}{\sqrt{n}}$$

6.1

In this formula for the standard error, the symbols denote:

- $\bar{x}$ = the sample mean (average);
- n = the sample size;
- S = the sample standard deviation.

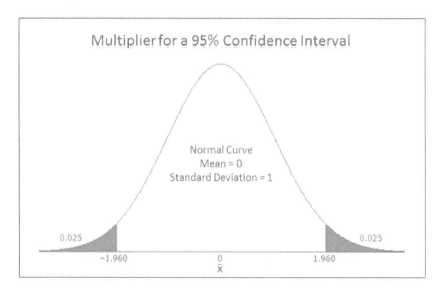

The formula for the $(1 - \alpha)\%$ confidence interval, when n is sufficiently large (about 100), is

$$\bar{x} \pm z_\alpha \text{SE}_{\bar{x}} \qquad\qquad 6.2$$

The margin of error in the formula is:

$$z_\alpha \text{SE}_{\bar{x}} \qquad\qquad 6.3$$

In these formulas, the symbols denote:

- $\bar{x}$ is the sample mean;
- z_α = the critical value from the standard normal distribution with confidence level α;
- $\text{SE}_{\bar{x}}$ = the standard error.

Microsoft Excel can be used to look up various values of z_α. Figure 6.6 illustrates three common values of z_α and shows the formula in Excel that can be used to compute other values.

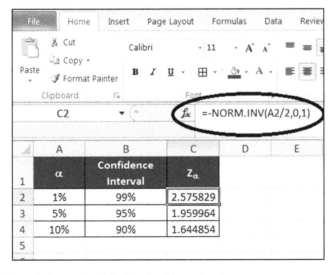

Figure 6.6: Excel Formula for *z* value at Certain Confidence Levels

The margin of error is the standard deviation of the raw observations divided by the square root of the sample size. Thus, a sample of size 400 has a margin of error of 1/20 of the standard deviation. A sample of size 100 would have a margin of error of 1/10 of the standard deviation. Therefore, a sample four times the size has a confidence interval that is one half as wide.

The margin of error and the level of confidence are tied together. A better (i.e., narrower) margin of error may be traded for a lesser level of confidence, or a greater level of confidence may be obtained by tolerating a larger margin of error (see Figure 6.7). The example has a sample size of 100, a mean of 100, and a standard deviation of 15.

The confidence level represents the chance that confidence intervals created in this way from repeated experiments will contain the true parameter 95% of the time. If we would like to have only 90% confidence, this will result in a narrower interval, but less confidence in the results.

Let's look at an example. Suppose that a data analyst is concerned with obtaining an estimate of the average number of burglaries in a certain retail chain. The analyst takes a sample of 50 stores, determines the number of burglaries in each store, and computes a sample mean of 24 and a standard deviation of 10. We wish to estimate the population parameter or true mean with a 95% confidence interval. The formula for a confidence interval is $\pm E$, where E is the margin of error. Furthermore, to calculate a 95% confidence interval, we use the following formula:

$$\text{confidence interval} = \bar{x} \pm z \times \frac{S}{\sqrt{n}}$$

6.4

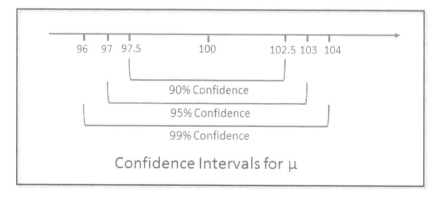

Figure 6.7: Confidence Intervals

* Standard error (SE_M) =
  o 10 (standard deviation) / 7.07107 (square root of the sample size)
    * 1.414
* Margin of error =
  o 1.96 (z score) × standard error
    * 2.771859
* Lower limit =
  o Mean $- z_{0.95}SE_M$
    * 24 $-$ 1.96 × 1.41
* Upper limit =
  o Mean $+ z_{0.95}SE_M$
    * 24 + 1.96 × 1.41
* 95% confidence interval $-$ 21.23 to 26.77

We are 95% confident that the true mean (μ) falls between 21.23 and 26.77. If you repeatedly obtained samples of size 50, then 95% of the resulting confidence intervals would contain the population mean. Keep in mind that as the sample size increases, the margin of error decreases, meaning that the larger your sample the more likely you are to better estimate the population parameter. This is true because n, the sample size, appears in the denominator. As an experiment, repeat the example using sample sizes of 100 and 1000.

Small Samples and *t* Distribution

If we are constructing a confidence interval for a smaller sample ($n < 100$), then we substitute a t distribution for the normal distribution. The t distribution is similar to the normal distribution, in that it is bell-shaped and symmetric about a mean of 0, but it tends to be heavier (i.e., have more observations) in the tails. The t distribution is defined by the number of degrees of freedom, which represents the sample size minus 1. As the number of degrees of freedom (sample size) increases, the t distribution becomes indistinguishable from the standard normal distribution.

The t distribution obtains its additional variance because we are not only estimating the mean, but we are also estimating the standard deviation. Since the standard deviation is part of the confidence interval equation, the t distribution takes into account that smaller sample sizes are going to introduce an additional source of variance with the estimation process for the standard deviation. We construct confidence intervals in the same way for small samples, but we use a t distribution in lieu of the z distribution.

The formula for the $(1 - \alpha)\%$ confidence interval, when n is small (less than 100), is:

$$t_{n-1,\alpha}$$

6.5

The margin of error in the formula is:

6.6

$$t_{n-1,} \pm SE_{\bar{x}}$$

In these formulas, the symbols denote:

- $\bar{x}$ is the sample mean;
- $t_{n-1,\alpha}$ = the critical value from the t distribution with confidence level α;
- $SE_{\bar{x}}$ = the standard error.

Figure 6.8 illustrates how values for the t distribution can be computed in Excel and also shows some of the more popular values when $n = 100$. Unlike the normal distribution, the t distribution values rely on the sample size. Values of the t distribution are obtained from the function "T.INV()" in Excel. The first argument is $\alpha/2$ and the second argument is the number of observations minus 1.

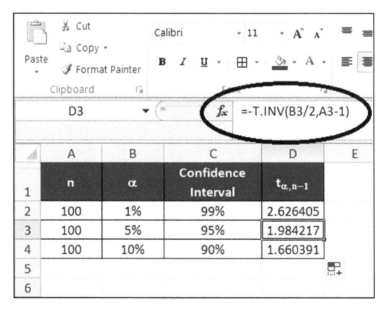

Figure 6.8: *t* distribution and Critical Values

Hypothesis Testing

A key element of inferential statistics is hypothesis testing. An example of a hypothesis that we may want to test is:

H_0 Men and women have equal probabilities of being hired for loss prevention.
H_1 Men and women do not have equal probabilities of being hired for loss prevention.

In this example, H_0 is known as the null hypothesis and H_1 is known as the alternative hypothesis. Based on data in our sample, we would like to say whether we think H_0 or H_1 is correct. In testing, we typically try to prove that there is an effect. At the end of the experiment, we will conclude that we should reject the null hypothesis in favor of the alternate hypothesis or we will fail to reject the null hypothesis. We never say that we are accepting the null hypothesis, only that our experiment failed to reject the null hypothesis.

For example, consider the loss prevention procedure of allowing only one employee to have the keys to a locked display and measuring the results of lower shrink. The statement about the reduction to shrink by limiting the key to only one employee would be stated in H_1. Alternatively, the null hypothesis (H_0) would be that there is no impact on shrink from the procedure. Our goal is to find enough proof to reject the null hypothesis and accept the alternative hypothesis, H_1, which would prove that limiting the key to only one employee reduces shrink.

Type I and Type II Errors

During a hypothesis test, two errors can occur. We could conclude that H_0 is true when H_1 is true or we could conclude that H_1 is true when H_0 is true. Table 6.2 illustrates these errors.

Hypothesis testing is about deciding which hypothesis is true, while trying to minimize Type I and Type II errors. When it comes to testing loss prevention

Table 6.2: Two Types of Error

Our Decision	Truth	
	H_0 *is Actually True*	H_1 *is Actually True*
We Say H_1 is True	Type I Error	Good Decision
We Say H_0 is True	Good Decision	Type II Error

programs, the null hypothesis (H_0) is usually saying that the program did not work and the alternative hypothesis (H_1) is saying that the program did work. Minimizing Type I errors is equivalent to "innocent until proven guilty" or "don't say a program works until you are very sure it actually works." Minimizing Type II errors is saying that you don't want to say that a loss prevention program does not work when it really does.

Table 6.3 is an analogy to court trial and jury. The jury is essentially making a hypothesis test.

In a jury trial, the jury unconsciously attempts to control Type I error by applying the criteria that the criminal must be found guilty "beyond a reasonable doubt." Therefore, we avoid sending an innocent person to prison. We could look at it the other way around and send everyone to jail who was reasonably suspicious. Then we would be controlling for Type II error. Just as controlling for Type II error in a jury trial is not the standard, neither is controlling for Type II error in hypothesis testing in other settings. In other words, we always try to minimize Type I error.

Test Statistics

Test statistics are the fundamental value used in testing hypotheses. For each statistical method, there are well-known test statistics that allow us to test hypotheses about our population. These test statistics are rooted in statistical theory, which determines which statistical distribution the test statistics follow. Often, several different test statistics can take on the same distribution in various situations. For example, the test statistic for independence in a contingency table and the test statistic for a significant parameter in the logistic regression model both have a chi-square distribution. In fact, many different tests will use a chi-square distribution for their test statistic.

Table 6.3: Analogy to the Jury System

Our Decision	*Truth*	
	The Person did not Commit the Crime	*The Person did Commit the Crime*
We Said the Person did Commit the Crime	Type I Error	Good Decision
We Said the Person did not Commit the Crime	Good Decision	Type II Error

Confidence Level and Statistical Power

Type I and Type II errors are connected to two important concepts in statistics; confidence level and statistical power. The probability of a Type I error is known as the confidence level of the test and is usually set to 1%, 5%, or 10%. This is the same as the confidence level for a confidence interval. During an experiment, we also want to minimize the probability of Type II error. 100% minus the probability of Type II error is known as the power of the statistical test. In other words, the power is how likely we are to reject the null hypothesis, assuming that it is actually false.

Using a concrete example, if EAS tags actually reduced shrink, then this would be the likelihood that our statistical test would show that the EAS tags actually reduced shrink. If the probability of Type II error were zero, this would mean that the power of our test was 100%. Power is adjusted in an experiment by increasing the sample size used in the experiment. The larger the sample size, the larger the power we can achieve. However, it is usually not feasible to have an unlimited sample size.

The sample size requirements are usually also controlled by the amount of difference we are trying to detect. For example, suppose we are trying to detect that a quarter is fair or unfair. If we are trying to detect whether a quarter is not fair by 10% or more, we will only require about 100 flips. However, if we are trying to detect a 1% deviation from being fair, it would take more than 10,000 coin flips to say there was a statistically significant difference that is not reasonable by chance alone (see Table 6.4 for the range of the percentages of heads on flipping a fair coin, based on simulated coin flip experiments and a hypothetical rate of 50% in the sample).

What Is a *p* Value?

Many of you, prior to reading this book, will have heard the phrase "*p* value." A *p* value is generated during a hypothesis test by using the distribution of a test statistic.

Table 6.4: 95% Confidence Intervals Showing the Percentage of "Heads" on Flipping a Fair Coin

Sample Size	Lower 95% Confidence Limit	Upper 95% Confidence Limit
50	0.361	0.639
100	0.402	0.598
500	0.456	0.544
1,000	0.469	0.531
10,000	0.490	0.510
100,000	0.497	0.533

The p value represents the probability of a Type I error given that H_0 is true. In layman's terms it is "the probability of observing the data we observed, given that H_0 is true." This means that small values for the p value lead us to believe that H_1 is true and that H_0 is not true; however, this can rarely be known with certainty. The p value will always take on values between 0 and 1. A standard cut-off to conclude that "the data tends to indicate that H_0 is not true" is a p value less than 0.05. This can be interpreted as: "there is less than a 5% chance that this data will occur if the null hypothesis is true."

Similarities Between Hypothesis Testing and Confidence Intervals

Confidence intervals and hypothesis testing are closely related. Confidence intervals tell you the likely range for values in the population, whereas hypothesis testing tests whether the true value in the population is equal to a value or range of values. It turns out that if the confidence interval does not contain the null hypothesis H_0, then we would reject the null hypothesis.

SAS Example

Consider the following example. A company claims that their new loss prevention tool will last for 9000 hours (call this H_0). Conversely, we have an alternative hypothesis that the tool does not last 9000 hours (call this H_1). A research group decided to test the claim. The group randomly selects 36 of the loss prevention tools. The data from this sample shows that the mean life of the loss prevention tool is 8000 hours, with a standard deviation of 1014 hours (see Figure 6.9). The following is an example in SAS to calculate this confidence interval:

```
proc univariate data=lp_tool cibasic;
    var lp;
run;
```

In this SAS code, the first line identifies the procedure we wish to use (proc univariate), the data we are using for the calculation (lp_tool), and the statistics we want SAS to produce (i.e., cibasic). The word "cibasic" in the data line will produce a confidence interval for the variable being analyzed (i.e., "lp"). The second row identifies the variable of interest ("lp"). The variable "lp" is an abbreviated name for the loss prevention tool that is being analyzed. The third row says "run," which tells SAS to execute the procedure. Figure 6.9 shows the results and SAS output.

```
                    The SAS System

                The UNIVARIATE Procedure
                    Variable:  lp

        Basic Confidence Limits Assuming Normality

    Parameter            Estimate     95% Confidence Limits

    Mean                   8000          7657        8343
    Std Deviation          1014
    Variance            1028571
```

Figure 6.9: SAS Output

Does this confidence interval support the claim for the company's new technology? Now, it can be seen in Figure 6.9 under "95% Confidence Limits" that the range is from 7657 to 8343. Furthermore, 9000 does not lie within the range of the 95% confidence interval, so we can reject the null hypothesis (H_0) at the 0.05 level in favor of the alternative hypothesis (H_1). That is, the loss prevention tool does not last 9000 hours, as purported by the company's claims.

What Is an Alpha Level?

An alpha level is calculated using the following formula: $\alpha = 1 - $ (confidence level/100) or confidence level $+ \alpha = 1$. Using a 95% confidence interval, we achieve an alpha level of 0.05 (see Figure 6.10).

We think of an alpha level as a significance level for our statistical tests. For example, if the results of our statistical test have a *p* value (i.e., probability of obtaining an effect) that is less than an alpha level of 0.05, then we can say that we are confident that our results are not due to chance (i.e., there is a true difference). Another way to interpret this is that if we conducted our study 100 times, we would get the same results 95 out of 100 times.

Some General Guidelines for Hypothesis Testing

As we have said, hypothesis testing works similar to the court system, "innocent until proven guilty." In hypothesis testing, H_0 is considered innocent and H_1 is considered guilty. Just as we would not like to send an innocent person to jail, we would not want to claim that a program works when it does not.

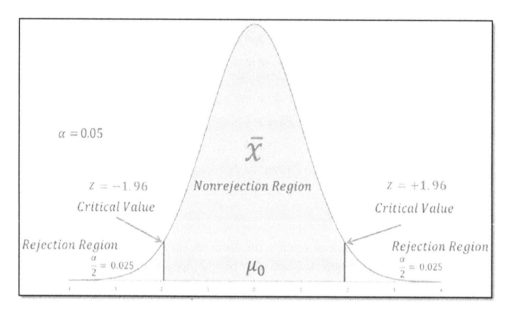

α = 0.05

z = −1.96
Critical Value

Nonrejection Region

$\bar{x}$

z = +1.96
Critical Value

Rejection Region
$\frac{a}{2}$ = 0.025

μ_0

Rejection Region
$\frac{a}{2}$ = 0.025

Figure 6.10: Alpha and Confidence Levels

Let's review the hypothesis testing from a few sections ago, regarding the hiring rates based on sex.

H_0 Men and women have equal probabilities of being hired for loss prevention.
H_1 Men and women do not have equal probabilities of being hired for loss prevention.

Controlling for Type I error, we do not want to claim that the retailer is discriminating based on sex if this is not the case. If we have a sample with a 70% hiring rate for women, and an 80% hiring rate for men, does this lead to the conclusion that the retailer discriminated against women? It might support that claim if certain conditions are met, but not necessarily.

The following three criteria are generally needed to support the claim:

1. Your sample needs to be representative of the population.
2. The sample needs to be of a sufficient size to eliminate random fluctuations that may occur in the data.
3. Other variables have been considered that may have an impact on the hypothesis.

If the data is not representative of the population, then the claim would be hard to substantiate. Suppose, for example, that more unqualified women (who are, therefore, more likely to be rejected) were sampled from the population; the sample would not represent the overall rate. This would bias the results toward H_1 even if H_0 were true.

Suppose the sample comprised ten men and ten women. If seven of the women were hired and eight of the men were hired, we would get the aforementioned hired rates, but the numbers of actual individuals hired differ only by 1. This sample would not be large enough to justify the claims. Conversely, if there were 10,000 men and 10,000 women, we would certainly have enough observations to make some statement about the hiring rate in the population, as long as the other criteria are satisfied. Statistical theory tells us the amount of variation expected from various sample sizes that will determine the sample size needed to say that 70% is statistically different from 80%.

Suppose the sample comprises 15,000 men and 15,000 women and our hiring rates were 80% and 70% respectively. Then one might conclude that women are not treated equally to men. Table 6.5 illustrates this situation.

Table 6.5: Hired and Nonhired Rates by Sex

	Men	*Women*
Number Applying	15,000	15,000
Number Hired	12,000	10,500
Number Not Hired	3,000	4,500
Hired Rate	80%	70%
Nonhired Rate	20%	30%

This conclusion would not be valid if there were another variable or variables that were related to the hiring rate and had an unequal sex distribution. For example, suppose that 2/3 of women applied for an in-store loss prevention analytics position and 1/3 of women applied for an armed security guard position. Further, suppose that 1/3 of men applied for the loss prevention analytics position and 2/3 of men applied for the armed security guard position. Tables 6.6 and 6.7 illustrate that there is no sex discrimination if we look at the results by type of loss prevention position.

Tables 6.6 and 6.7 show that the hiring rates are identical by type of job, but women apply more to the analytics position, which has a higher rejection rate. Therefore, the overall rejection rate for women is higher.

This is a classic example of why one should be careful when drawing conclusions about the population based on a sample without having prior knowledge about other relationships that exist in the data. Even if the data illustrates discrimination after analysis by job type, there may be other variables that could account for the differences in hired rates.

Table 6.6: Hired Rates by Sex for Loss Prevention Analyst Position

LP Analytics

	Men	Women
Number Applying	5,000	10,000
Number Hired	3,000	6,000
Number Not Hired	2,000	4,000
Hired Rate	60%	60%
Nonhired Rate	40%	40%

Table 6.7: Hired Rates by Sex for Armed Security Guard Position

Armed Guard

	Men	Women
Number Applying	10,000	5,000
Number Hired	9,000	4,500
Number Not Hired	1,000	500
Hired Rate	90%	90%
Nonhired Rate	10%	10%

Once criterion 1 and criterion 3 are satisfied, we can move on to hypothesis testing. Hypothesis testing essentially tests criterion 2, which asks, "Is there enough data to say that the population exhibits the relationship we see in the sample, or are we just seeing random fluctuations?"

Conclusions

In summary, this chapter provides the concepts and theories that create the foundation for statistical analysis. Statistics is grounded in the general theory of hypothesis testing and Type I and Type II errors. Understanding inferential statistics is key, since we rarely have the resources to study an entire population. Understanding and examining variable distributions is important, since many statistics rely on assumptions regarding variable distributions (see Chapter 8). Moreover, assessing distributions uncovers anomalies in the data.

Confidence intervals consider the variation in the population and give us an estimate for where the true population parameter lies. They provide a level of confidence in generalizing our results. Significance (alpha) levels and p values are closely linked to confidence intervals. If your alpha level is 0.05, then your confidence level is 95%. One confidence interval is equal to two margins of error, which is equal to four standard errors. If you want to decrease your margin of error by half, you need to quadruple your sample size. The standard error is the amount we expect the sample statistic to vary for a given sample size as a result of random sampling error.

The concepts and theories can be applied to many different statistics and situations in analytics. In the next chapter, we will dive into many specific areas where these concepts can be applied.

Glossary of Key Terms

Alternate hypothesis	One of the two hypotheses in hypothesis testing, it represents what the experimenter is trying to prove.
Confidence interval	An interval (range of values) that is calculated based on a parameter estimate plus and minus a margin of error. If repeated experiments are conducted, there is a $(1 - \alpha)\%$ likelihood that the interval will contain the true population parameter.
Confidence level $(1 - \alpha)$	The confidence level refers to two related concepts: (1) in forming confidence intervals, $(1 - \alpha)\%$ is the probability that with repeated samples the confidence interval will contain the population parameter; (2) when hypothesis testing, α is the probability of a Type I error.

Hypothesis testing	The process of (1) forming a null hypothesis and an alternate hypothesis and (2) conducting an experiment to test which of these hypotheses is correct. Following the experiment, we will either reject the null hypothesis in favor of the alternative hypothesis, or fail to reject the null hypothesis.
Margin of error	Represents the amount of error inherent in an estimate of the population parameter. The margin of error is typically represented in a confidence interval as

(parameter estimate) $\pm$ (margin of error)

	where the "$\pm$" symbol represents subtracting from the parameter estimate to get the lower bound of the confidence interval and adding to the parameter estimate to get the upper bound of the confidence interval.
Null hypothesis	One of the two hypotheses in hypothesis testing; it represents something opposite to what the experimenter is trying to prove.
Population	The universe of all objects about which we would like to make estimates.
Power	Equal to 100% minus the probability of Type II error. The power represents the probability of successfully rejecting the null hypothesis when it is actually false.
p value	The likelihood of observing a parameter estimate as extreme or more extreme than the value observed, given that the null hypothesis is true.
Sample	A sub-group of the population, which is collected to make inferences about the population.
Standard error	The standard deviation of a parameter estimate.
Statistical inference	The science of inferring information about a population based on a sample.
Type I error	An error that occurs in hypothesis testing when we reject the null hypothesis, but the null hypothesis is actually true. Minimizing this type of error is the primary focus in most hypothesis testing exercises.
Type II error	An error that occurs in hypothesis testing when we fail to reject the null hypothesis, but it is actually false.

Exercises

1. What is inferential statistics? How is it related to the concept of a population and a sample?
2. Why is sampling important?
3. What is a parameter? What is a statistic? How are the two concepts different?
4. What happens to the margin of error as the sample size increases? Why?
5. What is a confidence interval? What does it mean to have a 95% confidence interval?
6. a. Write the 95% confidence interval, assuming the following values (assume normal distribution: z score):

   - Sample size of 100;
   - Sample mean of 25;
   - Standard deviation of 7.

   b. Write the 95% confidence interval, assuming the following values (assume normal distribution: z score):

   - Sample size of 150;
   - Sample mean of 25;
   - Standard deviation of 7.

   c. Write the 95% confidence interval assuming the following values (assume normal distribution: z score):

   - Sample size of 100;
   - Sample mean of 25;
   - Standard deviation of 5.

   d. Compare the results from (a), (b), and (c). What happened to the confidence interval as the sample size increased? What happened to the confidence interval as the standard deviation decreased?
7. You think the age of the cashier is related to employee theft. Write null and alternative hypotheses to reflect your test.
8. What is a p value? What is the common p value where the researcher rejects the null hypothesis?
9. What is Type I error? What is Type II error? How are they related?

Chapter Seven

Common Statistical Hypothesis Tests

The null hypothesis is never proved or established, but is possibly disproved, in the course of experimentation. Every experiment may be said to exist only to give the facts a chance of disproving the null hypothesis.

—*R. A. Fisher*

Introduction

In the previous chapter, we covered the theory of hypothesis testing and confidence intervals. In this chapter, we cover common statistical tests that a practitioner can use for determining the statistical significance of an experiment. Statistical tests are designed to work for specific problems and with specific variables. We will explore some of the basic tests for comparing the means of two populations, evaluating the association of two category variables, comparing the proportions of two populations, and comparing the means across many categories.

Tests for Continuous Outcomes

Tests for continuous outcomes apply when there is a single numeric variable that we are interested in analyzing. Examples that are common in retail loss prevention of continuous outcomes include: (1) shrink, (2) return rate, (3) sales, (4) change in shrink, among many others. The first and simplest test that can be applied is known as the one-sample t test.

One-Sample t Test

Variable Type for Which This Is Appropriate: One Group on One Numeric Variable

The one-sample t test is appropriate when comparing the average of a variable within one group with a constant. This is considered by many to be one of the simplest statistical tests.

The one-sample t test is appropriate for the following examples:

- Comparing the average age of applicants for analytical loss prevention jobs against a constant (say 35);
- Comparing the average shrink this year with the National Retail Security Survey average;
- Comparing the average change in shrink between this year and last year with zero.

The null and alternative hypotheses for the one-sample t test are written as follows:

H_0 $\mu = \mu_0$ (the mean of the group is equal to the target value).
H_1 $\mu \neq \mu_0$ (the mean of the group is different from the target value).

The null hypothesis states that the mean of our variable in the population is equal to a known constant (μ_0). This constant can be any number. To perform the test, we need to compute the mean $(\overline{x})$ and the standard deviation (S) of the observations from our sample. The t statistic is computed as:

$$t = \frac{\overline{x} - \mu_0}{\frac{S}{\sqrt{n}}}$$

7.1

We evaluate the t statistic by comparing it with values of the t distribution with $n - 1$ degrees of freedom. With a criterion of (α), we can use Excel to compute the p value of the t statistic:

$$p = 2\star(1\text{-T.DIST}(t,n-1,\text{true}))$$

7.2

If the p value is less than 5%, we reject the null hypothesis (H_0) in favor of the alternate hypothesis (H_1). If the p value is greater than 5%, we fail to reject the null hypothesis.

Example: Is Store Shrink Different From the National Retail Security Survey Average?

The 2015 National Retail Security Survey (Moraca *et al.*, 2015) estimates that the average shrink across all retailers, based on those retailers surveyed, was 1.38%. The data (see Table 7.1) represents hypothetical shrink by store for a 25-store retailer. The retailer is interested to know if their shrink is statistically different from the average shrink rate in the National Retail Security Survey.

The average shrink for the 25 stores is 2.41% (0.0241) and the standard deviation is 0.51% (0.0051). The various calculations for the one-sample t test are shown in Figure 7.1. Excel does not have a one-sample t test built in, so we will input the calculations manually.

Here are the key functions to use in Excel:

- The function "AVERAGE()" is used to calculate the mean.
- The function "STDEV.S()" is used to calculate the sample standard deviation. Please note that "STDEV.P()" is for cases when you have the entire population and is not appropriate for statistical hypothesis testing.
- The p value is calculated using "T.DIST()"

Table 7.1: Hypothetical Shrink Rates from a 25-Store Retailer

Store Number	Shrink
1	2.60%
2	2.22%
3	2.62%
4	2.42%
5	2.14%
6	2.01%
7	2.63%
8	1.78%
9	2.71%
10	3.40%
11	1.87%
12	2.13%
13	2.91%
14	3.07%
15	2.02%
16	2.34%
17	2.39%
18	2.17%
19	2.19%
20	3.76%
21	1.98%
22	2.88%
23	1.48%
24	2.22%
25	2.43%

Based on the p value, $p = 0.00000000041385$, which is less than 0.05 or 5%, one would conclude that the average shrink in the store is significantly different from the National Retail Security Survey average of 1.38%.

This test can be run in SAS using the following code (assuming your dataset is named "shrink_data"):

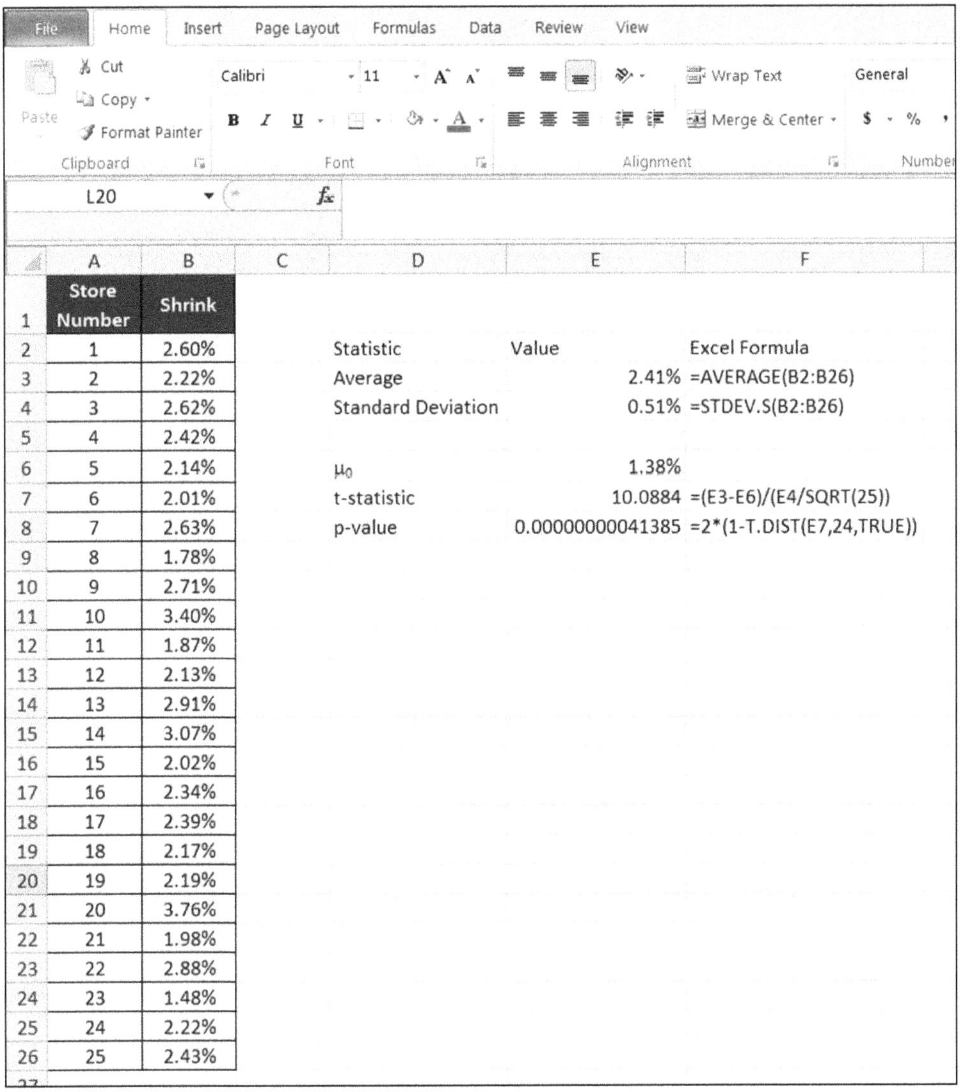

	A	B	C	D	E	F
1	Store Number	Shrink				
2	1	2.60%		Statistic	Value	Excel Formula
3	2	2.22%		Average	2.41%	=AVERAGE(B2:B26)
4	3	2.62%		Standard Deviation	0.51%	=STDEV.S(B2:B26)
5	4	2.42%				
6	5	2.14%		μ_0	1.38%	
7	6	2.01%		t-statistic	10.0884	=(E3-E6)/(E4/SQRT(25))
8	7	2.63%		p-value	0.00000000041385	=2*(1-T.DIST(E7,24,TRUE))
9	8	1.78%				
10	9	2.71%				
11	10	3.40%				
12	11	1.87%				
13	12	2.13%				
14	13	2.91%				
15	14	3.07%				
16	15	2.02%				
17	16	2.34%				
18	17	2.39%				
19	18	2.17%				
20	19	2.19%				
21	20	3.76%				
22	21	1.98%				
23	22	2.88%				
24	23	1.48%				
25	24	2.22%				
26	25	2.43%				

Figure 7.1: One-Sample *t* Test in Excel

```
proc ttest data=shrink_data sides=2 alpha=.01 h0=.0138;
    var shrink;
run;
```

In the SAS code, we set our null hypothesis to 0.0138 (which represents 1.38%) using the option "h0=.0138" and set the criterion level for rejecting the null hypothesis to 1% using the option "alpha=.01." Additionally, we use a two-sided test by specifying "sides=2," which we always recommend for hypothesis testing.

The output from the SAS system for the one-sample t test is shown in Figure 7.2. The value under the column header "Pr > |t|" represents the p value computed from the test statistic. In this example, the p value is shown to be "<.0001," which shows strong statistical significance and would result in the researcher rejecting the null hypothesis.

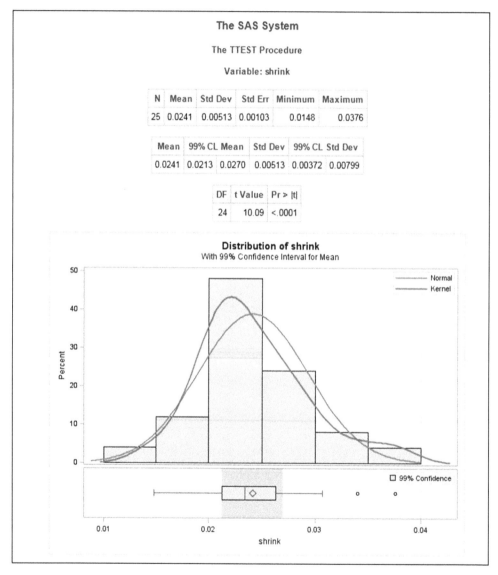

Figure 7.2: One-Sample t Test in SAS

Variable Type for Which This Is Appropriate: Two Groups Compared on One Numeric Variable

Two-sample *t* tests are appropriate for testing hypotheses about the average numeric values across two different groups. The two-sample *t* test is appropriate in the following examples:

- Comparing the average shrink of two groups of stores;
- Comparing the average age of applicants for analytical loss prevention jobs versus the average age of applicants for armed security jobs;
- Comparing the average processing time of an application received on Monday through Wednesday against the average processing time of an application received on Thursday through Friday;
- Comparing the average application processing times between two stores.

The two-sample *t* test will test one of the three following hypotheses:

Test 1

H_0 $\mu_1 = \mu_2$ (The average between Group 1 and Group 2 is equal).
H_1 $\mu_1 \neq \mu_2$ (The average between Group 1 and Group 2 is not equal).

Test 2

H_0 $\mu_1 \geq \mu_2$ (The average of Group 1 is greater than or equal to the average of Group 2).
H_1 $\mu_1 < \mu_2$ (The average of Group 1 is less than the average of Group 2).

Test 3

H_0 $\mu_1 \leq \mu_2$ (The average of Group 1 is less than or equal to the average of Group 2).
H_1 $\mu_1 > \mu_2$ (The average of Group 1 is greater than the average of Group 2).

Test 2 and Test 3 are known as one-sided *t* tests. We do not recommend these types of test, since they presuppose that the data can only be different in one direction. In practice, these tests are rarely used. Test 1 is the one used in most situations and will be used exclusively in this chapter.

The test statistic to conduct the two-sample t test (assuming the variances in the two groups are equal) is:

$$t = \frac{\bar{x}_1 - \bar{x}_2}{\left(\sqrt{\dfrac{(n_1 - 1)S_1^2 + (n_2 - 1)S_2^2}{n_1 + n_2 - 2}}\right)\left(\sqrt{\dfrac{1}{n_1} + \dfrac{1}{n_2}}\right)}$$

7.3

To perform the test, we will need to compute the mean of Group 1 ($\bar{x}_1$), the mean of Group 2 ($\bar{x}_2$), the standard deviation of Group 1 (S_1), and the standard deviation of Group 2 (S_2), and we need to know the sample size of each group (n_1 and n_2). The distribution of the t statistic of Equation 7.3 is a t distribution with $n_1 + n_2 - 2$ degrees of freedom. The p value can be calculated using Excel:

$$p \text{ value} = 2*(1\text{-}T.DIST(t, n_1+n_2-1, true))$$

7.4

The formula for the test that does not assume equal variance is slightly more complicated and we do not describe it in this book. Alternatively, Excel can be used to conduct the test of Equation 7.3 as well as the test where unequal variances are assumed. We will show later in this section how to use Excel to compute the other variants of the test. In practice, it is best to use the test with the unequal variance assumption to be more conservative. Generally, this test will make it slightly harder to reject the null hypothesis, and it is difficult to prove that the variances are actually equal. A two-sample t test looks for differences between the means of the two groups that are larger than normal deviation would dictate. The following example illustrates this point.

Two-Sample t Test Example

Suppose that we have two groups of applicants and we wish to compare their ages. We take the samples listed in Table 7.2.

Table 7.2: Ages of Applicants

Group 1	Group 2
35	40
30	28
39	30
48	34

Group 1 has an average age of 38 and Group 2 has an average age of 33. From this, a natural conclusion may be to assume that Group 2 has a lower average age in the population than Group 1. This sample, though, only has four observations from the population and each group shows considerable variation. Therefore, intuitively, it seems reasonable to see this level of difference in the average ages, just based on the random fluctuations in the data.

Suppose, however, that we have the situation shown in Table 7.3.

In this situation, Group 1 still has an average age of 38 and Group 2 still has an average age of 33, but now the random fluctuations are removed. In this situation, we would be more confident in concluding that Group 1 has a higher average age than Group 2.

This example shows the fundamental idea behind hypothesis testing. In the first example, the population could certainly contain two groups with equal means, and this dataset could have occurred simply by chance. In the second example, this seems far less likely since there is no variation in our data. Does this prove that the population has different means? No; it just contains more evidence that the means are different. Hypothesis testing is about weighing evidence. The second example provides far more evidence than the first example of different means.

A *t* test will produce a *p* value that measures the amount of evidence that your sample has against H_0. Typically, results will be displayed in the following format for the last two examples provided.

Nonsignificant Results (see Table 7.2)

Group 1 had an average age of 38 and Group 2 had an average age of 33. The difference in their ages was not statistically significant at the alpha level of 0.05 ($p = 0.452$). Therefore, we conclude that there is not enough evidence to show that Group 1 and Group 2 had different mean ages. The null hypothesis could not be rejected.

Table 7.3: Ages of Applicants

Group 1	Group 2
38	33
38	33
38	33
38	33

Group 1 had an average age of 38 and Group 2 had an average age of 33. The difference in their ages was statistically significant at the alpha level of 0.05 ($p = 0.034$). Therefore, we conclude that there is evidence that Group 1 and Group 2 do not have equal mean ages. We reject the null hypothesis and accept the alternate hypothesis.

Notice that in the statement of results, we never say for certain that either conclusion is true. Wording such as "there is evidence of" or "there is not enough evidence" is appropriate in statistical analysis. Wording such as "the means are different" or "the means are not different" is not appropriate in a statistical analysis.

Suppose there is a 50-store retailer with two distinct areas of the country (east and west) that would like to determine whether the two regions have different average shrink. The hypothesis that we are testing is:

H_0 $\mu_1 = \mu_2$ (The average of the east stores' shrink and that of the west stores' shrink are equal).

H_1 $\mu_1 \neq \mu_2$ (The average of the east stores' shrink and that of the west stores' shrink are not equal).

The data given in Table 7.4 shows the values for each store's shrink along with the region.

Using Excel, we can manually compute the t statistic and test the hypothesis (Figure 7.3).

Here are the key functions to use in Excel:

- The function "AVERAGE()" is used to calculate the mean.
- The function "STDEV.S()" is used to calculate the sample standard deviation. Please note that "STDEV.P()" is for cases when you have the entire population and is not appropriate for statistical hypothesis testing.
- The p value is calculated using "T.DIST()."

Based on the p value, $p = 0.00000226157297$, one would conclude that (at any practical confidence level, since the p value is less than one thousandth of one percent) the average shrink in the stores in the east is significantly different from the average shrink in the stores in the west.

Table 7.4: West and East Stores and Shrink Rates

West		East	
Store Number	*Shrink*	*Store Number*	*Shrink*
1	2.60%	26	1.82%
2	2.22%	27	1.17%
3	2.62%	28	2.10%
4	2.42%	29	1.27%
5	2.14%	30	1.36%
6	2.01%	31	1.96%
7	2.63%	32	2.42%
8	1.78%	33	1.25%
9	2.71%	34	2.07%
10	3.40%	35	2.24%
11	1.87%	36	1.64%
12	2.13%	37	1.07%
13	2.91%	38	1.58%
14	3.07%	39	1.77%
15	2.02%	40	1.69%
16	2.34%	41	2.16%
17	2.39%	42	2.08%
18	2.17%	43	1.83%
19	2.19%	44	1.53%
20	3.76%	45	1.89%
21	1.98%	46	1.65%
22	2.88%	47	1.68%
23	1.48%	48	2.11%
24	2.22%	49	1.56%
25	2.43%	50	1.77%

Excel has built-in utilities to execute the two-sample *t* test with equal variances, as illustrated in Figure 7.4.

The user must first enable the Analysis ToolPak add-in. Figure 7.5 shows the options when the user is choosing to conduct a two-sample *t* test with equal variances.

Once the top two entries in the form are filled in, click "OK" and Excel will compute the various statistics. The screenshot shown in Figure 7.6 shows the output from the test in Excel.

West		East	
Store Number	Shrink	Store Number	Shrink
1	2.60%	26	1.82%
2	2.22%	27	1.17%
3	2.62%	28	2.10%
4	2.42%	29	1.27%
5	2.14%	30	1.36%
6	2.01%	31	1.96%
7	2.63%	32	2.42%
8	1.78%	33	1.25%
9	2.71%	34	2.07%
10	3.40%	35	2.24%
11	1.87%	36	1.64%
12	2.13%	37	1.07%
13	2.91%	38	1.58%
14	3.07%	39	1.77%
15	2.02%	40	1.69%
16	2.34%	41	2.16%
17	2.39%	42	2.08%
18	2.17%	43	1.83%
19	2.19%	44	1.53%
20	3.76%	45	1.89%
21	1.98%	46	1.65%
22	2.88%	47	1.68%
23	1.48%	48	2.11%
24	2.22%	49	1.56%
25	2.43%	50	1.77%

Statistic	Value	Excel Formula
Average (West)	2.4148%	=AVERAGE(B2:B26)
Average (East)	1.7468%	=AVERAGE(E3:E27)
Standard Deviation (West)	0.5128687%	=STDEV.S(B2:B26)
Standard Deviation (East)	0.3518608%	=STDEV.S(E3:E27)
Average (West) - Average(East)	0.67%	=H4-H5
t-statistic	5.3700779820596	=H9/(SQRT((24*H6^2+24*H7^2)/(25+25-2))*SQRT(1/25+1/25))
p-value	0.00000226157297	=2*(1-T.DIST(H10,48,TRUE))

Figure 7.3: Two-Sample *t* Test in Excel

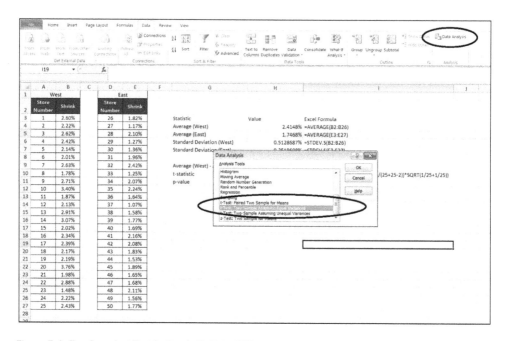

Figure 7.4: Two-Sample *t* Test in Excel; Built-in Utility

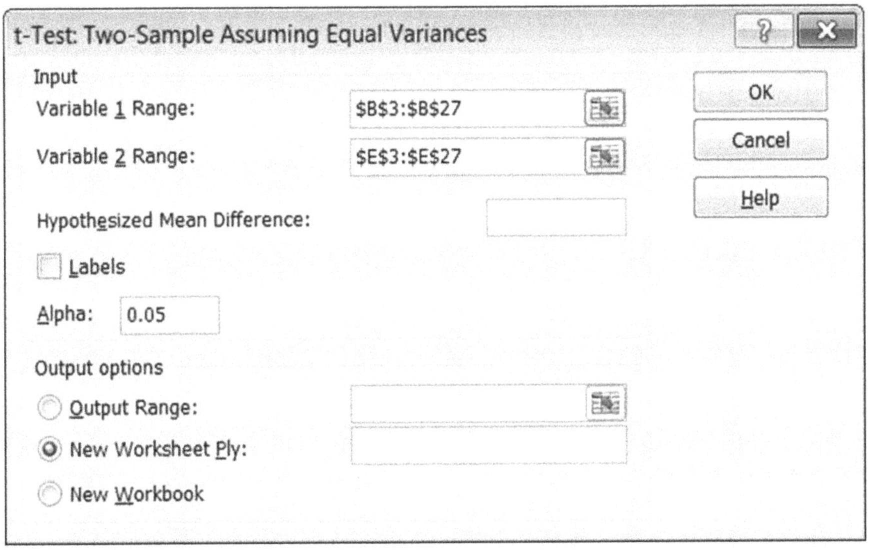

Figure 7.5: Two-Sample *t* Test Options in Excel

t Test: Two-Sample Assuming Equal Variances		
	Variable 1	*Variable 2*
Mean	0.024148	0.017468
Variance	2.63034E-05	1.23806E-05
Observations	25	25
Pooled Variance	1.9342E-05	
Hypothesized Mean Difference	0	
Df	48	
t Stat	5.370077982	
P(T<=t) One-Tail	1.13079E-06	
t Critical One-Tail	1.677224196	
P(T<=t) Two-Tail	2.26157E-06	
t Critical Two-Tail	2.010634758	

Figure 7.6: Two-Sample *t* Test in Excel—Output

You should use the highlighted *p* value to determine statistical significance. If the value is small, we will reject the null hypothesis. You should note that in the "Data Analysis" drop-down menu, there is an option to choose an unequal variance assumption on the data. While the *t* test with unequal variances will have significant results less often than the test with equal variances, it is preferable to use this test to be more conservative and because it is difficult to prove that the variances are actually equal.

This test can be run in SAS using the following code (assuming your dataset is named "shrink_data"):

```
proc ttest data=shrink_data sides=2 alpha=.01;
    var shrink;
    class group;
run;
```

In the SAS code, the null hypothesis when the "class" statement is used is that all of the means of the groups are equal. We set the criterion level for rejecting the null hypothesis to 1% using the option "alpha=.01." Additionally, we use a two-sided test by specifying "sides=2," which we always recommend for hypothesis testing.

The *t* test output from SAS is illustrated in Figure 7.7.

The results of the statistical test are shown under the column header "Pr > |t|." The top row under "Pr < |t|" assumes equal variances ("Pooled") and the bottom row assumes unequal variances ("Satterthwaite").

Paired *t* Test

A paired *t* test is appropriate if the groups have a natural pairing between each observation in each group. For example, if we observed the shrink one year in a group of stores and wanted to compare the shrink in the same stores the prior year, a paired *t* test would be appropriate. The paired *t* test is, in fact, equivalent to a one-sample test conducted on the differences between the two samples.

The null and alternative hypotheses for the two-sample paired *t* test are written as:

H_0 $\mu_1 = \mu_2$ (The average of Group 1 and the average of Group 2 are equal).
H_1 $\mu_1 \neq \mu_2$ (The average of Group 1 and the average of Group 2 are not equal).

The hypothesis is exactly the same as in the case of the typical two-sample *t* test (without pairing). To perform the test, we will subtract the values of one sample from the values of the other sample, one-by-one. For example, Figure 7.8 shows two groups of 20 stores that are measured before and after a change in the stores. We would like to test if the shrink changed in those stores.

The TTEST Procedure

Variable: shrink

group	N	Mean	Std Dev	Std Err	Minimum	Maximum
1	25	0.0241	0.00513	0.00103	0.0148	0.0376
2	25	0.0175	0.00352	0.000704	0.0107	0.0242
Diff (1-2)		0.00668	0.00440	0.00124		

group	Method	Mean	99% CL Mean		Std Dev	99% CL Std Dev	
1		0.0241	0.0213	0.0270	0.00513	0.00372	0.00799
2		0.0175	0.0155	0.0194	0.00352	0.00255	0.00548
Diff (1-2)	Pooled	0.00668	0.00334	0.0100	0.00440	0.00347	0.00592
Diff (1-2)	Satterthwaite	0.00668	0.00333	0.0100			

Method	Variances	DF	t Value	Pr > |t|
Pooled	Equal	48	5.37	<.0001
Satterthwaite	Unequal	42.495	5.37	<.0001

Equality of Variances

Method	Num DF	Den DF	F Value	Pr > F
Folded F	24	24	2.12	0.0709

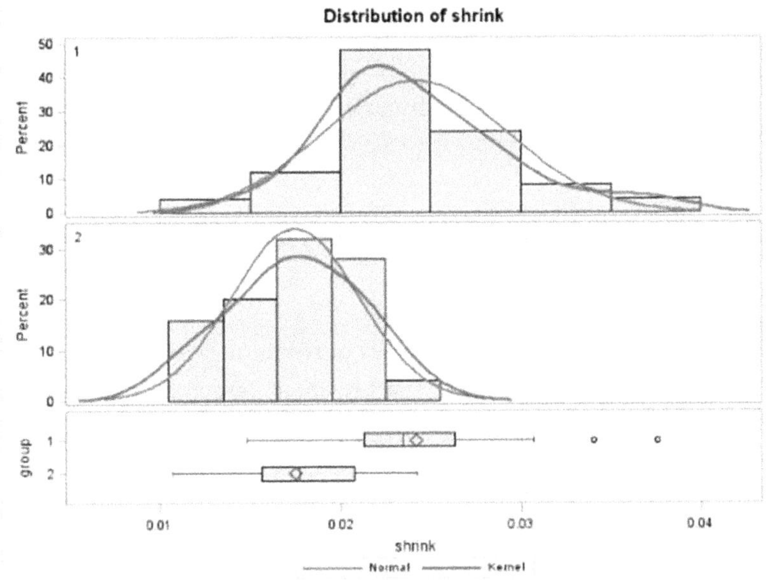

Distribution of shrink

Figure 7.7: SAS Output for *t* Test

Group	Store	Shrink Before	Shrink After	Difference
Test	1	0.011	0.024	0.013
Test	2	0.022	0.009	-0.013
Test	3	0.013	0.012	-0.001
Test	4	0.012	0.026	0.014
Test	5	0.023	0.011	-0.012
Test	6	0.014	0.014	0
Test	7	0.013	0.028	0.015
Test	8	0.024	0.013	-0.011
Test	9	0.015	0.016	0.001
Test	10	0.024	0.03	0.006
Test	11	0.009	0.015	0.006
Test	12	0.012	0.018	0.006
Test	13	0.025	0.032	0.007
Test	14	0.01	0.014	0.004
Test	15	0.013	0.013	0
Test	16	0.026	0.024	-0.002
Test	17	0.011	0.015	0.004
Test	18	0.014	0.015	0.001
Test	19	0.027	0.026	-0.001
Test	20	0.012	0.017	0.005

Average   0.0021000

Standard Deviation   0.0076085

Figure 7.8: Data and Calculations for a Paired *t* Test

The average difference ($\bar{x}_D$) is 0.0021 and the standard deviation of the difference (S_D) is 0.0076085. The *t* statistic is computed as:

$$t = \frac{\bar{x}_D}{\frac{S_D}{\sqrt{n}}}$$

7.5

For our data, $t = 1.234$. This statistic has a *t* distribution with $n - 1$ degrees of freedom and is identical to the one-sample *t* test presented earlier in this chapter. The *p* value for the test can be computed using the Excel formula:

$$p \text{ value} = 2*(1\text{-T.DIST}(t, n-1, true))$$

7.6

In this example, the *p* value = 0.232, which is higher than any typical cut-off for statistical significance. Therefore, we would fail to reject the null hypothesis that the shrink did not change year over year.

Suppose that we wanted to compare the shrink from this year to the shrink from last year on a store-by-store basis to determine if shrink had gone up or down over the year. Table 7.5 shows the shrink data for a 25-store retailer last year and this year.

Table 7.5: This Year's and Last Year's Shrink Rates

Last Year		This Year		Difference
Store Number	*Shrink*	*Store Number*	*Shrink*	*Shrink*
1	2.60%	1	1.82%	–0.78%
2	2.22%	2	1.17%	–1.05%
3	2.62%	3	2.10%	–0.52%
4	2.42%	4	1.27%	–1.15%
5	2.14%	5	1.36%	–0.78%
6	2.01%	6	1.96%	–0.05%
7	2.63%	7	2.42%	–0.21%
8	1.78%	8	1.25%	–0.53%
9	2.71%	9	2.07%	–0.64%
10	3.40%	10	2.24%	–1.16%
11	1.87%	11	1.64%	–0.23%
12	2.13%	12	1.07%	–1.06%
13	2.91%	13	1.58%	–1.33%
14	3.07%	14	1.77%	–1.30%
15	2.02%	15	1.69%	–0.33%
16	2.34%	16	2.16%	–0.18%
17	2.39%	17	2.08%	–0.31%
18	2.17%	18	1.83%	–0.34%
19	2.19%	19	1.53%	–0.66%
20	3.76%	20	1.89%	–1.87%
21	1.98%	21	1.65%	–0.33%
22	2.88%	22	1.68%	–1.20%
23	1.48%	23	2.11%	–0.63%
24	2.22%	24	1.56%	–0.66%
25	2.43%	25	1.77%	–0.66%

The Excel calculations shown in Figure 7.9, demonstrate the paired *t* test computed manually for the data.

Excel has a built-in function for computing the paired *t* test as well. Using the same data analysis option as in the prior section, choose the appropriate option (Figure 7.10) from the analysis menu.

The options are identical to the options in the previous two-sample *t* test. The output from the test is shown in Figure 7.11.

Last Year		This Year		Difference				
Store Number	Shrink	Store Number	Shrink	Shrink				
1	2.60%	1	1.82%	-0.78%	Statistic		Value	Excel Formula
2	2.22%	2	1.17%	-1.05%	Average (Last Year)		2.415%	=AVERAGE(B2:B26)
3	2.62%	3	2.10%	-0.52%	Average (This Year)		1.747%	=AVERAGE(E3:E27)
4	2.42%	4	1.27%	-1.15%	Standard Deviation (Difference)		0.523%	=STDEV.S(B2:B26)
5	2.14%	5	1.36%	-0.78%				
6	2.01%	6	1.96%	-0.05%	Average (This Year) - Average(Last Year)		-0.67%	=J5-J4
7	2.63%	7	2.42%	-0.21%	t-statistic		-6.3802	=J8/(J6/SQRT(25))
8	1.78%	8	1.25%	-0.53%	p-value		0.0000	=2*(1-T.DIST(ABS(J9),24,TRUE))
9	2.71%	9	2.07%	-0.64%				
10	3.40%	10	2.24%	-1.16%				
11	1.87%	11	1.64%	-0.23%				
12	2.13%	12	1.07%	-1.06%				
13	2.91%	13	1.58%	-1.33%				
14	3.07%	14	1.77%	-1.30%				
15	2.02%	15	1.69%	-0.33%				
16	2.34%	16	2.16%	-0.18%				
17	2.39%	17	2.08%	-0.31%				
18	2.17%	18	1.83%	-0.34%				
19	2.19%	19	1.53%	-0.66%				
20	3.76%	20	1.89%	-1.87%				
21	1.98%	21	1.65%	-0.33%				
22	2.88%	22	1.68%	-1.20%				
23	1.48%	23	2.11%	0.63%				
24	2.22%	24	1.56%	-0.66%				
25	2.43%	25	1.77%	-0.66%				

Figure 7.9: Paired *t* Test in Excel

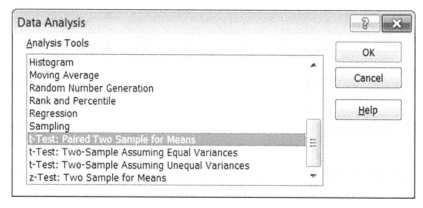

Figure 7.10: Paired *t* Test Options in Excel

t-Test: Paired Two Sample for Means		
	Last Year	*This Year*
Mean	0.024148	0.017468
Variance	2.63034E-05	1.23806E-05
Observations	25	25
Pearson Correlation	0.312510647	
Hypothesized Mean Difference	0	
df	24	
t Stat	6.380159906	
P(T<=t) one-tail	6.74074E-07	
t Critical one-tail	1.71088208	
P(T<=t) two-tail	1.34815E-06	
t Critical two-tail	2.063898562	

Figure 7.11: Paired *t* Test in Excel—Output

Use the highlighted p value to evaluate the hypothesis test. Based on the p value $= 1.348 \times 10^{-6} = 0.000001348$, there is strong evidence that the shrink is not the same as the prior year and is much less.

Tests for Categorical Outcomes

Tests for categorical outcomes apply when there are variables that take on categories of information rather than a continuous numerical outcome. Examples of categorical outcomes that are common in retail loss prevention are: (1) categories of shrink; (2) categories of return rate; (3) types of employee; (4) age group; (5) job type; and (6) hired or not hired. The first and simplest test that can be applied is known as the chi-square test of contingency tables.

Chi-Square Test of Contingency Tables

Variable Type for Which This Is Appropriate: Two Categorical Variables Measured on a Single Individual or Record

Contingency tables show the frequency distribution of two variables simultaneously. The purpose of a chi-square test of contingency tables is to demonstrate whether two categorical variables are related. Table 7.6 shows a contingency table between applicants' age group and job type.

A natural question from this analysis would be, "Is the type of job applied for related to the applicant's age?" A chi-square statistic can be formed from this table to test the hypothesis:

H_0 Job type is independent of applicant's age.
H_1 Job type is not independent of applicant's age.

To conduct a chi-square test, you must first determine the expected frequencies for each cell (i.e., the expected frequency for Cell A is calculated by multiplying the "Column 1 marginal" by "the Row 1 marginal" and dividing the result by the "grand total," or (Column 1 × Row 1)/grand total). Figure 7.12 illustrates the calculations in more detail. The first entry in the "Expected Data" table is computed as $1100 \times 745/3564 = 229.9$.

Then values are calculated for each cell based on the observed and expected frequencies in that cell. For example, for Cell A, the value is calculated by subtracting the expected frequency from the observed frequency and squaring the result, and then dividing the squared result by the expected frequency, that is: (observed − expected)^2/expected. Then the results are summed; this sum is the test statistic which has a chi-square distribution (χ^2) with the degrees of freedom equal to (number of rows − 1) × (number of columns − 1). In this example the degrees of freedom are $(5 - 1) \times (3 - 1) = 8$. See Figures 7.12 and 7.13 for all detailed calculations.

To compute the test statistic, sum all of the entries in the "(Observed − Expected)^2/ Expected" table. The total for the table in Figure 7.13 is 493.68, which has a chi-square distribution with eight degrees of freedom (written as $\chi^2(8)$). The p value is computed using the formula in Excel:

Table 7.6: Frequency of Job Applicants by Age Group and Job Type

Applicant's Age Group	Job Type		
	Analytics	*Security*	*Floor*
<25	400	300	45
25–35	300	450	25
35–45	250	500	19
45–55	100	500	15
55+	50	600	10

Actual Data					Expected Data (based on row and column frequencies)			
	Job Type					**Job Type**		
Applicant's Age Group	**Analytics**	**Security**	**Floor**	Row Totals	**Applicant's Age Group**	**Analytics**	**Security**	**Floor**
<25	400	300	45	745	<25	229.9	491.2	23.8
26-35	300	450	25	775	26-35	239.2	511.0	24.8
36-45	250	500	19	769	36-45	237.3	507.1	24.6
46-55	100	500	15	615	46-55	189.8	405.5	19.7
56+	50	600	10	660	56+	203.7	435.2	21.1
Column Totals	1100	2350	114	3564				

Figure 7.12: Actual and Expected Calculations

Observed – Expected				(Observed – Expected)^2/Expected			
	Job Type				**Job Type**		
Applicant's Age Group	**Analytics**	**Security**	**Floor**	**Applicant's Age Group**	**Analytics**	**Security**	**Floor**
<25	170.1	-191.2	21.2	<25	125.8	74.4	18.8
26-35	60.8	-61.0	0.2	26-35	15.5	7.3	0.0
36-45	12.7	-7.1	-5.6	36-45	0.7	0.1	1.3
46-55	-89.8	94.5	-4.7	46-55	42.5	22.0	1.1
56+	-153.7	164.8	-11.1	56+	116.0	62.4	5.8

Figure 7.13: Calculating the Chi-Square Statistic

$$p \text{ value} = 2\star(1\text{-CHISQ.DIST}(493.68, 8, \text{TRUE})) \hspace{2cm} 7.7$$

The results, in our example, give a great deal of evidence for the alternative hypothesis with $\chi^2(8) = 493.68, p < 0.00001$. We would conclude in this situation that there is significant evidence that the age of the applicant is related to the type of job applied for.

ANOVA

Variable Type for Which This Is Appropriate: A Numeric Variable Measured for Several Different Groups

ANOVA (analysis of variance) is a generalization of the two-sample t test to handle situations where there are more than two groups. An example for which ANOVA would be applicable is in comparing the average behavioral assessment scores between applicants by recruitment channel. Suppose that we collected data for applicants from recruiters, job site, college, and in-store to test the following hypothesis:

H_0 The average behavioral assessment score is the same for all four recruitment channels.

H_1 The average behavioral assessment score is different for at least one recruitment channel.

The following hypothetical example illustrates the type of data (see Table 7.7) for which ANOVA is appropriate.

An *F* test is used in ANOVA to test the hypothesis. Suppose that the *p* value for the example situation is $p = 0.23$. Then we would argue that there is not enough evidence to conclude that the behavioral assessment score is different between the four groups. We will not reject the null hypothesis.

If the *p* value is $p = 0.023$, then we would argue that there is evidence that the behavioral assessment score is different in at least one of the four groups. This conclusion leads to the question, "What group is different?" This question can be answered using the two-sample *t* test between all of the six different combinations of two groups.

Table 7.7: Average and Standard Deviation of Behavioral Assessment Scores across Four Recruitment Channels

Channel	Average BA Score	Std. Deviation of BA Score
Recruiter	730	35
Job Site	710	34
College	760	37
In-Store	680	33

ANOVA SAS Example

Next, we will illustrate an ANOVA procedure using SAS. In the following code, we will read in data and test the effectiveness of several different fictitious loss prevention tools (i.e., lpa, lpb, lpc, lpd, lpe, and lpf) in reducing store burglaries.

```
title1 'Testing LP Tools to Reduce Burglary';
data lp_data;
    input lp_tool $ store_burglary @@;
datalines;
```

```
        lpa  19 lpb  18 lpc  18 lpd  22 lpe  15 lpf  19
        lpa  33 lpb  25 lpc  19 lpd  21 lpe  16 lpf  19
        lpa  27 lpb  28 lpc  11 lpd  21 lpe  13 lpf  22
        lpa  33 lpb  25 lpc  16 lpd  19 lpe  14 lpf  18
        lpa  33 lpb  24 lpc  17 lpd  20 lpe  16 lpf  23;
Run;

Proc anova data = lp_data;
        Class lp_tool;
        Model store_burglary = lp_tool;
        means lp_tool / tukey;
run;
```

In the first section of SAS code, the syntax is creating a dataset called "lp_data" that includes our data for analysis. The input line specifies the independent variable name ("lp_tool") and dependent variable name ("store_burglary"). The "datalines" are the actual raw data that creates the dataset for analysis. Lastly, "run" executes the syntax.

In the next section of SAS code, the first sentence identifies the procedure we wish to use ("Proc anova") and the data we are using for the calculation ("lp_data"). The second row is a class statement, which is where the independent variable ("lp_tool") is specified. The third row specifies what we are modeling; here we state the dependent variable first, then an "=" sign and the independent variable. If our analysis produces significant results, we want to see which of the loss prevention tools is most effective, so want to conduct an ad-hoc test. The "means" row tells SAS to produce a Tukey test, which allows us to assess which of the loss prevention tools are significantly different from each other. While we won't go into the details behind the calculations in the Tukey test, we will describe how to interpret SAS's output. The last row says "run," which tells SAS to execute the procedure.

Figure 7.14 is an output that SAS produces that includes the statistics of interest. As you can see in the output, the ANOVA procedure was significant, $F = 11.76$, $p < 0.0001$. Therefore, we can say that there is a significant mean difference across the levels of the independent variable. Now, we want to know the details regarding the differences, so the SAS output shown in Figure 7.15 reports the mean differences. As we can see in the Tukey test, there are several significant mean differences. Figure 7.15 shows that lpd has fewer burglaries than lpa, lpf has fewer burglaries than lpa, lpc has fewer burglaries than lpb or lpa, and, lastly, lpe has fewer burglaries than lpb or lpa.

Testing LP Tools to Reduce Burglary

The ANOVA Procedure

Dependent Variable: store_burglary

Source	DF	Sum of Squares	Mean Square	F Value	Pr > F
Model	5	675.2000000	135.0400000	11.76	<.0001
Error	24	275.6000000	11.4833333		
Corrected Total	29	950.8000000			

R-Square	Coeff Var	Root MSE	store_burglary Mean
0.710139	16.29186	3.388707	20.80000

Source	DF	Anova SS	Mean Square	F Value	Pr > F
lp_tool	5	675.2000000	135.0400000	11.76	<.0001

Figure 7.14: ANOVA SAS Output

Means with the same letter are not significantly different.

Tukey Grouping		Mean	N	lp_tool
	A	29.000	5	lpa
	A			
B	A	24.000	5	lpb
B				
B	C	20.600	5	lpd
B	C			
B	C	20.200	5	lpf
	C			
	C	16.200	5	lpc
	C			
	C	14.800	5	lpe

Figure 7.15: Tukey Test SAS Output

MANOVA is a generalization of ANOVA to handle multiple numeric variables across a number of groups. The hypothesis test is an extension of the ANOVA H_0, that is, the means of all variables are equal across all groups.

An example of MANOVA is comparing behavioral assessment score and age simultaneously across all job channels. Just as in ANOVA, a significant result is usually followed up with specific tests between two groups at a time to learn more about where differences exist between the groups.

Conclusion

The tests shown in this chapter are useful in determining whether improvements in key metrics like shrink, return rate, and employee turnover from various loss prevention initiatives are really different or whether the difference is simply due to random noise. Given mounting pressure, time, and resource restrictions, it is easy to understand why many leaders are seeking guidance on how to evaluate the effectiveness of loss prevention programs. Statistical analyses are critical for determining whether certain programs and tools are impactful and in helping to guide program improvements. The good news is that developing an understanding of the concepts of statistical significance and the statistical procedures can help with efforts to assess the validity of program value and their impact on shrink. In the next chapter, we will explore the ideas presented so far to describe how to conduct in-store experiments.

Exercises

The dataset given in Table 7.8 shows the monthly shrink rates in stores 1 and 2. Use this dataset (Table 7.8) for these exercises.

1. Conduct a two-sample t test on the data (assume equal variances):

    a. Write the null and alternative hypotheses.
    b. What is the mean shrink for Store 1? For Store 2?
    c. What is the two-tailed p value?
    d. Can you reject the null hypothesis?

Table 7.8: Sample Data

Store 1	Store 2
1.80%	1.43%
1.70%	1.55%
1.75%	1.66%
1.66%	1.68%
1.68%	1.55%
1.90%	1.44%
1.84%	1.65%
1.85%	1.70%
1.65%	1.70%
1.55%	1.65%
1.55%	1.65%
1.90%	11.43%

2. Conduct a two-sample t test on the data, but assume unequal variances. How did the results change? Why?
3. Conduct a paired t test using the data:
   a. Write the null and alternative hypotheses.
   b. What is the two-tailed p value?
   c. Can you reject the null hypothesis?

In our lust for measurement, we frequently measure that which we can rather than that which we wish to measure ... and forget that there is a difference.

—*George Udny Yule*

Introduction

The previous chapters have covered a variety of topics that serve as the foundation for evaluating loss prevention programs. We covered the basics of criminological theory, provided an overview of some relevant areas of retail security, and introduced you to the fundamental statistical procedures needed to conduct experiments in stores. In this chapter, we explore some of the basic concepts in designing an experiment and measuring results in retail stores or in the retail headquarters.

Retail is constantly changing and so are the threats to retailers. While this year it is booster bags, next year it may be a problem with forged receipts or counterfeit merchandise. To best deploy programs to your stores, each program needs to be evaluated and tested to determine if it actually works or just seems like it might work. To this end, we will discuss the concepts of an experiment and how to conduct one. Additionally, we will cover the process of measuring the effects of the experiment. If the experiment is successful, we will provide some considerations for deploying and monitoring of the program.

Types of Loss Prevention Programs That Can be Evaluated

Loss prevention initiatives are intended to prevent losses to the retailer without interfering with normal operating procedures and sales generation. The initiatives that may be implemented can span a range of types, like policies, procedures, in-store solutions, product protection solutions, home-office solutions, solutions developed in house, solutions purchased from a vendor, software solutions, and many more. The specific goals of these solutions may be different, but they are typically to remove some loss or mitigate a risk. Figure 8.1 lists some common loss prevention solutions.

Each of these solutions is aimed at reducing loss directly or through a deterrent effect on the shopper or employee. As these programs are rolled into stores or into use in a back-office capacity, we recommend testing them, when possible, with the outlined methods.

Metrics to be Tracked When Evaluating Loss Prevention Programs

Loss prevention programs are intended to reduce losses to the retailer while not having an adverse effect on the normal operation of the business. With these two equally important yet opposing goals, there will be metrics that represent the reduction to losses and metrics that represent impacts to normal operation of the business. Figure 8.2 lists some of the metrics that can be used to determine improvements in loss-related areas.

While we will want to see the corresponding loss-related metrics improve with the implementation of a loss prevention program, we have to be equally focused on not impacting core sales-related metrics, which may indicate that our loss prevention

Loss Prevention Initiative
Camera system
Armed security guard in store
Product in secure case
Return counter in front of store
Locks on doors
In-store greeters or other unarmed security guards
Tender policies on returns
Policies on gift card sales
Exception reporting
Organized retail crime investigation team
EAS tags on merchandise
Return authorization system
Alarm systems in stores
Keeping less than $X in the store at any time
Counterfeit bill detector
RFID tags on merchandise
Sending staff to training for dealing with shoplifters

Figure 8.1: Common Loss Prevention Solutions

program has impacted normal business. Figure 8.3 illustrates some of the values we may track when conducting experiments on loss prevention programs.

Overall, we would like the decrease in loss to be larger than any impact to the normal operations of the store. For example, if we typically lose $200,000 annually on iPads because of theft and we are able to reduce that amount by 20% (a $40,000 savings) that may seem like a good result. However, if we typically sell $10,000,000 annually in iPads and the sales were reduced by 2% (for a total of $200,000) by our program, then our program should not be implemented.

Metrics Related to Loss
Shrink
Number of shoplifting incidences
Number of employees terminated for cause
Number of stolen items
Number of break-ins
Number of armed robberies
Return rate
Percentage of returns without a receipt
Number of times the cash drawer was short
Employee turnover
Percentage of transactions with a manual reduction to price
Transaction voids or line item voids

Figure 8.2: Loss Reduction Metrics

Metrics Related to Normal Operations
Sales (actual and according to plan)
Number of visitors to a store
Conversion rates
Sales of a specific product
Net promoter score; other customer service metrics
Employee satisfaction metrics
Gross profit ($ or %)
Net profit

Figure 8.3: Normal Operations Metrics

What Is an Experiment and the Scientific Method?

When you think of an experiment, you may think of a lab, where people are busy at work with beakers, lab coats, and strange chemicals. However, an experiment is really a part of the scientific method where we are testing our hypothesis and trying to determine if what we thought was true was actually true. While that method can sometimes refer to chemists in a lab, it can also refer to loss prevention professionals trying to minimize loss.

Figure 8.4 illustrates the normal flow in the scientific method's process. First, the researcher will ask a question. An example question is, "Why do the iPads in the display area of the store always get stolen?" Next, the loss prevention professional would research the question. For example, an inspection of the display area in the store may reveal that the iPads are only secured to the table with a very weak device that can be easily broken. Next, the loss prevention professional would form a hypothesis: "If the iPads are secured to the table with a more secure device (Acme device ABC), they will not get stolen as often." At this point in the scientific method, some type of experiment

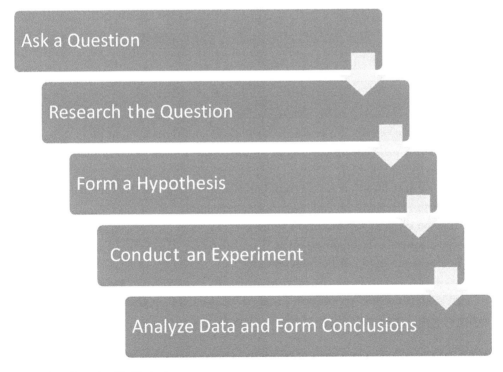

Figure 8.4: The Scientific Method

should be conducted to determine whether the hypothesis is correct. In the rest of the chapter, we discuss the considerations when designing an experiment as well as how to analyze loss prevention experiments.

Conducting Experiments

When conducting an experiment, the primary goal is to answer the research hypothesis without any doubt as to the validity of your experiment. In this section, we will discuss some of the ways to avoid threats to the validity of the experiment and to isolate the information you are trying to measure.

The Ideal Experiment

1. The experiment is conducted on a very large number of experimental records.
2. The test subjects are representative of the entire population.
3. The test factor is applied exactly as it is planned to be deployed.
4. The only change in the test subjects would be the test factor.
5. There is a control group.
6. The test and control subjects are randomly assigned.
7. The test subjects and test administrators do not know to which group each test subject was assigned.
8. The proper analytical techniques are used and are appropriate to the data and experiment.

In real life, it is usually impossible to have ideal conditions in all of these areas. In loss prevention and with testing in-store programs, there will be many limitations:

- There are usually limits on the number of stores, customers, and managers.
- Store employees will be well aware of any changes.
- It may be difficult to randomize subjects.
- Other changes may be going on at the same time.
- The test stores may not be representative.

That said, if the loss prevention professional is careful in the experimental design, many of these ideal conditions can be achieved.

Figure 8.5 shows some common threats to experimental validity. Some of these are the opposite of what was in the list of ideal conditions for an experiment.

Each of these items can interfere with an experiment and make the results and conclusions unreliable. We will discuss each of the items and strategies for avoiding these issues.

Threats to the Validity of an Experiment	Description of Issue
Confounding variables	There are other variables in the experiment that are related to the outcome and change the results.
Biased sample; not representative	The sample selected for experimentation is not representative of the population.
Hawthorne or observer effect	The observers of an experiment are biased in favor of a certain result and influence the study.
Regression to the mean	The most extreme values are used as a test sample. Extreme values will naturally gravitate toward the mean even without a treatment and this can invalidate the results.
Experiment is not representative	The experiment itself is not representative of how the method would be used in real life.
Improper analysis	The analysis failed to consider certain important elements.
No control subjects	All subjects received the treatment and therefore we do not have anyone who did not get the treatment to compare them with.
Sample size too small	There are not enough records to make a conclusion.
Execution errors	The subjects who were chosen for the experiment did not actually participate in the experiment or participated in a way that was incorrect.

Figure 8.5: Threats to Validity

Consider the example earlier in this chapter of a lot of stolen iPads; we hypothesized that this was due to the poor device securing them to the display counter. Suppose further that you were attempting to measure the effects of a more secure device to determine that device's effect on theft rates. If, at the same time as your experiment, there was a separate initiative that placed a guard in the area with the iPads, this would be a confounding factor, which would make measuring the effects of the more secure device impossible. Since both prevention factors are present at the same time in the same stores, it will be impossible to separate the effects of the guard from the effects of the more secure devices.

A second example has to do with the selection of the test stores. If test stores were significantly different from the control stores on key variables, like shrink, crime, or other factors, then the effects of the program might be influenced by these outside factors. When testing loss prevention programs, it is important that only one factor is changed at a time in the store. Additionally, whenever possible, the stores should be assigned to test and control groups randomly so that all other potential confounding variables will be distributed equally in both the test and the control groups. If there are suspected confounding variables after the experiment is completed, the researcher can include those variables as control variables in a regression analysis (see Chapter 9) to remove the effects of the confounding variables. This approach is discussed in more detail in Chapters 10 and 11.

Biased Sample

Biased samples refer to cases where the test or control samples contain records that are not representative of the entire population. For example, suppose that only the stores with the highest shrink were used for an experiment. There are a few issues with using stores that are different from a typical store. Any conclusions would be limited to only high-risk stores and not applicable to an average store or a low-risk store. The second issue is that shrink and crime tend to fluctuate over time, owing to natural random variation. If a store is classified as high risk, it may be selected by random chance and its normal state of risk may be much lower. So there will be a natural tendency known as *regression to the mean*, which will tend to pull those stores back to their normal state (which is lower than their outlier state).

Hawthorne or Observer Effect

Communications to the store associates during a test can influence the results of the study. Imagine that the following message goes out to store associates and managers: "iPads are being stolen at an unacceptable rate from the display areas so the loss prevention team is deploying new measures to reduce theft rates." It is a very natural reaction for those receiving this communication to pay more attention to the display area and watch for potential thieves. This increased attention would probably influence the theft rates downward and would make it hard to separate the effects of the communication from the effects of the new security devices.

Experiment is not Representative

If the loss prevention solution or the way in which the experiment is conducted is not representative of what the loss prevention professional intends to do when the solution is deployed, the results may not be valid. For example, if we hypothesize that securing the iPads with Acme device ABC will help, but then we test Acme device XYZ, our results may not be applicable to Acme device ABC. Similarly, if the experiment is conducted using different types of screw or on a different countertop or in any way differs from the true usage, then the results will only apply to the tested case and may not be extrapolated to more general uses.

Improper Analysis

Another potential threat to an experiment's validity and the conclusions from the experiment is improper or incomplete analysis. If the wrong statistical tests are used, if confounding variables that should have been considered are not considered, or if another explanation for the effect was not analyzed, then the results may be invalid. To avoid validity issues with improper analysis, confounding variables, seasonality, open and closing stores, control stores, and proper statistical tests should be used in the analysis.

No Control Group

A control group is a group that has everything similar to the test group and does not get the proposed loss prevention solution. If a test is run without a control group, there will be serious validity issues, especially in retail testing. Since there are constant changes to a retail environment, it will be impossible to separate any effects from the normal day-to-day changes and the loss prevention solution. For example, product mix, seasonal shopping patterns, economic trends, and customer shopping patterns may change any of the loss-related metrics independently of the loss prevention solution.

Sample Size Too Small

Even if a proposed hypothesis is true, without an adequate sample size, we may not be able to prove the hypothesis (and reject the null hypothesis in the statistical test). This becomes increasingly important when the size of the effect is small. For example, suppose we are trying to detect whether shrink has decreased. With only ten stores in a sample and with the natural variation of shrink, we will be unable to detect small changes in shrink due to natural fluctuations in the data. However, if we use 100 stores, this will probably overcome the variation in shrink. Using another example that was shown earlier, suppose we are trying to detect whether a quarter is fair or unfair. With only 100 flips, we could say that a quarter with a true 40% heads rate represented an unfair coin. However, it would take 10,000 coin flips to say that a coin with a true 49% heads rate is an unfair coin (meaning that the 49% head count is not reasonable by chance alone). Table 8.1 shows the range of the percentage of heads on a fair coin based on simulated coin flip experiments and a hypothetical rate of 50% in the sample.

Execution Error

With retail testing, the loss prevention practitioner is often at the mercy of the store managers, store associates, and district loss prevention personnel to execute on the test. For example, if all the stores are shipped the Acme device ABC to better secure iPads

Table 8.1: Sample Size and Confidence Limits

Sample Size	Lower 95% Confidence Limit	Upper 95% Confidence Limit
50	0.361	0.639
100	0.402	0.598
500	0.456	0.544
1,000	0.469	0.531
10,000	0.490	0.510
100,000	0.497	0.503

to the display counter, but the staff in one or two of the stores neglect to install the equipment, then that store's results are not going to be reflective of the new security measures. Likewise, if there is a test on EAS (electronic article surveillance) tags and no employee is responding when the alarm pedestals by the door sound, then the EAS tags will not be very effective. For any experiment that is conducted, it is important to make sure that it is well executed for the experimental unit. Metrics should be developed to determine how well each experimental unit actually complies with the program.

Steps for Conducting an Experiment

In this section, we will go step by step through what to do when conducting a test for a loss prevention solution. There are many types of loss prevention solutions that were listed previously and many more that were not listed. Each type may have different specific approaches to conducting the experiment, but general guidelines will be provided for best practices at each step.

Step 1: Determining What to Test and for How Long

The first step is to determine what program should be tested. Many loss prevention departments will have a long list of potential initiatives, each of which may require a test to determine its effectiveness for reducing losses. Each one should be categorized by type and a rough estimate of the potential value and cost should be calculated to determine the prioritization. Types should be categories that make sense to the department's objectives. Some examples are (but this list is certainly not complete): initiatives that involve changes to the store layout; initiatives that provide physical security protections to products; camera-related initiatives; loss prevention software tools; real time authorization solutions; and coupon security initiatives.

Step 2: Determining Key Metrics to Track

Once the list of key potential initiatives is dissected and a single initiative is picked, the key metrics to be tracked must be picked. The metrics should be divided into the primary metrics and the other metrics you will track and measure. All of the focus on the design of the experiment should be focused on the primary metrics. The primary metrics should be easy to translate into an overall program value if the initiative is rolled out on a larger scale. The primary metrics should be easy to measure and should be divided into loss improvement metrics as well as sales impact metrics. Figure 8.6 lists some potential key metrics by initiative.

Loss Prevention Initiative	Loss–Related Metrics	Operational Metrics
Camera system	Overall shrink, shoplifting incidence	Sales, store traffic, conversion
Armed security guard in store	Overall shrink, shoplifting incidence	Sales, store traffic, conversion
Product in glass case	Shrink of the specific products in the case, and shoplifting incidence	Sales of specific products
Return counter in front of store	Return rate, shrink, shoplifting incidence	Overall sales, store traffic
Tender policies on returns	Return rate, nonreceipted return rate	Overall sales
Policies on gift card sales	Chargeback incidence	Gift card sales
Exception reporting	Employee fraud cases caught, value of case, shrink	Employee turnover
EAS tags on merchandise	Overall shrink, shoplifting incidence	Sales, store traffic, conversion, sales of tagged products
Return authorization system	Return rate, shrink, nonreceipted rate	Sales, sales for returners
Counterfeit bill detector	Incidence of counterfeit bills	Sales
RFID tags on merchandise	Overall shrink, shoplifting incidence	Sales, store traffic, conversion, sales of tagged products

Figure 8.6: Loss Prevention Initiatives and Related Metrics to Measure

Step 3: Selecting Test and Control Subjects

Selecting test and control subjects first requires the loss prevention professional to ask "What is a test subject?" When possible, test subjects should be chosen to maximize the number of experimental units. If there are more experimental units, there will be a more accurate estimate of the effect. For most loss prevention programs, the experimental unit will be the store, but this is not always the case. Figure 8.7 provides some possible experimental units for several loss prevention programs.

In the cases where the store is the unit of measurement, a subset of stores will be chosen that will implement the program, and the remaining stores will not implement the program. Whenever possible, the stores with the program should be chosen using a process known as *randomization*. Randomization means that the test stores are chosen from the total population in a random way so that each store has an equal chance of being selected.

In some cases, entire districts must remain together as test units or control units and only one or a few districts can be chosen. In these cases, it is more important to choose a district or small set of districts that is representative of the entire chain in the primary test metrics.

Loss Prevention Initiative	Test Units	Notes
Camera system	Stores	
Armed security guard in store	Stores	
Product in glass case	Products, stores	
Return counter in front of store	Stores	
Tender policies on returns	Districts or stores	
Policies on gift card sales	Stores, registers, transactions	Since this can be driven by the point of sale, many options exist
Exception reporting for employees	Stores, employees	
EAS tags on merchandise	Products, stores	
Return authorization system	Stores	
Counterfeit bill detector	Stores	
RFID tags on merchandise	Products, stores	

Figure 8.7: Test Units

Having a control group that is as close as possible to the test group, in terms of the key variables being measured and any possible confounding variables, is critical in the analysis. If the test and control groups are large enough, randomization will guarantee that the distribution of possible confounding variables will be statistically similar in the test and control groups. "Large enough" is not always well defined, but it is likely to be a hundred or a few hundred units for the test and the control groups. If the test and control groups have different distributions for key confounding variables, the results can be influenced significantly.

Step 4: Sample Size Determination

An important step in setting up your experiment is to determine how many stores (or other experimental units) you will need to have to measure the effects. If the store is the test unit, the most optimal test will have one half of the stores as test stores and one half of the stores as control stores. The desirable sample size for testing the difference between the mean of a variable between two groups, for each group (at a confidence level of 95%), is determined by the following formula:

$$\text{expected difference} > 1.96 \frac{S}{\sqrt{n}}$$

8.1

Equation 8.1 says that the margin of error (or confidence interval half-width) should be less than the expected difference between the groups with and without the test program. If we rearrange the formula a little, the suggested sample size is

$$n > \left(\frac{1.96\ S}{\text{expected difference}} \right)^2$$

8.2

To calculate this sample size, an estimate of the standard deviation of the metric you are measuring, and also the expected change in the mean of the variable due to the loss prevention program, is required. There are similar functions to this one that determine the sample size for tests of proportion and many other statistical tests.

Step 5: Conducting the Experiment

Once the experimental units and the control units have been chosen, the next step is to start the experiment. For this step, the program will be rolled out to the test units. It is important that no other significant changes are made during the test, which might interfere with the results. Additionally, during the test, it will be important to monitor the execution of the program implementation. The experimental design should be such that the test and control stores are as identical as possible for some period prior to the test and at the point the test begins, the only thing changed being the implementation of the loss prevention program.

Another important consideration in conducting the experiment is the timing of measurement on the key metrics. For sales, returns, and the various incidence-related metrics that were mentioned in the previous sections, these variables can be readily obtained from point of sale data or incidence reports from the stores. If the key outcome metric is shrink, additional care must be taken in coordinating an inventory measurement before and after the test is completed.

Step 6: Analysis and Reporting of the Results

Once the program is completed, an analysis should be conducted to measure the impact of the new loss prevention program on the key metrics. A few key factors should be addressed in the analysis, which are unique to retail.

Seasonality   A key reasons to use a control sample is seasonality. Most retailers have very different sales and loss patterns depending on the time of the year. There are a few techniques that we can use in the analysis to protect against seasonal fluctuations falsely influencing results.

Year–over–year trends before the test If stores are trending higher or lower on a key metric year over year just before the test, it may be important to consider these trends in the analysis. A way to deal with both the year-over-year trends and seasonality is to use the following metric for each store:

$$\text{net change} = (\text{metric}_{\text{test period this year}} - \text{metric}_{\text{test period last year}}) - (\text{metric}_{\text{before period this year}} - \text{metric}_{\text{before period last year}}) \qquad 8.3$$

Each store in the test and control sample converted to this measurement captures the net change in the key metric considering trends before and during the test compared with the prior year.

Same–store measurement If the experimental units are stores, and those stores are newly opened, it may be impossible to adjust for seasonality and year-over-year trends as shown in Equation 8.3. It is usually best to exclude newly opened or recently closed stores for this reason.

Once these considerations have been taken into account, the next step will be to perform some type of statistical test. The type of statistical test will generally depend on the metric, but in most of the examples shown in this chapter, the outcome is a continuous outcome. If that is the case, a two-sample *t* test should be performed on the net change shown in Equation 8.3. Tests should be repeated for any variables that are being tracked for the experiment.

Step 7: Deployment and Ongoing Analysis

If the results of the experiment are good and the program is to be rolled out to all stores for a retailer, there are some rollout considerations.

Execution of the program The program should be executed similarly to how it was executed for the test. It is also important to

Ongoing measurement

establish execution reports to determine whether the program is being executed properly as the program matures.

If ongoing measurement is required, it may be useful to maintain a control group of stores that never get the program and can be used as a baseline group to compare against. Alternatively, the program's removal can be tested at some point. This means that for some period the program is removed from a random sample of stores and now our test program is the removal of the program. This type of test would be conducted like the original test but in reverse.

Demonstrating Return on Investment

The goal of an experiment and an analysis is to determine whether the loss prevention initiative creates value beyond the cost of the program. Let's take the iPad example and build a return-on-investment case that can be presented to executive-level management for the deployment of Acme security device ABC.

To follow the suggestions from the previous section, we have made the following determinations:

- The primary metric is shrink rate. The secondary metric is sales.
- We analyzed all stores' shrink rates from May 2015 to April 2016. The median shrink rate chainwide was 1.38%. We identified 200 stores in districts 8 and 12 that are representative of the chain. During the same period, 95% of these stores had a shrink rate ranging from 1.34% to 1.42%.
- We randomly selected 100 stores to test the security device. The remaining 100 stores represent our control stores.
- When the test was conducted, we ensured the Acme security devices were installed correctly and using the same installation method that would be used should the program be implemented fully.

To measure return on investment, we first need to analyze the data in a manner that accounts for seasonality and normal data fluctuations. For this reason, we would measure the shrink rate in the test stores and control stores before the test, during the test, and during the same two periods in the previous year. Let's assume, for this test, that we can obtain shrink within a specific time window using a manual method of measurement. Figure 8.8 illustrates hypothetical results (note that rounding affects the final program impact):

		Shrink Rate							
Group	Number of Stores	Prior to Test (May to June)			Test Period / With Device (July to August)			Net Change	Program Impact
		2016	2015	Change	2016	2015	Change		
Test Stores	100	1.38%	1.31%	0.07%	1.40%	1.43%	−0.03%	−0.10%	−0.09%
Control Stores	100	1.37%	1.36%	0.01%	1.42%	1.43%	0.00%	−0.02%	

Figure 8.8: Hypothetical Results Showing Shrink Rate Impact of Security Device ABC

A few things to note about the analysis:

- If we did not compare the results year over year, it would look like the security device resulted in higher shrink rates. In the test stores, the shrink rate prior to the test was 1.38%, and during the test the shrink rate increased to 1.40%. Similarly, with the control stores, without the year-over-year comparison, it would seem as though shrink rate increased from 1.37% to 1.42%.
- If we did not include a "prior period," we would not account for the trend in shrink rate prior to the installation of the security devices. This means that if we looked only at the test stores and the test period, it would seem that, year over year, shrink rate decreased 0.03%. However, this does not account for the fact that shrink rate was already up 0.07% year over year, prior to the install. Using the prior period and the test period we can determine that the impact of the device in the test stores was actually −0.10%, not 0.03%.
- If we did not include the control stores, we would attribute too much impact to the security device. You can see in Figure 8.8 that simply based on normal fluctuations, the net change in shrink rate was −0.02% in the control stores. This means that we should not attribute the full −0.10% reduction we see in the test stores as the impact of the device. Some of the decrease may be fluctuations in the shrink rate, as demonstrated in the control stores.
- The program impact is obtained by taking the test stores' net impact minus the control stores' net impact. The net impact is accounting for seasonality with a year-over-year approach and any existing trends with a before-and-after approach, as described.

The next step is to measure the impact of the test loss prevention initiative on a granular basis to ensure that the impact we saw in Figure 8.8 was not attributable to only a few select larger stores. To that end, we can calculate the percentage of stores in both groups (test and control) that had a shrink rate reduction year over year, comparing the test period with the control period. Figure 8.9 is an example of the underlying data need for the analysis; we would need a row for each store to complete the analysis.

We can test whether the results are significant at the store-level in two ways:

- A paired t test using the "Net Change" column, comparing the mean net change of the test stores with the mean net change of the control stores;
- A chi-square test using the "Improve" column, comparing the proportion of stores improving for both store groups (data illustrated in Figure 8.10).

The result of the paired t test from Excel is shown in Figure 8.11 (remember that the data is fictional). The test stores had an average net impact of -0.12% while the control stores average net impact was 0.00%. The p value is much less than 0.05; therefore, the results are significant and we can claim that the impact of the security device is associated with lower shrink rates beyond those expected due to normal fluctuations.

The chi-square test results are illustrated in Figure 8.12. The first row in each square represents the observed count, the second row illustrates the expected count, and the

Store	Group	Prior to Test (May to June)			Test Period / With Device (July to August)			Net Change	Improve
		2016	2015	Change	2016	2015	Change		
1	Test	1.38%	1.37%	0.01%	1.40%	1.40%	0.00%	−0.01%	1
2	Test	1.38%	1.39%	−0.01%	1.41%	1.38%	0.03%	0.04%	0
3	Test	1.65%	1.45%	0.20%	1.38%	1.39%	−0.01%	−0.21%	1
4	Test	1.33%	1.32%	0.01%	1.37%	1.37%	0.00%	−0.01%	1
5	Test	1.33%	1.32%	0.01%	1.36%	1.36%	0.00%	−0.01%	1
10	Control	1.41%	1.40%	0.01%	1.41%	1.40%	0.01%	0.00%	0
11	Control	1.14%	1.10%	0.04%	1.41%	1.42%	−0.01%	−0.05%	1
12	Control	1.44%	1.42%	0.02%	1.42%	1.41%	0.01%	−0.01%	1
13	Control	1.43%	1.22%	0.21%	1.33%	1.33%	0.00%	−0.21%	1
14	Control	1.42%	1.43%	−0.01%	1.32%	1.32%	0.00%	0.01%	0

Figure 8.9: Analysis of Store-Level Impact

Group	# / % of Stores that Improved (Lower Shrink)	# / % of Stores that Didn't Improve (Same or Higher Shrink)	Total Stores
Test	68 / 68%	32 / 32%	100 / 100%
Control	52 / 52%	48 / 48%	100 / 100%

Figure 8.10: Data Used for Store-Level Analysis—Chi-Square Test

t-Test: Paired Two Sample for Means

	Test Stores	Control Stores
Mean	-0.12%	0.00%
Variance	2.95661E-06	3.10886E-07
Observations	100	100
Pearson Correlation	0.556968874	
Hypothesized Mean Difference	0	
df	99	
t Stat	-7.780771632	
P(T<=t) one-tail	3.52759E-12	
t Critical one-tail	1.660391157	
P(T<=t) two-tail	7.05518E-12	
t Critical two-tail	1.9842169	

Figure 8.11: Excel Output for a Paired *t* Test

Group	Improved	Same/Decline	Total
Test	68 (actual) 60 (expected) -1.07 (χ^2)	32 40 -1.6	100
Control	52 60 -1.07	48 40 -1.6	100
Total	120	80	200

χ^2 = 5.333, df = 1, χ^2/df = 5.33 , $p(\chi^2 > 5.333)$ = 0.0209

Figure 8.12: Chi-Square Results

third row shows the chi-square statistic. Again, the p value is 0.02 (less than 0.05); therefore, the results are significant.

Following the results illustrated in Figures 8.11 and 8.12, we would want to ensure that Acme security device ABC did not negatively affect sales. Using exactly the same design, we would measure the average store's monthly net sales, as illustrated in Figure 8.13. As illustrated, net sales remained relatively flat and both the test stores and the control stores have similar results.

Per Store Monthly Net Sales

Group	Number of Stores	Prior to Test (May to June)			Test Period / With Device (July to August)			Net Change	Program Impact
		2016	2015	Change	2016	2015	Change		
Test Stores	100	$ 60,000	$ 58,800	2.0%	$ 61,000	$ 59,500	2.5%	0.48%	0.02%
Control Stores	100	$ 61,000	$ 60,000	1.7%	$ 62,300	$ 61,000	2.1%	0.46%	

Figure 8.13: Analysis of Sales Trends During the Test

Although we do not show it in this book, identical statistical tests were performed on the sales and no significant differences were found.

To extrapolate the results of an experiment to the full chain, we need to tie the analyzed metric to the overall business objective. For example, shrink has a direct impact on profit margin, whereas return rate reduction is typically associated with a reduction in return dollars. Continuing with our analysis, we have now illustrated that Acme device ABC had a significant impact on shrink of a 0.09% reduction (Figure 8.8). We also know that each store would require five ABC devices, each costing $35 for the item and installation. For this example, we will assume that all devices need to be replaced once a year. For a retailer with 500 stores, this would result in an $87,500 annual investment (cost). Return on investment is calculated by using the difference between the current shrink dollars and the expected shrink dollars, given the 0.09% reduction in shrink from Acme security device ABC, and comparing the savings with the cost as a ratio (savings/cost). The full return-on-investment calculation is presented in Figure 8.14.

In Figure 8.14, the program is estimated to save the retailer $324,000 annually and cost $87,500 annually. This results in a return on investment = $324,000/$87,500 = 3.7. This implies that for every dollar invested in the program, the retailer will save $3.70.

Conclusion

The processes for conducting experiments in this chapter should help the loss prevention professional test and evaluate which programs will have the greatest effect in controlling losses. Many of the methods described here are not limited to loss prevention and can be applied to testing a number of different hypotheses in areas other than loss prevention within retail or even outside of retail. In the next chapter, we will expand on testing methods and modeling techniques that can help managers further assess loss prevention tools and ensure that a case can be made that money invested yields acceptable results.

Investment Cost

Number of stores	500
Number of devices per store	5
Cost per device	$35.00
Total cost of the program	$87,500

Return on Investment

Annual sales	$360,000,000
Average shrink rate	1.38%
Shrink dollars	$4,968,000
Reduction to shrink rate	−0.09%
Expected shrink rate	1.29%
Expected shrink dollars	$4,644,000
Reduction to shrink dollars	$324,000

Return on investment	3.7 to 1

Figure 8.14: Return on Investment for Acme Security Device ABC

Exercises

1. Name four threats to validity.
2. What are confounding variables? How do they influence the experiment? What can you do to remove the impact of confounding variables?
3. Why is sample size important in an experiment?
4. What are the steps of an experiment?
5. What is randomization? How is it important in testing? What does it help mitigate?
6. Why should an experiment use a control sample?

Chapter Nine

Introduction to Modeling

> Essentially, all models are wrong, but some are useful.
>
> —*George E. P. Box*

Introduction

In this chapter, we will discuss the basic principles of statistical modeling. In general, the goal of a statistical model is to define the relationship between one or many explanatory variables (which are also referred to as predictor variables or independent variables) and one or more outcome variables (which are also referred to as response variables or dependent variables). In this book, we only discuss the case with a single outcome variable with one or more explanatory variables. There are many types of models, which will be discussed in chapters to come. The type of model that is appropriate for various circumstances will depend on the types of response and predictor variables that are of interest, the complexity of the relationship between the variables, and the intended purpose of the models.

In general, a statistical model is a combination of (1) a fixed mathematical formula and (2) a component that captures the random fluctuations in the observations. Figure 9.1 shows an illustration of a model's components.

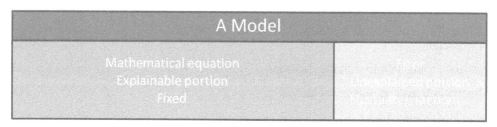

Figure 9.1: A Statistical Model

The fixed mathematical formula can range from fairly simple to extremely complex. The fixed mathematical formula within the model is what is known as the explainable portion of the model and the random fluctuations represent the unexplainable part of the model. A statistical model's intent is not so much to describe the world accurately, as it is to describe as much of the world as it can and then estimate the distribution of the error that is remaining (including how much that error will fluctuate).

A statistical model is typically built for one of two reasons (sometimes both). Either the modeler would like to describe the relationship between the predictor variables and the response variable, or the modeler would like to make predictions. In either case, the model development process can be identical; however, the choice of model may be different to accommodate these goals. For example, some of the more advanced modeling methods have very complex structures for the explainable part of the model and it may become difficult to explain the relationship between the predictor variables and the response variable.

General Formulation for a Statistical Model

As we stated in the prior section, a statistical model has two main components, a fixed component and a random component. A very general model structure is

$$\text{response} = g\big(\text{predictor variables}\big) + \text{error} \qquad\qquad 9.1$$

A model is a function of the predictor variables to predict or explain a response. In Equation 9.1, the explainable portion of the model is the function "$g()$," which combines the predictor variables to explain as much as it can about the response variable. Since we are rarely able to explain everything perfectly, there is an error term, which represents the unexplainable part of the model. The error term is not always a simple added term, as shown in Equation 9.1, but many of the models we will discuss have this exact structure.

In the following chapters, as we discuss models, we will typically use "Y" to represent the response variable and $X_1, X_2, \ldots, X_k$ to represent k predictor variables, where k represents an arbitrary number of possible variables that we may use. The general formula of Equation 9.1 can be rewritten using this alternate formulation:

$$Y = g\big(X_1, X_2, \ldots, X_k\big) + \text{error} \qquad\qquad 9.2$$

Many different models fall into this class of model. The following are some well-known models that have the structure above for $g()$:

Linear regression models $\qquad \beta_0 + X_1\beta_1 + X_2\beta_2 + \ldots + X_k\beta_k$

Additive models $\qquad \beta_0 + f_1(X_1) + f_2(X_2) + \ldots + f_k(X_k)$

Neural networks $\qquad f\left(\alpha_0 + \sum_{i=1}^{M}\alpha_i s\big(\beta_{0j} + X_1\beta_{1j} + X_2\beta_{2j} + \ldots + X_k\beta_{kj}\big)\right)$

Extreme gradient-boosting models $\quad \sum_{i}^{M} f_i\big(X_1, X_2, \ldots, X_k\big)$ where f_i is a regression tree fit on

$$Y - \sum_{j=1}^{i-1} f_j\big(X_1, X_2, \ldots, X_k\big)$$

Each of these models is attempting to estimate the function "$g()$" reliably using a different approach. The models listed fall into two distinct classes of model: (1) parametric models and (2) nonparametric models. Linear regression models, neural networks, and extreme gradient boosting are parametric models; the parameters in the model are notated using the symbols α and β. The additive models are typically fit as nonparametric, where each function $f_i()$ will be estimated. In general, the more parameters in a model, the more computationally complex it is to fit. Completely nonparametric methods are usually the most complicated to fit.

Predictive Models vs. Inferential Models

Statistical models are divided into two main classifications, inferential and predictive. In both types of models, the structure is identical and there is a set of values, known as parameters, that need to be estimated. Estimation is often referred to as fitting the model. The processes for fitting an inferential and a statistical model are the same, but the usage of the model may be dramatically different. An inferential model is intended to be used for inferring information about a population based on a sample, whereas a predictive model is generally concerned with making predictions about Y from future observations based on knowing only the values $X_1, X_2, ..., X_k$.

Just as with Chapter 6, on inferential statistics, we assume that some model exists in the population and that we are using data from a sample to estimate the parameters of the model. The error of the parameter estimates dictates if the parameter is statistically significant, which in turn will tell you something about the underlying predictor variable and its relationship to the response variable. Another component of inferential modeling is that of explaining and interpreting the model parameters in a way that can be explained to other people. For example, we may want to conclude that for every year of tenure for a store manager, the shrink decreases in the store by 5%. This type of conclusion can be easy to demonstrate with a linear model and very difficult with a neural network. In the following chapters, we will explore the inferential aspects and predictive aspects of each model type.

How Models are Fitted

The models shown in this chapter each have a mathematical equation, which represents the explainable portion of the model between the explanatory and predictor variables and an error component of the model. When models are fit, we are typically trying first to estimate the parameters of the explainable portion of the model and then to estimate the distribution of the remaining error term.

When fitting any model, there is a mathematical problem being solved, in that we would like the model to *best* explain the data we have observed. The key word in that last sentence is *best*. *Best* is determined by measuring the quality of the fit of the model and then trying to maximize that quality of fit. This measure is always some mathematical equation, which needs to be maximized for many different values of the parameters we would like to estimate. For some models, like the linear regression model, *best* is actually determined by a formula that is well known and always has the same answer. For more complex models, like neural networks, finding the best is a complex search into multidimensional space to find the exact spot where a maximum occurs. We won't get into the minutiae of the fitting algorithms, but will tell you that it is a complex mathematical process, which is usually invisible to the end user of the statistical routine.

Overfitting

As models become more complex, either through the addition of many variables or through the complexity of the model structure $g()$, the practitioner needs to be concerned with overfitting. There is a fine balance between fitting the explainable portion of the model and fitting the data. The objective with any model fitting is that the explainable portion of the model contains the true relationship of the predictor variables to the response variable in the population. This means that if we draw another sample and fit another model repeatedly, we should get roughly the same answer for the explainable portion of the model each time. Overfitting occurs when the model is fitted to the data more than it should be; if repeated sampling is done, the model does not fit as well on subsequent samples.

Figure 9.2 illustrates a model fitted to two variables to obtain the relationship between the variables. Some of the relationship is explainable—"This is the curved black line"—and some of the relationship is unexplainable—the deviation of the dots from the line. It is unrealistic to expect that we can explain random fluctuations.

With a very complex model structure, in some cases, the fitting process can actually begin to fit the unexplainable parts of the model. Figure 9.3 illustrates a case where the model is being overfitted to some of the noise.

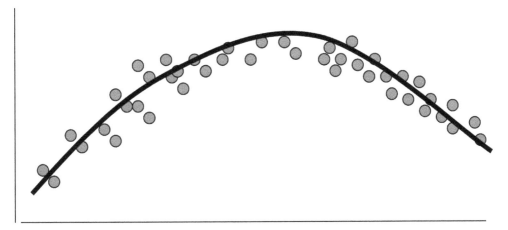

Figure 9.2: Correctly Fit Model

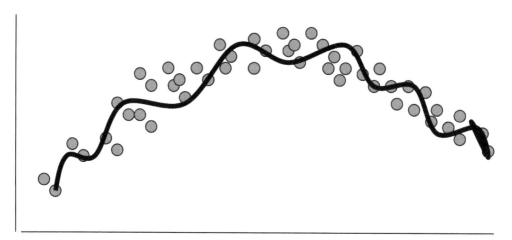

Figure 9.3: Overfitted Model

There are a few issues with overfitting the data:

(1) While the model will fit the data very well, the model will not be explaining the *true* relationship that exists in the population between the predictor variables and the response variables.
(2) If another sample is taken and a new model is fitted on the same variables, it will have a very different shape from the first model.
(3) If the model were used to make predictions about a new record, the model shown in Figure 9.3 would not be as accurate, on average, as the model shown in Figure 9.2.

Cross-Validation

One way to guard against overfitting is to use a cross-validation approach to modeling. There are several variations of the cross-validation approach, but the concept is similar, and is illustrated in Figure 9.4.

The goal in cross-validation is to remove some of the observations from the fitting process; when the model is fit, the model will be tested only on the sample that was withheld from the process. This approach will ensure that the model is not overfitted to the data, because we are checking the model's accuracy on a sample that was not used during the fitting process.

There are two common methods of splitting the data between the portion used for model fitting and that used for model validation.

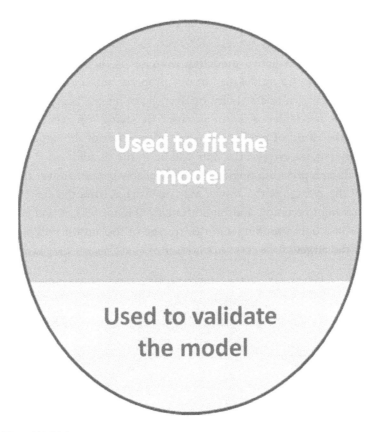

Figure 9.4: Fit and Validate

Time-based Data up to some date is used for fitting the model and all data after that time is used for model validation. For example, use data from 1/1/2015 to 12/31/2015 for model fitting and from 1/1/2016 to 6/30/2016 for model validation.

Random selection Use some selection process (we highly recommend random selection) to determine whether the observation in question belongs to the "model-fitting" pool of data or the "model-validation" pool of data. For example, add a random number to each observation and assume that all observations with random numbers between 0 and 0.750 belong to the model-fitting section while those with random numbers between 0.751 and 1 belong to the model-validation section.

Accuracy vs. Precision

One key concept in predictive modeling exercises is the concept of accuracy and precision. In some cases, a model may fit one property but not the other (Figure 9.5).

Accuracy refers to a model's ability, on average, to hit the center of the target. The key phrase in the last sentence is "on average." By saying "on average" we mean that the **center** of the cloud of predictions is near the center of the target. Each dot may fluctuate wildly but, on average, the dots will be in the middle.

Models with high precision (Figure 9.6) will reliably give an answer that is in a **tight** grouping, but the average of the answer may, on average, **miss** the center of the target. If a model has high precision and high accuracy (Figure 9.7), it will reliably give an answer that is in a tight grouping and the average of the answer will be very close to the center of the target.

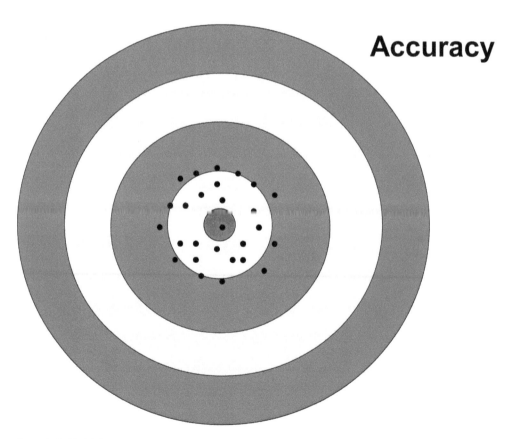

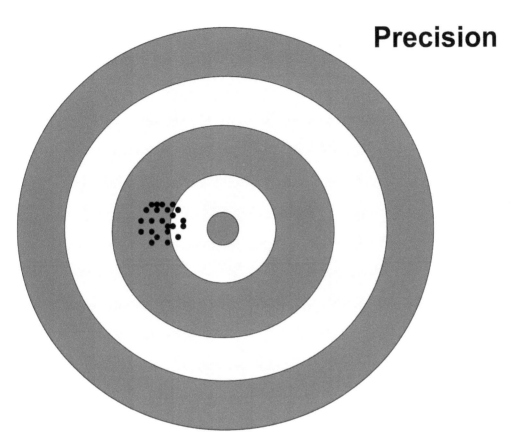

Precision

Figure 9.6: Model Precision

What are Predictive Models, Machine Learning Approaches, and Artificial Intelligence?

Many readers will have heard the buzzwords and phrases that frequently surround analytical methods. Phrases like "machine learning," "predictive models," "prescriptive models," "artificial intelligence," "big data," "unsupervised learning," and the like, are constantly evolving and reappearing over time. In fact, "artificial intelligence" has made its appearance many times over the decades in various forms and contexts. In this section, we will attempt to put context around these different phrases to help you understand what these terms really refer to.

The term "predictive models" refers to a general class of solutions that are designed to generate predictions using mathematical equations. The mathematical equations are like the $g()$ function described earlier. Predictive models are estimated using

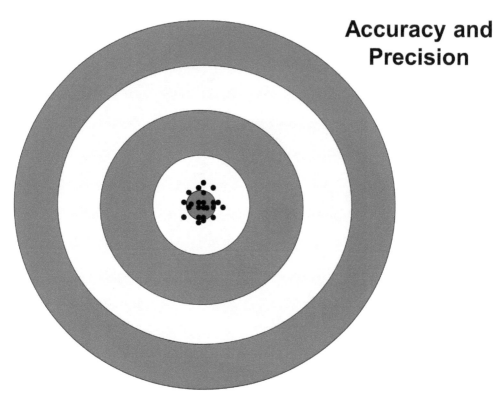

Accuracy and Precision

Figure 9.7: Model Accuracy and Precision

statistical methods that utilize examples (data) from the past in order to estimate events in the future or for unknown records. Linear regression and logistic regression, as well as many machine learning approaches, fall into this category of model.

The term "machine learning" refers to models that have a more general structure for $g()$, which can automatically estimate the relationship between the predictor variables and the response variables. Gradient-boosting models, random forests, and neural networks fall into this class of model. In Chapter 12 (see Figure 12.6), we show how these types of model structure are able to fit a complex shape without additional instruction from the modeler on what shape to expect. While the shape in Figure 12.6 can be fit with linear models, the modeler will be required to add an interaction term and a squared term to the model.

The term "artificial intelligence" refers to machines making decisions based on algorithms and models that can mimic human behavior. Within the artificial intelligence category, predictive models, some of which are based on machine learning, are often part of the algorithm. Usually, artificial intelligence refers to more human-like decisions, such as machine vision, voice recognition, facial recognition, audio transcription, and the like, but can be broader than this. Some recent advances on the artificial intelligence front would be self-driving cars and personal assistants, like Apple's Siri. Artificial intelligence (AI) is often sub-divided into narrow AI and artificial general intelligence (AGI). Narrow AI refers to solutions that are engineered to tackle a specific problem. All of the examples in this section are highly engineered by human beings and fall into the category of narrow AI. Most experts agree that AGI is decades away; AGI refers to an artificial intelligence that is able to learn completely on its own.

The term "big data" refers to enormous datasets that can often serve as the basis for predictive models, machine learning, or artificial intelligence. This term has come about recently on the tails of petabyte and higher data collection engines like Google. Additionally, it also often refers to the exercise of combining data across different data sources to learn something new. For example, we may combine Google searches for things relating to colds and flu with analysis of flu cases from the US Centers for Disease Control and Prevention to create a model that forecasts upcoming epidemics.

The term "prescriptive models" usually refers to predictive models that have another layer of logic added to provide specific instructions on how to "fix" or "prescribe" a set of actions for the user to take. An example would be a model that recognizes that your house's air conditioner is acting inefficiently and asks you to check for closed vents in the living room.

The term "unsupervised learning" refers to modeling and analytical techniques that attempt to determine features of the data without having an outcome variable. Clustering is a popular form of unsupervised learning where the data is segmented into groups based only on the characteristics of the predictor variables.

While there are different meanings for some of these phrases, there are also many similarities. Most of the procedures involve taking data and attempting to solve problems with that data. Usually, the solution involves taking predictor variables and response variables and finding out how they are related so that we can utilize that model in some type of system that helps human beings do their jobs better. In some sense, while the context of each phrase's usage is often different, they are far more similar than they are different ("A rose by any other name would smell as sweet," Shakespeare).

Typical Steps in a Model Development Project

A model development project typically follows a fairly consistent path. In this section, we will discuss the model planning phase and model lifecycle.

Planning Phase

The first step in developing a predictive model is actually determining what the problem is that you would like to solve. We refer to this step as the planning phase of the predictive modeling project. The following key questions should be answered during this phase of the project:

- What problem is the modeler trying to solve or improve?
- What is the current process?
- What is the desired process for the future?
- How would data flow into the model(s)?
- What data will be used in the initial model(s)?
- What are the future directions for model development and improvement?
- Who is the end user of the model output?
- How will the model output be delivered?
- What model output will be returned to the users?
- Where will the model be hosted and what software platform will be used?
- What reports will be needed to monitor and assess model performance?
- How will the model fit into the workflow for that process?
- What is the process and timing for model updates (and how will timing be determined)?

Once these questions are answered, the model developer has a good idea of what data will be needed to solve the issue at hand, where the data is, how to use the data for modeling, what model output is needed, who will use the model and how, how to monitor model performance, and how often to assess the model for updates. Armed with these answers, the model developer can begin the actual model building process, described next.

Predictive Model Lifecycle

The model lifecycle is illustrated in Figure 9.8. It includes four main milestones:

1. Gathering and cleaning of data;
2. Model development and testing;
3. Model integration;
4. Model monitoring and updating.

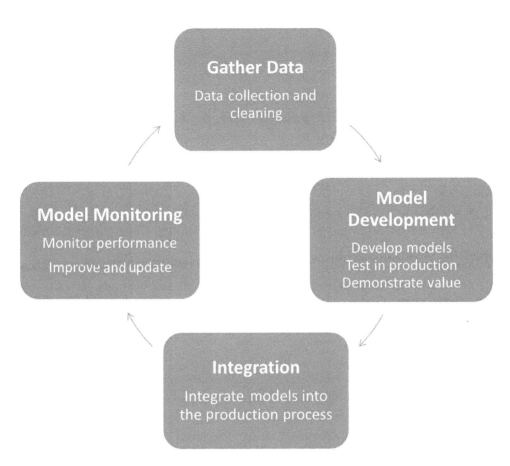

Figure 9.8: Model Lifecycle

Gather Data

The first step in Figure 9.8 is to gather data. Gathering data means collecting data from various databases and other data sources to be assembled for building the model. Data can be classified as follows:

- Internal data:
  - From easy-to-access sources;
  - From hard-to-access sources.
- External data:
  - Census data;

- Economic trend data;
- Individual-level trend data.

- Other data sources.

Data may be easy or hard to obtain. We classify the difficulty of data collection with the following outline. Most of these data processing categories are commonly known as data ETL (extract, transform, and load).

- Easiest:
  - In the format for the software you will be working with (e.g., SAS tables);
  - Can use the modeling software to read in the data you will be using for modeling from the storage database.
- Moderately hard:
  - In raw tables created using an operating system you are familiar with (e.g., ASCII files);
  - Requires user to write programs to read in the raw data and get it into the format required by the modeling software.
- Very hard:
  - In many different poorly defined file formats that you have to deduce;
  - In a format that is from a different operating system (e.g., mainframe, Extended Binary Coded Decimal Interchange Code);
  - Requires user to write more advanced programs to read in the raw data and deal with anomalies to get it into the format required by the modeling software.

Ultimately, for processing in most statistical software, data will have to be all in a single row for each observation. Data from multiple sources will need to be combined to create a modeling dataset and transaction data will have to be summarized at points in time when predictions are to be made. External data will need to be combined using a key (e.g., ZIP code, first or last name). Data from distinct internal tables will need to be combined and de-normalized. The ultimate dataset may have multiple rows per person at different points in time. Many modeling techniques will require sampling to meet model assumptions.

Once the data is all together, many clean-up steps are needed to prepare the data for model fitting. Explore each variable in the data and look for issues using the graphical methods and the descriptive statistics described earlier in the book. This process will also help begin the modeling process, since you will be getting to know your variables. You will want to compute frequency distributions for category variables for variables with a reasonable number of levels. For variables such as ZIP code, name, or address, which have too many levels to observe, look at the percentage missing, distribution of the length of the field, and the percentage of invalid values. For numeric variables, compute a percentile distribution (deciles). For dates, look at the frequency of key dates over time to look for gaps in the data. At this point, cross-check important key variables with dates to look at percentile distributions and frequency distributions to identify changes over time.

At this time, investigate such common data problems as missing values for variables, sparse data, inconsistencies, coding errors, or time-related changes in the data. Identify and define key variables, which will ultimately be used in raw format or a transformed format for modeling and response definition. Apply variable cleaning when it is appropriate. Some key techniques for cleaning data are categorized next:

- Handling missing values:
  - Simple solution: replace the missing values with the mean.
  - Advanced solutions: some more advanced missing data handling techniques exist, which can impute the values during the modeling process.
- Sparse data:
  - Sparse data occurs when there are many values of a categorical value, but some of them have only a few observations represented. For example, only a few people living in a certain ZIP code, or only a few of stock keeping unit 123 being sold in a certain month.
  - Combining sparse categories into a single category. For example, combine several stock keeping units into one category.
- Inconsistent definitions:
  - You will need to map the definitions to a common definition.
  - For example: if flag = "error" is now flag = "broken," you will need to map both "error" and "broken" into flag2 = "problem."
- Time-related changes:
  - Changes to the database over time need to be considered. This may require imputing missing values or dropping variables with inadequate history.
- Coding errors in specific fields (e.g., poorly typed names and addresses):
  - Once issues are identified, strategies need to be developed to handle problem variables.

Model Development

Once the data is assembled and basic investigations have been made on the data, it is time to begin the model development process. There may be a need to iterate between steps, as new issues are uncovered.

Step 1 Identify a response variable. This variable should be directly related to what you are trying to predict. For example, if you would like to forecast shrink, you might pick a variable that represents the change in shrink year over year as a percentage difference or an absolute difference. Additionally, you might simply want a response variable that is binary, such as "Did the shrink increase; Y/N?"

Step 2 The response variable will dictate the type of model to use. In the following chapters, we will discuss which type of model is appropriate for various response variables.

Step 3 Determine whether different segments of the data require different models (e.g., models by region or category of customer). Sometimes, different variables will be available for different segments. For example, "behavior of past customers in response to a loss prevention initiative" might have different variables from "behavior of new customers in response to a loss prevention initiative."

Step 4 Begin exploring the potential predictor variables to determine each predictor variable's relationship to the response variable. The methods in the previous chapters can be used to display these relationships. The modeler should also identify the need for transformations. If variables are right skewed or have sparse cells (category variables), the modeler may want to transform the underlying data to be more useful in a model. For example, right-skewed variables are probably best handled with a log transformation. Throughout this process, the modeler will want to identify the best candidate variables for modeling. The best variables will be those that have a clear relationship with the response variable.

Step 5 Begin fitting the model with one variable at a time to determine the variables with the best predictive power.

Step 6 The raw data variables are only the beginning of predictor variables. Derive other variables from the primary variables to increase your predictor variable's selection pool. For example, you may include a raw variable as well as variables based on different transformations (log scale, square, etc.). You may want to include interaction terms and variables calculated over different periods (e.g., activity in the past 30 days or in the past year). Variables that calculate the difference between other variables may also be useful (e.g., time between activities, distance between locations). Compound variables are often the most predictive (e.g., using the total amount stolen divided by the total number of transactions processed to create "theft dollars per transaction"). Add variables from external data (e.g., census records, crime records) to see if they are also predictive.

Step 7 Determine how to assess model fit (on the validation data). There are a number of methods, which will be discussed in the next section and following chapters. Once you determine what model evaluation metric to use (several are covered in the upcoming chapters), begin to remove and add variables and note how the model performs at each step. Note that some previously "good" variables may become nonsignificant once other variables are added.

In the following chapters, the choice of the proper modeling technique will be described in more detail. While fitting the appropriate model, the variable selection and the model fit measurement are key components, which we will leave to those chapters. The following outline illustrates some key components of assessing model fit and performance. Many of the concepts will be covered in their appropriate modeling chapters.

- Evaluation of model's predictive performance:
  - Cross-validation:
    - Choose a portion of the sample to exclude from modeling. Evaluate the model fitting using this sample.
    - Several cross-validation samples can be used for more robust estimation.
  - Select performance statistics:
    - Examples: Kolmogorov Smirnoff statistic for binary responses and R^2 (R squared) for continuous outcome.
    - Compound model structures will require other metrics. Choose a metric that is related to the purpose for which the model will be used.
- Evaluation of model fit:
  - Residual analysis, analysis of outliers, and analysis of influential observations:

- Residuals:

  - Residuals measure the difference between a prediction and the actual value.
  - Most routines and software allow for the output of standard residuals (these residuals have a standard normal distribution, which is a normal distribution with a mean of zero and a standard deviation of one).

- Outliers:

  - Outliers are typically observations that are 2–3 standard deviations or more from the predicted value (a value of 2 or 3+ on a standard residual).
  - These observations should be investigated for errors and for influence.
  - For logistic regression, evaluate observations that are high predictions or low predictions, but have the actual value in the opposite direction. Issues with extrapolation or with appropriate model structures (i.e., the need for a squared term) can often be discovered.

- Influential observations:

  - An outlier that is positioned far from the center of the data will often have a large influence over the parameter estimates.
  - PRESS (predicted residual error sum of squares) statistics in regression models can help identify large influence observations. These are calculated by refitting the regression model with each observation removed one at a time, and calculating that observation's residual from the resulting model.
  - Large influence observations should be investigated for removal.

- Comparison of different model structures with each other;
- Review model results with stakeholders;
- Iterate, while improving performance.

Typically, a presentation of results follows model development. During this presentation, your peers and supervisors will generally have many critiques on many steps in the process. It's most likely that, based on the feedback, you will iterate through the modeling steps prior to arriving at a final model.

Model Integration and Deployment

Once the model is developed and finalized, there may or may not be a need to integrate and deploy the model. At a minimum, the process for model development needs to be well documented and repeatable. Model deployment will involve creating and testing a module that can calculate the model variables for each customer, store, or whatever unit the models are built on. The module should be able to produce raw model calculations (also known as scores or predictions), and apply any post-model rules or transformations to the models. The module must be validated to ensure that the predictions are the same as those produced during model development.

For the model to be used in an operational manner, the raw data must be available in a timely manner and the model predictions must be provided quickly and efficiently. The best way to ensure that data is available is to automate the data feed to the model. This means that the data is there whenever a prediction or model estimate needs to be calculated. The deployment team should create automated scripts or real time programs that read in the data, clean it, prepare it for data derivation, and run the module to create the model predictions.

Model Monitoring

Once a model is being used, there are necessary steps for model monitoring, which will ensure that the model is performing properly. Model monitoring includes such things as: (1) analyzing the model input variables to ensure that variables are consistently defined over time; (2) analyzing the model output to ensure that the prediction distributions are consistent and stable over time; and (3) evaluating the model's accuracy using control samples. Over time, the modeler should determine the model's loss in accuracy that arises as the model becomes more out of date. These monitoring efforts will involve the use of automated reports and manual review processes. Periodic model refits accomplish several goals. First, new components can be added that utilize new data or learning from initial deployments. Second, the model refit brings model accuracy to original (or higher) levels.

Conclusion

The concepts in this chapter apply to most of the modeling algorithms described throughout the remainder of the book. It is important to note, however, that the model fitting itself is only one of the steps in the process of getting a model from concept to usage in a real-world situation. The best models are always developed not only by considering the model structure, but also by paying careful attention to the variables that go into the model. Even the best modeling algorithms will do poorly if the wrong variables are not in the model to begin with.

Exercises

1. What is a model? What are the two components?
2. What is the difference between predictive and inferential models?
3. How can you reduce the chance of overfitting the model? What does it mean to cross-validate the model?
4. What is the difference between accuracy and precision?
5. What are the steps in the predictive modeling lifecycle?
6. What are some methods to check model fit?
7. What are some methods to check model performance?

Linear Regression

Statistical thinking will one day be as necessary for efficient citizenship as the ability to read and write.

—*H. G. Wells*

Introduction

If the purpose of our research is to predict or explain Y (the dependent variable) on the basis or knowledge of one or more values of X (the independent variables or predictor variables) then we are interested in statistical modeling, a topic we started to review in Chapter 9. In this chapter and the next, we will cover a specific category of models, called regression models. Chapter 10 is limited to linear regression and Chapter 11 covers logistic regression. After finishing this chapter and the next, you should be able to make models for solving problems like, "Will shrink go up or down?", "Will employees terminate their employment?", and many more. Predicting the future course of shrink or predicting other trends in the data could save you a lot of money and help you allocate a limited amount of resources.

Modeling Basics

As covered in the previous chapter, a model is a function of the predictor variables to predict a response. There is usually an error term, since we can never predict an outcome perfectly. Here is an equation that depicts the structure of a model:

$$\text{response} = g(\text{predictor variables}) + \text{error} \qquad\qquad 10.1$$

Many models assume a "linear" model structure. Linear means that each of the predictor variables is simply multiplied by a coefficient, like a slope in the equation of a line. A linear relationship can be depicted by a line; as X increases or decreases by some factor, Y will increase or decrease by a fixed amount. For example, let's assume that our independent variable (X) is the number of security guards at the store. The dependent variable (Y) is the shrink rate. We may find a linear relationship between the two variables such that whenever the number of security guards is increased by 10%, the shrink rate decreases by 0.5%.

If the relationship between the independent variables and the dependent variables is linear, a linear model has the advantage of being relatively simple to interpret and the algorithms for fitting models are fast. However, it is essential for the relationship to be linear, otherwise the model may not be the best fit for the data.

Linear Regression

What is regression useful for? Describing relationships between one or many predictor variables and one response variable and creating a prediction equation. A simple linear regression can be defined by the equation $Y = \alpha + \beta \times X + \text{error}$, where β is the slope of the line, the amount by which Y changes when X increases by one unit, and α is the intercept of the line, the value of Y when $X = 0$. The typical assumptions for this model will be discussed in more depth in the following sections, but it is assumed that the error has a normal distribution with mean 0 and variance σ^2.

The development of a tool for prediction, called a regression equation, is based on Equation 10.1. The regression line enables one to predict the value of the dependent variable (Y) from that of the independent variable (X). To use the equation for prediction, substitute the value of X in the equation and compute the resulting value of Y. For example, after a linear regression has been conducted, one would be able to predict a person's weight (dependent variable) from his or her height (independent variable). Figure 10.1 illustrates a scatter plot and corresponding regression line and equation for the relationship between weight and height.

The regression coefficient (β) provides a way to measure the impact of the independent variable (X) on explaining the dependent variable (Y). If the independent variable is continuous (here, height in feet), then the regression coefficient denotes the change in the dependent variable (here, weight in pounds) per unit of change in the independent variable (here, height in feet). It is important to note that correct understanding of the regression coefficient requires particular attention to the units of measurement.

Regression Assumptions

Regression has many applications, such as determining relationships or making estimates and predictions, but, like all statistical procedures, it also has prerequisites or

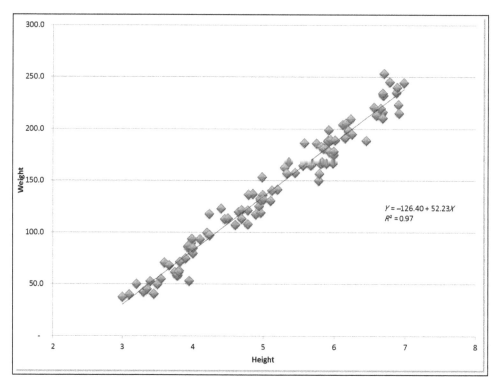

Figure 10.1: Regression Line Showing Linear Relationship Between Height and Weight

assumptions that need to be met prior to analysis. The results of the regression analysis are only reliable when the following four assumptions are met:

1. Linearity;
2. Independence;
3. Homogeneity of variance;
4. Normality.

Linearity

The assumption of linearity is that the relationship between the independent variables and the dependent variable is linear. In other words, each increase by one unit in an independent variable is associated with a fixed increase or decrease in the dependent variable. If linearity is violated, the analysis will not properly represent the true relationship.

The linearity assumption can be assessed by plotting the independent variables against the dependent variables (with a scatter plot, for example) to assess whether the relationship does indeed seem linear (see Figure 10.1). Also, it can be assessed by examining a scatter plot of the residuals; specifically, a scatter plot of the standardized residuals as a function of standardized predicted values. The scatter plot should indicate a linear trend; if the scatter plot shows a nonlinear trend, transformation of the variable is suggested. We will review linearity and provide an example of a residual plot later in the chapter (Figure 10.9).

Independence

The assumption of independence is that the observations are not related or correlated to one another or do not influence one another once the value of X is considered. For example, if we take a random sample of stores and measure the shrink of those stores, the stores can be thought of as independent units in that the shrink in one store does not necessarily influence the other store. Two variables are independent if knowing the value of one variable will not tell you anything about the value of the other variable.

Homogeneity of Variance

The assumption of homogeneity of variance is that the variance of the error term in the model is the same across all levels of the independent variable. This is also known as homoscedasticity. A residual plot, a plot of standardized residuals as a function of standardized predicted values, is a good way to test for homogeneity (this will be discussed later in the chapter, see Figure 10.9). The opposite of homoscedasticity is heteroscedasticity. If heteroscedasticity is detected, log transformation of the variable is suggested.

Normality

The assumption of normality is that the error terms will be normally distributed. A histogram of the residuals and a normality plot can be assessed to test the assumption of normality. Look for outliers, as they may distort relationships in the analysis. If the histogram indicates a skewed distribution, we suggest transforming the response variable, Y, and using the new variable in the analysis.

Checking assumptions is important and has significant benefits to the analyst. When assumptions are met, Type II error is reduced and the results of the analysis are more powerful.

Excel Example

In a fictitious study, data were obtained from 100 women and men aged 18 to 40. The association between height and weight was examined. Their height, our X variable, ranged from 3 feet to 7 feet. Weight in pounds, our Y variable, was the dependent variable, which was to be estimated from the independent variable (i.e., height in feet).

Figure 10.2 is a regression summary output from Excel. To conduct a regression analysis in Excel, take the following steps:

1. In an Excel spreadsheet, label the independent variable (Height) column and the dependent variable (Weight) column.
2. Click the "Data" tab → select "Data Analysis" → choose "Regression."
3. For the input Y range, select the column that includes the dependent variable; for the input X range, select the column that includes the independent variable.
4. Select other options (e.g., Excel provides plots to assess the residuals) and click "OK."

Based on the data, the following regression line was determined: $Y = -126.40 + 52.23 \times X$, where X is height in feet and Y is weight in pounds. The intercept ($\alpha = -126.40$) is the value of the dependent variable when $X = 0$. In this case, it does not make much sense that someone could have a height of 0; thus, explanation of the constant is often not valuable. The regression coefficient of 52.23 means that, in this model, a person's weight increases by 52.23 pounds with each additional foot of height.

SUMMARY OUTPUT								
Regression Statistics								
Multiple R	0.98							
R Square	0.97							
Adjusted R Square	0.97							
Standard Error	10.73							
Observations	100							

ANOVA						
	df	*SS*	*MS*	*F*	*Significance F*	
Regression	1	338476.27	338476.27	2939.08	0.000	
Residual	98	11286.07	115.16			
Total	99	349762.34				

	Coefficients	*Standard Error*	*t Stat*	*P-value*	*Lower 95%*	*Upper 95%*	*Lower 95.0%*	*Upper 95.0%*
Intercept	-126.40	5.06	-24.97	0.00	-136.45	-116.35	-136.45	-116.35
Height	52.23	0.96	54.21	0.00	50.32	54.14	50.32	54.14

Figure 10.2: Excel Regression Summary Output

For a person whose height is 6 feet, the predicted weight is 187 pounds ($Y = -126.40 + 52.23 \times 6$ feet).

As illustrated in Figure 10.2, the second table, labeled "ANOVA," tests the hypothesis ($H_0: \beta = 0$) and, in the summary, provides an F statistic and a significance level. Based on previous chapters, we know that our results are significant if $p < 0.05$ and in this case $p < 0.0001$ ("*Significance F*") indicates significant results. In the third table, we can see the intercept (i.e., the constant) and the regression coefficient (i.e., for every unit change in height, 52.23 is the change in weight), which form the regression equation. Both rows test the hypotheses $H_0: \alpha = 0$ and $H_0: \beta = 0$, respectively. You should note that, in the simple linear regression case, squaring the t statistic for the Y value (54.21) gives the F statistic in the table above.

As you can see in the top table in Figure 10.2, the adjusted R-square and R-square are similar (97%), since we only have one independent variable. The adjusted R-square adjusts the R-square using the number of independent variables. Think of the adjusted R-square as a penalty; the more independent variables, the lower the adjusted R-square. The adjusted R-square of 0.97 means that 97% of the variation in weight can be explained by the variation in height.

Example: Strong and Weak Relationships Between Variables

Figures 10.3 and 10.4 illustrate strong relationships between X and Y and no relationship between the two variables, respectively. The line in Figure 10.3 would be

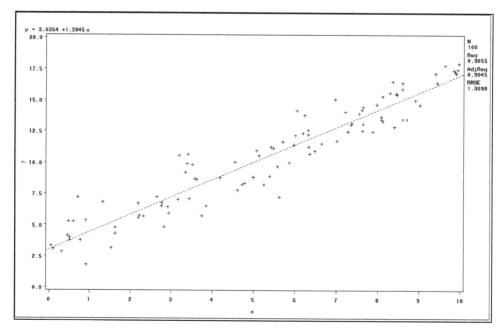

associated with a high *R*-square (close to 1), while the line in Figure 10.4 would be associated with a low *R*-square (close to 0).

SPSS Example

We conducted the same data analysis in SPSS. In addition, we opted to create a residual plot and histogram to investigate the assumptions of homogeneity of variance and normality. To run the linear regression model go to "Analyze" → "Regression" → "Linear" (see Figure 10.5).

When the next window opens, use the arrow to move "Weight" to the "Dependent" box and "Height" to the "Independent(s)" box (see left side of Figure 10.6). Select the "Plots" option to create the residual and histogram plots, as illustrated on the right side of Figure 10.6.

The results of the analysis are illustrated in Figure 10.7. The adjusted R^2, the overall model significance ($p < 0.05$), the constant and height coefficients, and the significance of the height variable are circled. As expected, the results are identical to those illustrated in Excel.

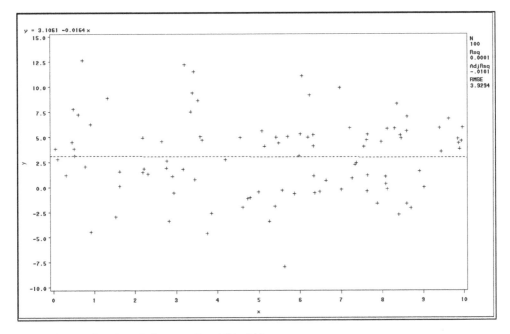

Figure 10.4: No Relationship Between *X* and *Y* in SAS

The histogram in Figure 10.8 illustrates a reasonable normal distribution and the residual scatter plot in Figure 10.9 confirms that the variance is homogenous (no heteroscedasticity). When the residuals look like a "bird's nest" or when the residuals seem almost randomly distributed in the plot, the assumption of homogenous variance is valid. If, however, the residual plot has a "fan pattern," where the residuals are more tightly clustered given certain values of the predicted variable and "fan out" given other predicted values, we are faced with the issue of heteroscedasticity. Figure 10.10 illustrates an example of heteroscedasticity.

Estimation and Hypothesis Testing

We hypothesize that a relationship exists in the population: average$(Y) = E(Y) = \beta_0 + \beta_1 \times X$.

Based on a sample, we estimate the parameters describing that relationship. This parallels the preceding discussions relating to a population mean and the sample mean. Repeated sampling will show the variance of the estimates.

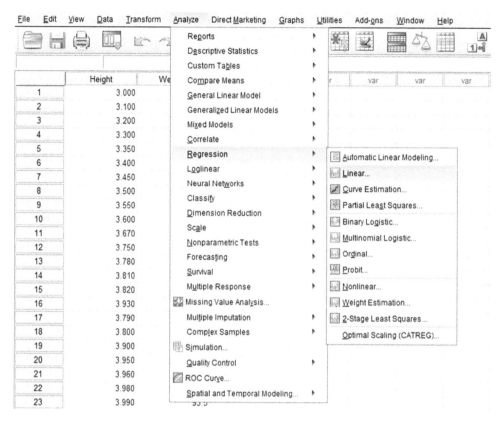

Figure 10.5: Running Linear Regression in SPSS

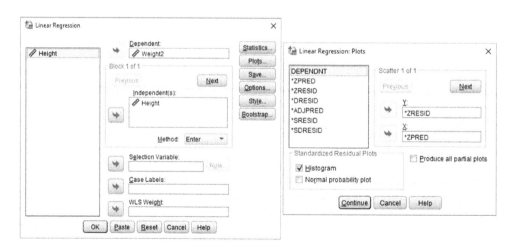

Figure 10.6: Running Linear Regression and Residual Plots in SPSS

Model Summary[b]

Model	R	R Square	Adjusted R Square	Std. Error of the Estimate
1	.984[a]	.968	.967	10.7314

a. Predictors: (Constant), Height

b. Dependent Variable: Weight2

ANOVA[a]

Model		Sum of Squares	df	Mean Square	F	Sig.
1	Regression	338476.268	1	338476.268	2939.081	.000[b]
	Residual	11286.071	98	115.164		
	Total	349762.339	99			

a. Dependent Variable: Weight2

b. Predictors: (Constant), Height

Coefficients[a]

Model		Unstandardized Coefficients		Standardized Coefficients	t	Sig.
		B	Std. Error	Beta		
1	(Constant)	-126.402	5.063		-24.966	.000
	Height	52.231	.963	.984	54.213	.000

a. Dependent Variable: Weight2

Residuals Statistics[a]

	Minimum	Maximum	Mean	Std. Deviation	N
Predicted Value	30.292	238.172	141.844	58.4718	100
Residual	-27.0240	29.7165	.0000	10.6771	100
Std. Predicted Value	-1.908	1.647	.000	1.000	100
Std. Residual	-2.518	2.769	.000	.995	100

a. Dependent Variable: Weight2

Figure 10.7: Linear Regression Output SPSS

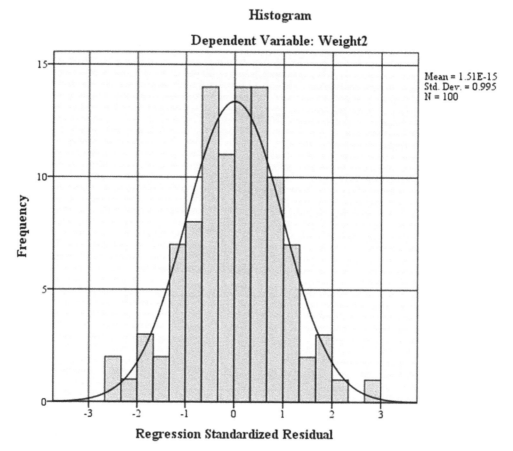

Figure 10.8: Residual Plot in SPSS

In simple linear regression, we test for a relationship between Y and X. This is the same as testing $H_0: \beta_1 = 0$. This hypothesis tests whether the slope of the line is zero or not. Figure 10.12 shows an SAS output that shows the regression coefficient and the p value. Based on the output, we can reject the null hypotheses that $\beta_1 = 0$, since $p < 0.0001$.

Residuals

Residuals deal with comparing predictions with actual responses. The equation for the residuals is $e_i = y_i - \hat{y}_i$. In other words, residuals are the difference between the actual values and the predicted values. We want the line to be as close to the data points as

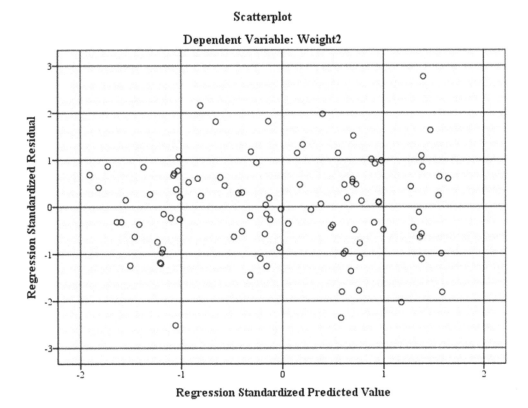

Figure 10.9: Histogram in SPSS—Testing Normality

possible; the smaller the error or residual, the better our prediction (see Figure 10.1 for a good example).

Residual plots can reveal unwanted patterns that indicate biased results or weak relationships. The residuals should be random (see Figure 10.13). If the residuals suggest that your error distribution is not homogeneous (Figure 10.10), you have an opportunity to improve your model. The residuals should not be either systematically high or low. The residuals should be centered on zero throughout the range of fitted values. In other words, the model is correct on average for all fitted values. Further, residuals should be normally distributed.

For continuous responses, look for observations that are very far from the prediction. Standardize the residual to account for natural fluctuations. This technique is a common output in most regression outputs from popular statistical software packages. When you examine the residuals, determine if: (1) observations need to be removed; (2) observations are important even though they are outliers; or (3) a term in the model is missing.

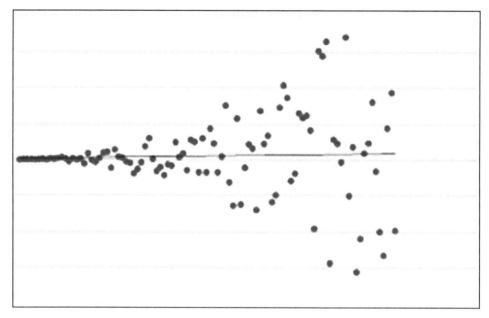

Figure 10.10: Example of Heteroscedasticity

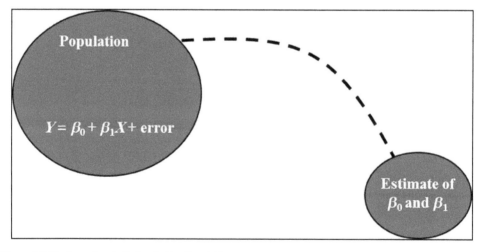

Figure 10.11: Sampling to Estimate the Population

How are Regression Models Fitted: Least Squares

The ordinary least squares method estimates the slope and intercept of the regression line so that the residuals are as small as possible. Figure 10.14 shows an assessment of residuals.

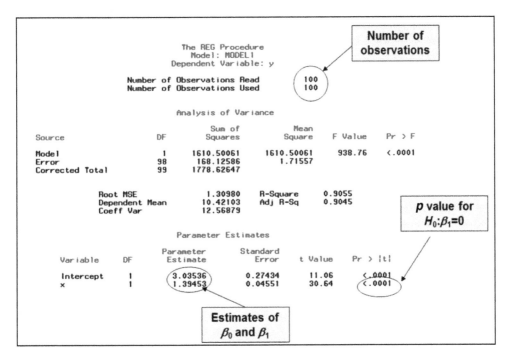

Figure 10.12: Strong Relationship Between *X* and *Y* in SAS

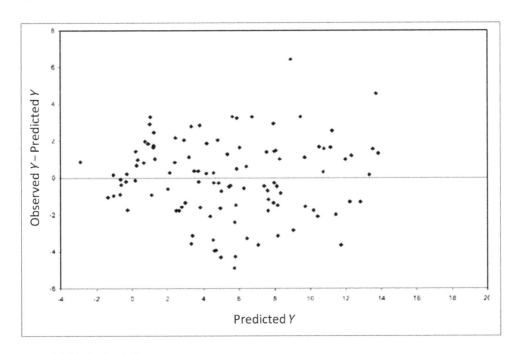

Figure 10.13: Residual Plot

The least squares method minimizes the difference between the prediction and the actual value. To choose a line, minimize the sum of squared distances between the line and the data points (see Figure 10.15). The advantages of this method are that it is simple, easy to understand, and computationally easy to fit.

The values of β_0 and β_1 that minimize the sum of the squared errors will intuitively fit in the middle of the cloud of dots on the scatter plot of Figure 10.15.

R Squared

The coefficient of determination, R^2 (R squared), is the fraction of the overall variance that can be attributed to the independent variables in a regression model; it ranges from 0 to 1 (see Equation 10.2). The closer the regression model's estimated values ($\hat{y}_i$) are to the actual values (y_i), the closer the coefficient of determination is to 1 and the better the model fits the data (the more variance that is accounted for by the model). R^2 is also the correlation of the actual observations (Y) to the predicted values of Y squared. R^2 provides an estimate of the strength between the independent variables and

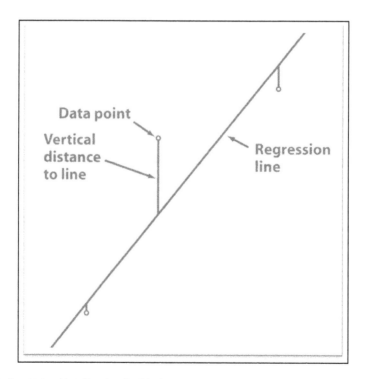

Figure 10.14: Regression Line Showing Residuals

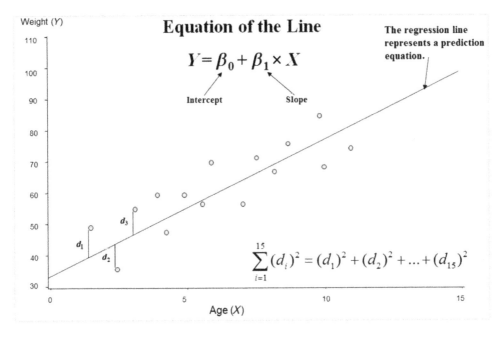

Figure 10.15: Regression Line Represents a Prediction Equation

the dependent variable. Another way to think of R^2 is that it reflects the scatter around a regression line; the tighter the scatter is to the line, the less variability, and hence the higher R^2. R^2 is handy, but it cannot tell you whether your estimates are biased or not. A good rule of thumb is to evaluate your residual plots.

$$R^2 = \frac{\sum_{i=1}^{n}(\hat{y}_i - \bar{y})^2}{\sum_{i=1}^{n}(y_i - \bar{y})^2} = \frac{\text{explained variance}}{\text{overall variance}} = \frac{\text{explained variation}}{\text{overall variation}}$$

10.2

The coefficient of determination is a measure of the validity of a regression model. It reflects the variation in the values of the dependent variable that is explained by the independent variable. It is important to note that the more independent variables in your model, the larger the coefficient of determination becomes. This, in turn, lowers the precision of the estimation of the regression coefficients (β_i). A noteworthy solution is to use the adjusted coefficient of determination, which takes the number of independent variables in your regression model into account and provides a better picture of the model's accuracy. Additionally, the modeler can measure R^2 on a cross-validation sample, which will indicate if the data is overfitted.

Predictions

The regression model can be used to make predictions of Y for new cases of X. When making predictions, the user will use a type of confidence interval known as a prediction interval. Prediction intervals are used because of the uncertainty of making predictions based on the distribution or scatter of a number of previous observations. In other words, prediction intervals represent the range in which a new observation is likely to fall, given specified characteristics of the predictors.

Prediction intervals take into account not only the margin of error around the mean prediction but also the actual error inherent in an individual observation. A narrower prediction interval represents more accurate predictions. For example, let's use shoplifting arrests to predict shrink rate. Based on the results, we see that 26 arrests produce a prediction interval of 4.25–5% shrink rate. We can, therefore, be 95% confident that an observation with a value of $X = 26$ will, from repeated sampling, have a value in the range 4.25% to 5%, 95% of the time. Prediction intervals can be interpreted and assessed based on working knowledge of the subject matter being studied.

Dangers with Extrapolation

When we make predictions for Y based on values of X, we want to stay within the range of our values for X used in the data, otherwise we may get answers that have little support from the data. Going outside the range of the X variables to make a prediction about Y is known as extrapolation. Consider, for example, a model is built that relates discarded packages to shrink for liquor stores. Applying such a model to big box stores, or even clothing stores, would be illogical, since the relationship between discarded packages and shrink is not consistent for all types of retailer. Similarly, if I built a model to compare height (Y) and age (X) for children aged 5 to 17, I would not want to use that model to predict the heights of individuals who are 50. I would probably estimate their height to be extremely high in these cases.

Multiple Regression

In the previous sections, we discussed simple linear regression. Multiple regression builds on simple linear regression. The main difference is that in multiple regression the dependent variable is modeled against several independent variables instead of one. In other words, multiple regression seeks to describe the relationship between one dependent variable (Y) and many predictors or independent variables ($X_1, ..., X_k$). If we let $Y = f(X_1, ..., X_k) + error$ we have a generalization of simple linear regression.

The error has a normal distribution with mean 0 and variance σ^2. But what is $f(X_1, ..., X_k)$? This is a function of all of the predictor variables $X_1, ..., X_k$. For multiple linear regression, $f(X_1, ..., X_k) = \beta_0 + \beta_1 X_1 + \beta_2 X_2 + ... + \beta_k X_k$. In three dimensions (i.e., $p = 2$), this equation represents a plane. In more than three dimensions, we call this a hyperplane.

What are $X_1, ..., X_k$? These represent predictor or independent variables. We write it like this to symbolize that there are an arbitrary number of them (k). They can represent either continuous or categorical variables. If a category variable has S categories, then it will use $S - 1$ predictor variables and parameters to represent it.

Multiple regression will provide the independent contribution of each explanatory variable to the prediction of the outcome while controlling for the influence of the other explanatory variables.

$$Y = \beta_0 + \beta_1 X_1 + \beta_2 X_2 + \beta_3 X_3 + \beta_4 X_4 + \varepsilon$$

10.3

So, where do estimates come from? Recall that in simple linear regression we wanted to minimize the sum of the squared distances of each observation from the line. This distance is written for the ith observation as d_i = predicted value$_i$ − actual value$_i$. We can do the same in multiple regression, also using least squares estimation. Estimation using the ordinary least squares method in multiple regression is the same as simple linear regression, in that it minimizes the squared distances between the observed and predicted values for the dependent variable. In other words, ordinary least squares estimates the values of $\beta_0, \beta_1, ..., \beta_k$ to minimize the sum of the squared residuals. That is, given multiple independent variables, $X_1, ..., X_k$, the estimates are selected simultaneously to make $\sum_{i=1}^{n}(Y_i - \hat{\beta}_0 - \hat{\beta}_1 X_{1i} - \hat{\beta}_2 X_{2i})^2$ as small as possible. Finding the minimum of this equation has a definite answer and does not require a searching algorithm, like some of the other models covered later in this book.

Example Output from SAS for Multiple Regression

See Figure 10.16 for an annotated example of a multiple regression analysis using SAS. Here are a few things to observe in the output:

- β_1, β_2, and β_4 are significant ($p < 0.05$). Therefore, we can reject the null hypotheses regarding β_1, β_2, and β_4 (their slopes are not equal to zero).
- β_3 is not significant.
- The parameter estimate for β_1 is negative. This means that for every unit increase in X_1, the dependent variable will decrease 5.3 units (holding other variables constant).

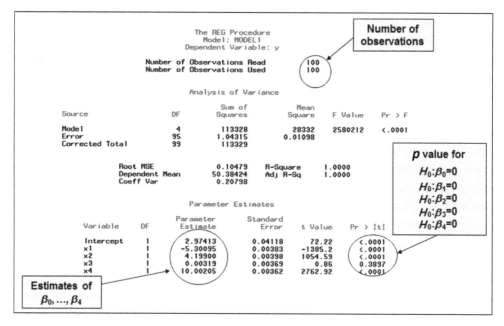

Figure 10.16: Example SAS Output for Multiple Regression Y vs. X_1, X_2, ..., X_4

- The parameter estimates for β_2 and β_4 are positive. This means that for every unit increase in X_2, the dependent variable will increase 4.199 units and for every unit increase in X_4, the dependent variable will increase 10.002 units (holding other variables constant).
- The model fits the data well. R^2 and adjusted R^2 are both 1 (an unreasonably good fit, but the data is fictional).

Excel Example

In a fictitious study, data were obtained from 25 retail stores. The loss prevention team collected data on internal theft incidences, organized retail crime theft incidences, and manager tenure for each store and wanted to build a multiple regression model to predict shrink. Shrink is the dependent variable and ranges from 4% to 21%. The data is presented in Table 10.1.

Figure 10.17 shows a multiple regression summary output that Excel produces. To conduct a multiple regression analysis in Excel, follow these steps:

1. In an Excel spreadsheet, label your independent variable columns and dependent variable column.
2. Click the "Data" tab, select "Data Analysis," and choose "Regression."

Table 10.1: Fictional Retail Store Data

Store Number	Inter Theft	ORC Theft	Manager Tenure	Shrink
1	104	109	1	0.210
2	100	106	2	0.190
3	98	99	4	0.185
4	95	92	5	0.180
5	87	88	5	0.170
6	86	81	6	0.165
7	79	76	9	0.160
8	72	70	10	0.155
9	70	68	11	0.150
10	66	67	11	0.148
11	64	62	12	0.140
12	61	60	13	0.132
13	55	59	14	0.131
14	54	57	15	0.124
15	51	54	16	0.121
16	45	49	16	0.110
17	40	44	17	0.105
18	32	33	18	0.090
19	31	32	23	0.085
20	25	28	24	0.077
21	21	24	25	0.068
22	18	19	26	0.064
23	15	18	27	0.058
24	9	17	29	0.056
25	5	9	32	0.042

3. For the input *Y* range, highlight the column that includes the dependent variable. For the input *X* range, highlight all of the columns that include the independent variables.
4. Click "OK."

We are interested in the effect of internal theft, organized retail crime theft, and manager tenure on store shrink. So, we build our multiple regression model and get the results (see Figure 10.17). The prediction model is: *predicted* shrink = 0.0817 + 0.0007

SUMMARY OUTPUT								
Regression Statistics								
Multiple R	1.00							
R Square	0.99							
Adjusted R Square	0.99							
Standard Error	0.00							
Observations	25.00							
ANOVA								
	df	*SS*	*MS*	*F*	*Significance F*			
Regression	3	0.05	0.02	1,102.11	0.00			
Residual	21	0.00	0.00					
Total	24	0.05						
	Coefficients	*Standard Error*	*t Stat*	*P-value*	*Lower 95%*	*Upper 95%*	*Lower 95.0%*	*Upper 95.0%*
Intercept	0.082	0.020	4.044	0.001	0.040	0.124	0.040	0.124
Internal_Theft	0.001	0.000	2.092	0.049	0.000	0.001	0.000	0.001
ORC_Theft	0.000	0.000	1.695	0.105	(0.000)	0.001	(0.000)	0.001
Manager_Tenure	(0.001)	0.001	(2.241)	0.036	(0.003)	(0.000)	(0.003)	(0.000)

Figure 10.17: Summary Output for Multiple Regression in Excel

$\times$ internal theft + 0.0005 $\times$ organized retail crime theft + $-0.0015 \times$ manager tenure. The intercept ($\beta_0 = 0.0817$) is the value of the dependent variable when X_1, X_2, ..., X_k are all equal to 0. Predicted shrink when internal theft, organized retail crime theft, and manager tenure are all zero equals 0.0817.

The interpretation of regression coefficients in multiple regression is: for every unit increase in the value of independent variable X_1, the dependent variable Y will increase by the regression coefficient (β_1), controlling for the effect of the other independent variables. If β_1 is negative, we would say for every unit increase in the value of independent variable (X_1) the dependent variable Y will decrease by the regression coefficient ($|\beta_1|$), controlling for the effect of the other independent variables. Here are some examples from our model in Excel:

- For every additional internal theft incident we see, we predict that shrink will increase by 0.0007, controlling for the other two independent variables.
- For every additional organized retail crime theft incident we see, we predict that shrink will increase by 0.0005, controlling for the other two independent variables.
- For every additional year of manager experience we have, we expect shrink to decrease by 0.0015, controlling for the other two independent variables.

Now imagine that you want to predict the shrink for a store given the variables in your model. You know that Store 100 has 47 internal theft incidents, 46 organized retail crime theft incidents, and a manager with 19 years of experience. With this data, you can predict that Store 100 will have:

$$\text{predicted shrink} = 0.0817 + (0.0007 \times 47) + (0.0005 \times 46) + (-0.0015 \times 19) = 0.108 \qquad 10.4$$

As you can see in Figure 10.17, the adjusted $R^2 = 0.99$. The coefficient of determination measures the proportion of variability in the dependent variability explained by the model ($0 \leq R^2 \leq 1$). Adjusted R^2 takes into consideration the degrees of freedom and provides a more accurate picture of the model's accuracy. Adjusted R^2 of 0.99 means that 99% of the variation in shrink can be explained by internal theft, organized retail crime theft, and manager tenure.

The second table in Figure 10.17 provides an F statistic and a significance level for a compound hypothesis, $H_0: \beta_1 = 0, \beta_2 = 0,$ and $\beta_3 = 0$, vs. the alternative hypothesis that at least one of the parameters is nonzero. Based on previous chapters, we know that our results are significant if $p < 0.05$ and in this case $p < 0.0001$ (*significance F*), indicating significant results. In the third table, we can see the intercept (i.e., the con-

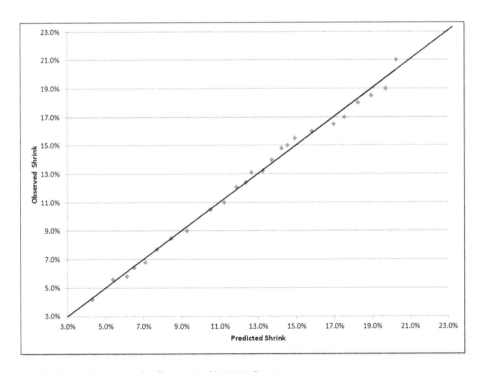

Figure 10.18: Prediction Line for Regression Model in Excel

stant) and the regression coefficients, which form the regression equation for prediction. Figure 10.18 illustrates how well our model predicts shrink (note how close the data points are to the fitted line). Note: the data are not real and you should not expect results this strong in real life.

To run the same analysis in SAS, input the data into SAS with "proc import," an infile statement, or using this data-step:

```
title1 'Multiple Regression in SAS';
data shrink_data;
input Store Internal_Theft ORC_Theft Manager_Tenure Shrink;
datalines;
```

1	104	109	1	0.210
2	100	106	2	0.190
3	98	99	4	0.185
4	95	92	5	0.180
5	87	88	5	0.170
6	86	81	6	0.165
7	79	76	9	0.160
8	72	70	10	0.155
9	70	68	11	0.150
10	66	67	11	0.140
11	64	62	12	0.140
12	61	60	13	0.132
13	55	59	14	0.131
14	54	57	15	0.124
15	51	54	16	0.121
16	45	49	16	0.110
17	40	44	17	0.105
18	32	33	18	0.090
19	31	32	23	0.085
20	25	28	24	0.077

21	21	24	25	0.068
22	18	19	26	0.064
23	15	18	27	0.058
24	9	17	29	0.056
25	5	9	32	0.042;

Run;

To create a regression model, use a "model" statement, such as
model <dependent variable> = <list of independent variables>
The code is:

```
ods output ParameterEstimates=Parameter_Estimates;
proc reg data=shrink_data;
    model shrink = internal_theft orc_theft manager_tenure;
    output out=shrink_predict predicted=predicted r=resid;
run;
ods output close;
quit;
```

The output is shown in Figure 10.19. Figures 10.19 and 10.20 illustrate the same example as in Figures 10.17 and 10.18 using SAS vs. Excel. You can see that the results are identical between the two procedures.

Another aspect to highlight in the SAS output of Figure 10.19 is the root mean square error, which is another way to represent the accuracy of the model or the error of the model. It measures the absolute fit of the model to the data (i.e., how close the observed data points are to the model's predicted values). It is the square root of the variance of the residuals; therefore, the smaller the root mean square error, the better. A good way to assess your model fit is to compare the root mean square errors in your training dataset and your test dataset. The root mean square error should be similar in both datasets.

SPSS Example

To run a multiple regression model in SPSS, go to "Analyze" → "Regression" → "Linear" (see Figure 10.21). In the box that opens, use the arrow to move "Shrink"

The SAS System

The REG Procedure
Model: MODEL1
Dependent Variable: Shrink

Number of Observations Read	25
Number of Observations Used	25

Analysis of Variance

Source	DF	Sum of Squares	Mean Square	F Value	Pr > F
Model	3	0.05382	0.01794	1102.11	<.0001
Error	21	0.00034186	0.00001628		
Corrected Total	24	0.05417			

Root MSE	0.00403	R-Square	0.9937
Dependent Mean	0.12464	Adj R-Sq	0.9928
Coeff Var	3.23711		

Parameter Estimates

Variable	DF	Parameter Estimate	Standard Error	t Value	Pr > |t|
Intercept	1	0.08174	0.02021	4.04	0.0006
Internal_Theft	1	0.00066735	0.00031896	2.09	0.0487
ORC_Theft	1	0.00048583	0.00028667	1.69	0.1049
Manager_Tenure	1	-0.00146	0.00065047	-2.24	0.0360

Figure 10.19: Summary Output for Multiple Regression in SAS

to the "Dependent" area, and the three independent variables to the area called "Independent(s)" (see Figure 10.22). The resulting output is illustrated in Figure 10.23.

As noted, all three programs (Excel, SAS, and SPSS) produce the same results. The overall model is significant ($p < 0.05$). The internal theft variable is significant ($p < 0.05$) and the manager tenure variable is significant as well ($p < 0.05$). The organized retail crime theft variable, however, is not significant.

Variable Selection

For your regression model to be strong and valid and to explain the dependent variable as well as possible, it should only include independent variables that explain a large portion of the variance in the dependent variable and are significant. In a case where

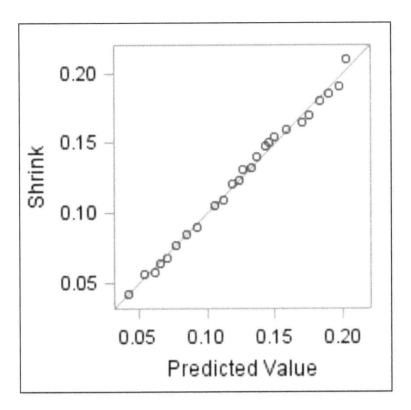

Figure 10.20: Prediction Line for Regression Model in SAS

you have included many independent variables based on theory and subject knowledge, but want to only include those predictors that are contributing positively to the model, there are several options. Most software packages include several different types of variable selection, so that only the best predictors are included in the final model. The variable selection process, essentially, enables the analyst to remove unnecessary predictors and enhance predictive accuracy. There are various methods of selecting the best variables for your model.

Forward Selection

Forward selection begins with an empty model and variables are added one at a time. Variables are added to the model one by one, choosing the variable with the highest contribution each time. Entry into the model requires some level of statistical significance, which is set by the modeler. This is an iterative process and it is complete when there are no variables left that contribute to explaining the variance in the dependent

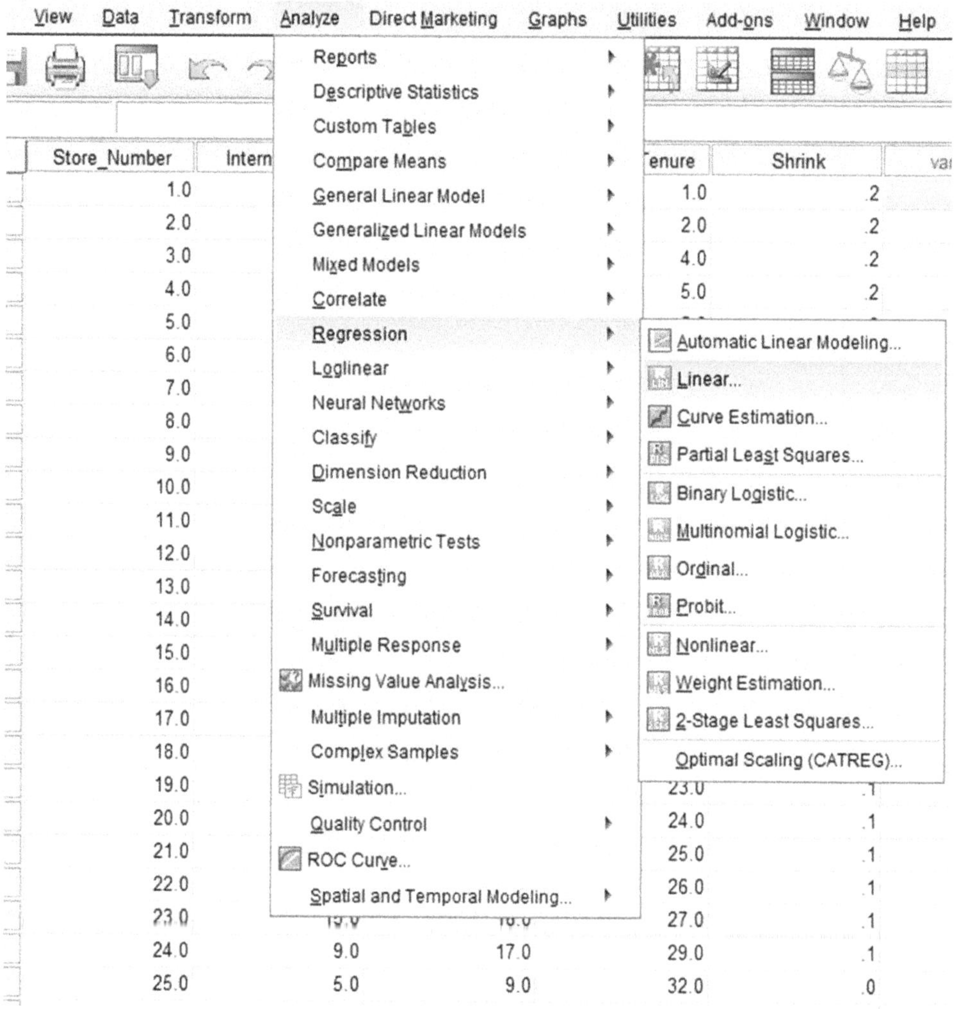

Figure 10.21: Multiple Linear Regression in SPSS

variable and are statistically significant. A disadvantage to this method is that variables added to the model cannot be taken out. Often, once new variables are added, a variable that entered in a previous step will no longer be significant.

Backward Selection

Backward selection is the opposite process. It begins with a model that contains all possible relevant independent variables. Variables are removed from the model based

238

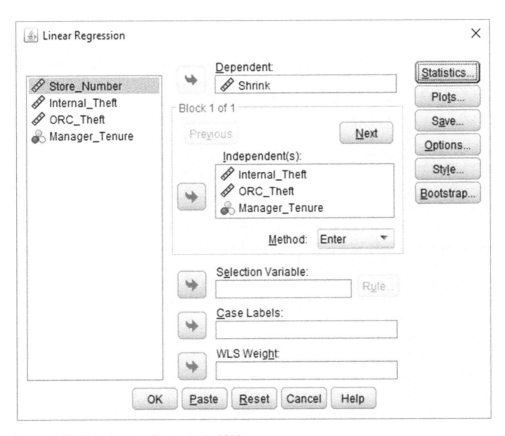

Figure 10.22: Multiple Linear Regression in SPSS

on their lack of incremental contribution to the model and their lack of statistical significance; then the model is refit (i.e., the parameters are re-estimated without the dropped variable). In other words, the independent variables with the smallest contribution to the model, which are also not statistically significant, are removed one by one. This is an iterative process and is done until no independent variables are left that are nonsignificant. A disadvantage to this method is that variables taken out of the model cannot be added back in.

Stepwise Selection

Stepwise regression is a variation of both the forward and backward selection processes. It begins with an empty model and adds an independent variable that best contributes to the model, and then iterates the process. Additionally, variables are removed from the

Model Summary

Model	R	R Square	Adjusted R Square	Std. Error of the Estimate
1	.997[a]	.994	.993	.0040

a. Predictors: (Constant), Manager_Tenure, ORC_Theft, Internal_Theft

ANOVA[a]

Model		Sum of Squares	df	Mean Square	F	Sig.
1	Regression	.054	3	.018	1102.106	.000[b]
	Residual	.000	21	.000		
	Total	.054	24			

a. Dependent Variable: Shrink

b. Predictors: (Constant), Manager_Tenure, ORC_Theft, Internal_Theft

Coefficients[a]

Model		Unstandardized Coefficients		Standardized Coefficients	t	Sig.
		B	Std. Error	Beta		
1	(Constant)	.082	.020		4.044	.001
	Internal_Theft	.001	.000	.428	2.092	.049
	ORC_Theft	.000	.000	.300	1.695	.105
	Manager_Tenure	-.001	.001	-.272	-2.241	.036

a. Dependent Variable: Shrink

Figure 10.23: Multiple Linear Regression in SPSS

model at each step if they become nonsignificant as other independent variables are added. That is, at each step in the modeling process, variables that previously entered the model but are no longer significant are removed. The process stops when no additional variables can be added that are significant or can be removed due to lack of significance.

Cross-Validated Stepwise

The cross-validation stepwise process starts with no variables and adds one variable at a time. The variable with the best property for some metric evaluated on a cross-validation sample is added. Entry requires some level of statistical significance. Variables that are no longer significant are removed. Continue adding variables until no variable meets the criteria for entry or removal.

Here are the SAS model options for the means of selection and elimination:

- model y = x1 x2 x3 / forward;   /* forward selection */;
- model y = x1 x2 x3 / backward;   /* backward elimination */;
- model y = x1 x2 x3 / stepwise slentry=0.05 slstay=0.1; /* stepwise selection */.

   You should note in the stepwise selection procedure that the options "slentry" and "slstay" control the significance level at which a variable is able to enter and leave the model, respectively.

In SPSS, variable selection is achieved by selecting "Method" after designating the dependent and independent variables (see Figure 10.24).

Outliers in Regression

Regression is very sensitive to outliers; outliers can distort the regression line and the predictive values. When an outlier is included in the analysis, the outlier pulls the regression line toward itself. This can result in a solution that is more accurate for the outlier, but less accurate for all of the other cases in the dataset. The problems of satisfying assumptions and detecting outliers are intertwined. For example, if an observation has a value on the dependent variable that is an outlier, it will affect the skew and hence the error distribution. Removing an outlier may improve the distribution of a variable. Transforming a variable may reduce the likelihood that the value for a case will be characterized as an outlier.

   Let's look at an example of the effect of an outlier on the regression equation. Previously in this chapter, we illustrated a linear regression equation using height to predict weight; our regression equation was $Y = -126.40 + 52.23 \times X$. In Figure 10.25, the data is exactly the same with the exception of one additional data point. The new data point changes the regression equation to $Y = -85.50 + 43.86 \times X$. In addition, R^2 dropped from 97% to 81% with the new data point included in the model. As can be seen, when an outlier is in the model it can have negative effects on the predictive power and relationships in your model.

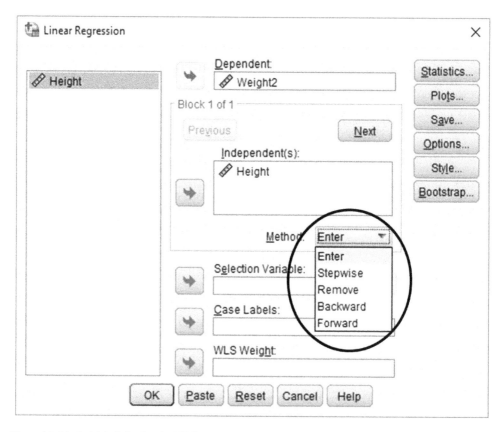

Figure 10.24: Variable Selection in SPSS

The influence of an observation can be interpreted as how much the predicted score for the other observations would change if the observation in question were removed from the analysis.

If the dataset that you are using for modeling has outliers, this can in turn affect the least squares fit. For example, if a data point or observation is moved up or down, the corresponding predicted value will move up and down as well. The amount of change is dependent on the distance the observation is from the line and the mean of the X values. This effect on the overall regression line is called leverage and we get a value of the leverage for each observation. The greater an observation's leverage, the greater influence it has. Additionally, an observation with a value equal to the mean on the independent variable has no influence on the slope of the line, regardless of its value on the dependent variable. However, an extreme observation on the independent variable has the potential to affect the slope of the regression significantly.

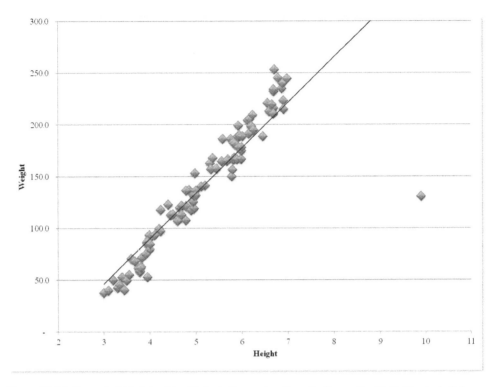

Figure 10.25: Example SAS Output for Multiple Regression Y vs. X_1, X_2, ..., X_3 with Outlier Included

Cook's D is a viable measure regarding the influence of an observation. It is proportional to the sum of the squared differences between predictions, taking into consideration all observations in the model as well as predictions made after removing the observation in question. If both of the predictions are the same, including or excluding the observation in question, then the observation has no influence on the model. However, the observation has influence if the predictions differ greatly when the observation is excluded from the analysis. A common rule of thumb is that an observation has too much influence if it has a Cook's D value over 1.0.

Interactions and Nonlinear Relationships

What is a variable interaction? An interaction is when an independent variable has a different effect on the dependent variable depending on the values of another independent variable. Suppose we have two variables:

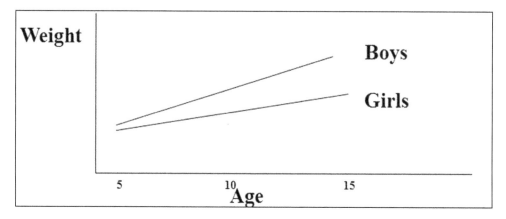

- X_1 = 1 if the subject is female and 0 if male.
- X_2 = age of the subject.
- Y = weight of the subject (dependent variable).

To evaluate the effect of an interaction, we can assess the p value for that interaction. To see the interaction and get a better picture of the relationship, we can look at an interaction plot. In the plot in Figure 10.26, a different line describes each sex. This illustrates how sex interacts with the effect that age has on weight. We can see that weight appears to be very similar for boys and girls at age 5. However, at age 15, boys weigh much more than girls, and the slope of the increase from 5 to 15 is much higher in boys than in girls.

Nonlinear relationships occur when the true relationship with the Y and X variables is not a line, but a curve. In many cases, simple curves like the one shown in Figure 10.27 can be handled by adding a term to the model, which is the square of the original X variable, as well as the X variable itself.

Figure 10.27 illustrates an example of a nonlinear relationship between age and weight.

Overfitting

As covered in the general modeling section, overfitting can affect linear regression models as well. By including too many variables in your regression equation, you can begin to fit the noise. This is basically like fitting noise (see the discussion in Chapter 9). A large number of parameters can lead to overfitting in linear regression, just as in more complex model structures. Figure 10.28 represents overfitting of this data.

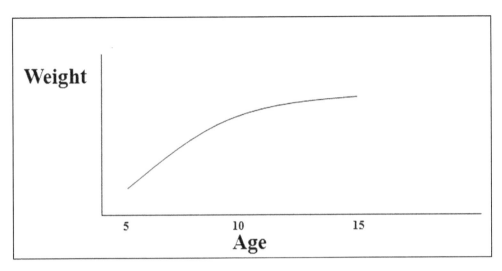

Figure 10.27: Nonlinear Relationship Between Weight and Age

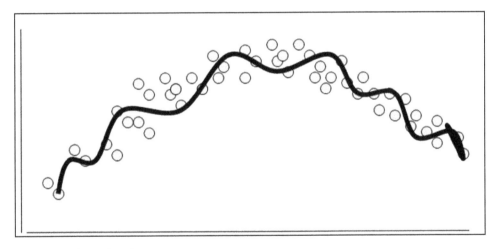

Figure 10.28: Overfitting of Data

Figure 10.29 shows the line if there is no overfitting; this line represents a proper description of the data.

To avoid overfitting your model, make sure to collect a sample that is large enough that you can include all of your predictors or independent variables. Additionally, the modeler should utilize cross-validation samples to determine whether the addition or exclusion of a variable improves both the fit sample and the cross-validation sample.

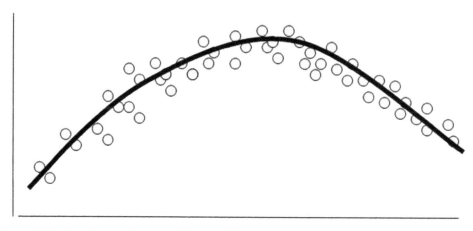

Figure 10.29: Line Representing Correct Picture of Data

Multicollinearity

Another important consideration when fitting regression models is multicollinearity. Multicollinearity occurs when the X variables are correlated to one another; this can cause issues with model fitting and variable interpretation. A correlation matrix can be used to test the amount of multicollinearity. The amount of multicollinearity can be assessed by using the variation inflation factor (VIF). This is a measure that computes the amount that the variance is increased in an estimate due to collinearity. The VIF is an indication of how large the standard error is, compared with what it would be if the variables in your model were uncorrelated with each other. The square root of the VIF is interpreted as the number of times larger the standard deviation of the estimate is than a case with no collinearity. It is always greater than or equal to 1. It is calculated for each independent variable; those variables with high VIF values can be removed. A good rule of thumb is that if values of your VIF exceed 5 (which means that the standard deviation due to multicollinearity is $\sqrt{5} = 2.2$ times larger than with no multicollinearity), this often indicates multicollinearity. A related variable, tolerance, which is 1/VIF, is calculated for each independent variable by regressing it on other independent variables. Low values of tolerance indicate possible multicollinearity. If your tolerance value is below 0.2, you probably have a problem with multicollinearity. Think of it as $1 - R^2$, because if R^2 is high then your independent variables would be highly correlated.

Power for Regression

Recall from earlier chapters that statistical power is the ability to detect a relationship, if it exists. We want to ensure that we have sufficient power to detect relationships and have precise estimates. To ensure statistical power, we must have a large enough sample size. Also, as the number of independent variables increases in our model, we must accordingly increase our sample size. If your sample size is not large enough, you will not be able to fit a model that adequately estimates the true model for your dependent variable. While it is beyond the scope of this book, there are many sources on power calculation for linear models (e.g., Dupont & Plummer, 1998).

Estimating Parameters and Cross-Validation

How are parameters estimated? A good rule of thumb is to estimate parameters on a training dataset and assess the model performance on the test dataset (also called "fitting" and "evaluation" datasets, discussed in Chapter 9). In other words, the general idea is to fit your model on one set of data and evaluate it on a completely different set of data. This means that a portion of the data is not used in estimating the parameters and is used to check the quality of the predictions.

Keep in mind that if there are too few cases in the training or fitting dataset, a poor estimate is created, while if there are too few observations in the test or evaluation dataset, the test error is not an accurate approximation of generalization error. For example, a good rule of thumb is to use 75% of the data for fitting or estimation and 25% to validate, test, or check for overfitting. Initially, the squared error is calculated on both sets of data at the same time. As new variables are added or when we try interactions or squared terms in the model, when the 25% sample has no decrease in error, this indicates good additions to the data and good parameter estimates (see Figure 10.30).

Cross-validation can also be done on several cross-validation samples to improve stability. For example, you can divide the data into four groups of 25% each. Fit the model on 75% and evaluate on the remaining 25% for each of the four cases. As variables are added, if all four sub-samples of 25% do not improve, the new variable would

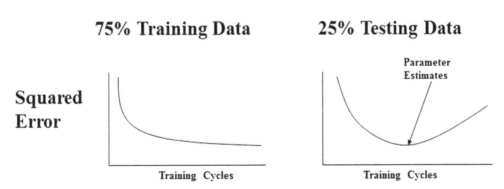

Figure 10.30: Training and Test Data

not be added. In Figure 10.30, a training cycle is used to represent the various changes, additions, and subtractions the modeler will have to make to or from the data.

Conclusions

Linear regression is a very useful tool in solving many problems in loss prevention. This chapter explored the fundamental steps for applying linear regression models to your day-to-day work. Additionally, best practices were described that should be followed in a model project. With the tools described in this chapter, combined with prior chapters, loss prevention personnel can build models to describe shrink, model returns, evaluate factors affecting employee tenure, estimate the number of incidences in a given period of time, and many more models.

Exercises

1. What is linear regression? What kind of variable are you trying to predict?
2. In a simple linear regression (one X variable and one Y variable), what does the coefficient represent?
3. Assume that you have the output shown in Figure 10.31 for a regression model:

Variables in the Equation

Variable	DF	Parameter Estimate	Standard Error	$Pr > |t|$
Intercept	1	0.15	0.02	0.006
Var1	1	0.05	0.003	0.008
Var2	1	0.28	0.0004	0.045

Figure 10.31: Regression Output

    a. Which variables are significant?
    b. How do you interpret the coefficient for Var1?
    c. Predict the value of Y, when Var1 = 100 and Var2 = 146.

4. Name some of the variable selection options available when building a regression model.
5. What is the difference between R^2 and adjusted R^2? Which should you use if you have many independent variables in your model?

Logistic Regression

In God we trust. All others must bring data.

—W. Edwards Deming

Introduction

In the previous chapter, we covered the basics of linear regression models. With regression analysis, the dependent variable Y is a numeric variable, which can take on a range of values on the real number line. In this chapter, we cover a different type of modeling framework, known as logistic regression. With logistic regression, the response variable Y can only take on two possible values, 1 and 0. To handle such cases appropriately, we use a logistic regression model to model the relationship between Y and X (or a series of X values) in a similar way to how we used linear regression models. We will start with the case where there is a response variable (or dependent variable) Y, and one predictor variable (one independent variable) X. Then we will move on and expand this model to find the relationship of a response variable Y to a series of predictor variables $X_1, X_2, ..., X_k$.

We will describe some of the basic concepts associated with logistic regression, such as the relationship of probability and odds, and the concept of an odds ratio. We won't go too deeply into the mathematics of fitting logistic regression models, but we will show you how to fit a logistic regression model in SAS and SPSS and how to read the output from the model.

Some Examples of Problems Appropriate for Logistic Regression

Logistic regression models are appropriate when modeling cases with binary (yes or no) type outcomes. Many problems in loss prevention can be directly modeled with logistic regression. Additionally, even some numeric problems can be converted into binary problems by looking at extreme values of the numbers. One example of converting a numeric problem into a binary problem would be if shrink is greater than some threshold. We may be interested in modeling cases where the shrink exceeds (or will exceed) 4% or some other extreme value.

The following list provides some additional examples that can be modeled using a logistic regression model:

Employee is fraudulent

The binary response will indicate whether the employee has been fired for fraud or some other related issue.

Store will have a break-in in the next 6 months

The binary response indicates that a store was broken into in a 6-month time window and we may use data from the prior 6 months to create predictor variables to predict this outcome.

Person in the self-checkout lane is not processing all items
The binary response will be to identify known transactions where the customer has intentionally not processed portions of their transaction in the self-checkout lane.

Credit card transaction is fraudulent in the next 30 days
The binary response indicates whether a specific credit card transaction is known to be fraudulent or is known to be legitimate or not known to be fraudulent, the latter two being grouped together.

Customer will make a purchase
The binary response represents whether a specific customer to a retailer will make a purchase in the store in the next 30 days from a specific point in time.

Customer will return merchandise just purchased
The response will be whether the customer returns the merchandise in some time window.

Probability, Odds, and Odds Ratios

For logistic regression, we are concerned about a binary outcome of "1," which usually denotes a case of interest, and "0," which usually denotes a noncase. We say usually, because it actually does not matter what the "1" and "0" represent. The only important thing here is that there are two outcomes. With binary outcomes, probability is the natural way to express the likelihood of a "1" or the likelihood of a "0." In this chapter, we use the notation $P(Y = 1)$ to represent the probability that Y will take on a value of "1." Since Y can only take on two possible values, we know that the following relationship holds:

$$P(Y = 0) = 1 - P(Y = 1) \qquad \text{11.1}$$

This means that the probability that Y will take on the value "0" can be determined if we know the probability that Y will take on the value of "1" by subtracting that probability from 1. For example, if $P(Y = 1) = 0.4$ (or 40%), then the probability that Y will take on the value "0" or $P(Y = 0) = 0.6$ (or 60%).

The odds are the chance of an event occurring divided by the chance that the event won't occur. Odds are often expressed as a ratio. For example, if there is a 66.666...% chance of rain, then the chance of no rain is 33.333...%. Therefore, the odds of rain are 2 to 1, meaning that it is twice as likely to rain as it is not to rain. For another example, assume that a coin has a 50% chance of landing heads. Then the odds are 1 to 1 that the coin will land on heads (also known as even odds). In logistic regression models, using the odds is the fundamental way the model is expressed.

Odds Ratios

Odds ratios are an extension of odds to compare two groups. The odds ratio between groups 1 and 2 of a specific event occurring is:

$$\text{odds ratio} = \frac{\text{odds}_1}{\text{odds}_2}$$

11.2

$$\text{odds ratio} = \frac{\dfrac{P_1}{\left(1 - P_1\right)}}{\dfrac{P_2}{\left(1 - P_2\right)}}$$

11.3

Let's assume that, in stores in Group 1, there is a 4% chance that, at any given time, there is a criminal in a store in Group 1. Similarly, assume that Group 2 has a 3% chance that, at any given time, there is a criminal in a store in Group 2. Then the odds of a criminal being in Group 1 are $(0.04/0.96) = 0.041667$ and the odds of a criminal being in Group 2 are $(0.03/0.97) = 0.030928$. The odds ratio is:

$$\text{odds ratio} = \frac{0.041667}{0.030928} = 1.35$$

11.4

This means that Group 1 stores are 35% more likely (or have 1.35 times the odds) than Group 2 to have a criminal in the store.

Simple Logistic Regression Model

In this section, we are going to discuss the most simplified version of a logistic regression model to illustrate the features of the model. Assume that we have one predictor variable X, and one response variable Y, which can take on a value of "0" or "1." The logistic regression model is written as:

$$\ln\left(\text{odds}\left(Y = 1|\,X\right)\right) = \ \alpha + \beta X$$

11.5

This model is exactly the same as the simple linear regression model, where the Y is replaced by the log of the odds that Y takes on the value of "1." This model can also be rewritten as (applying a little algebra to the first equation):

$$P\left(Y = 1|\,X\right) = \ \frac{e^{\alpha+\beta X}}{1 + e^{\alpha+\beta X}}$$

11.6

The formula on the right side of this equation is known as the logistic function; this is why the logistic regression model is named as it is. The logistic function is unique in that it

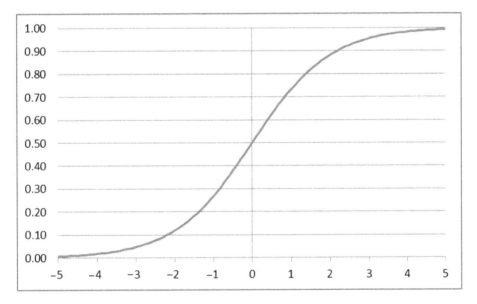

Figure 11.1: Logistic Function

only takes on values from 0 to 1, which makes it well suited to modeling probabilities. The logistic function, $f(x) = e^x/(1 + e^x)$ is shown in Figure 11.1 for values of X from -5 to 5.

The logistic function has values approaching 0 as X decreases and approaching 1 as X increases. This means that no matter what the values are for $\alpha + \beta X$ in the model, the predictions can never be smaller than 0 or greater than 1. You should contrast this functional form with the linear regression model, which has no boundaries on the values for the predictions. The simple linear model can be fit to binary data, but the predictions may not make sense and it is recommended therefore to fit the logistic regression model.

Fitting the Logistic Regression Model

What does it mean to "fit" a logistic regression model? Put simply, fitting the logistic regression model involves finding estimates for α and β that align with the data the best. With simple linear regression in the last chapter, this amounted to finding a line that fitted best to a scatter plot. It is fairly easy to visualize which line would work best. Unlike the simple linear regression model, there is no simple formula for fitting the logistic regression model. A method known as maximum likelihood estimation is used for estimating the parameters of the logistic regression model. This approach takes advantage of the theoretical properties of the logistic regression model to create something called a likelihood function. The likelihood function measures the likelihood of our data given certain values of α and β. Using the likelihood function, we find the values of α and β that make our data the most likely (i.e., maximize the likelihood function) and those values are our estimates of α and β.

When α and β are estimated using the maximum likelihood approach, the parameter estimates have well-known properties that allow for hypothesis testing and confidence intervals for each parameter and will also allow us to compute predictions and confidence intervals for the predictions.

Model Estimates Output

When a logistic regression model is fitted to data, most software will produce several output tables with key results on the model fit as well as hypothesis tests. In this section, we will describe a simple example dataset and fit a logistic regression model to the dataset.

Example: Manager Turnover vs. Crime Score

The set of 100 observations given in Table 11.1 represents fictitious data containing the crime index (X) for the store where the manager works and a binary variable indicating whether the manager terminated employment in the calendar year 2015 (Y).

Table 11.1: Simulated Crime Index and Manager Termination Data

Observation	Crime Index	Manager Left in 2015
1	67.536	0
2	150.820	0
3	186.697	0
4	245.918	1
5	230.193	0
6	231.772	0
7	197.683	0
8	143.089	0
9	222.393	1
10	216.709	0
11	118.689	0
12	162.610	1
13	186.239	1
14	195.471	0
15	123.001	0
16	232.320	0
17	211.405	0
18	219.215	0
19	187.099	0
20	101.784	1
21	253.313	0
22	57.125	0
23	236.390	1
24	304.861	1
25	203.847	1
26	103.438	1
27	218.524	0
28	211.457	0
29	199.993	1
30	295.792	1
31	267.715	1
32	183.428	0

(Continued)

Table 11.1 (Continued)

Observation	Crime Index	Manager Left in 2015
33	221.173	0
34	118.475	0
35	206.467	0
36	238.942	0
37	189.583	0
38	260.866	0
39	187.594	0
40	167.280	0
41	185.359	0
42	188.167	0
43	165.193	1
44	157.763	0
45	165.452	0
46	238.578	1
47	218.098	0
48	190.436	0
49	144.180	0
50	193.967	0
51	149.676	1
52	185.971	0
53	109.236	0
54	109.691	1
55	235.432	1
56	217.673	0
57	224.411	1
58	131.792	0
59	240.344	1
60	212.866	0
61	133.281	0
62	180.991	0

(Continued)

Table 11.1 (Continued)

Observation	Crime Index	Manager Left in 2015
63	169.894	0
64	155.885	0
65	196.326	1
66	170.035	0
67	199.141	0
68	217.479	0
69	307.409	0
70	211.661	0
71	202.297	0
72	205.543	0
73	208.486	0
74	159.595	0
75	259.671	0
76	285.658	1
77	251.984	0
78	161.924	0
79	197.715	0
80	232.112	0
81	151.226	1
82	299.065	1
83	223.033	0
84	162.151	0
85	186.728	0
86	208.491	0
87	153.955	0
88	208.992	0
89	253.927	1
90	128.847	0
91	172.869	0
92	256.070	0

(Continued)

Table 11.1 (Continued)

Observation	Crime Index	Manager Left in 2015
93	113.909	0
94	136.688	0
95	177.067	0
96	121.675	0
97	198.154	0
98	127.460	0
99	160.027	0
100	246.285	1

The following SAS code was used to fit a logistic regression model to the data:

```
proc logistic data=madeupdata descending plots=ALL;
    model managerleft = crimeindex;
run;
```

The option "descending" tells SAS to model $P(Y = 1)$ vs. $P(Y = 0)$. SAS will fit $P(Y = 0)$ by default if this options is not specified.

Figure 11.2 illustrates the output produced with this SAS code. Within the SAS output, we will focus on two of the sections, which have been numbered and circled.

Section 1   This shows that the fit of the model with SAS was successful. While this seems like a basic step, that the software should function properly and fit the model, it is not always able to fit the model. If certain anomalies occur in the data, from time to time, the model will not be able to be fitted and the estimates provided by the software will be inaccurate.

Section 2   This section of the output is testing the significance of both the α ("intercept") and β ("crimeindex") statistics.

Here are the column descriptions for Section 2.

Estimate   This is the parameter estimate. Remember, this is an estimate of the population parameter based on a sample of the data. In the SAS code that preceded the output, the simulation of the data is shown. The true parameter for α is -2.4. Similarly, the true parameter for β is 0.005.

Standard error   This column is the estimated standard deviation of the estimate for α and β. This can be used to compute confidence intervals for the parameters.

Wald chi-square   This is the chi-square statistic that is used to test the null hypotheses ($H_0: \alpha = 0$ and $H_0: \beta = 0$).

Pr > ChiSq   This is the p value from the statistical test. In both cases in this example, the p value is less than 0.05, which indicates statistically significant results.

To fit the same model in SPSS, go to "Analyze" $\rightarrow$ "Regression" $\rightarrow$ "Binary Logistic" (see Figure 11.3).

In the window that opens, use the arrow to move "Manager Left" to the "Dependent" box and "CrimeIndex" to the "Covariates" box (see Figure 11.4). The output is shown in Figure 11.5. Note the bottom table in Figure 11.5 showing the parameter estimate, standard error, and overall significance. As expected, the results are the same as those shown using SAS.

Interpreting the Model Parameters

The parameters in the model, α and β, represent the slope and the intercept of the log-odds. Since most people don't think in the log-odds scale, we will attempt to interpret the parameters. The α parameter represents the baseline log-odds if $X = 0$. Put slightly differently: to remove the log part of the equation, e^{α} represents the odds of having $Y = 1$ when $X = 0$. In linear regression, the β parameter is known as the slope of the line. In logistic regression, it is the slope of the log-odds line. In linear regression, we say that β represents the expected change in Y given a unit change in X. In logistic regression, we say that β represents the expected change in the log-odds that $Y = 1$, given a unit change in X. Alternatively, e^{β} represents the change in odds of $Y = 1$, given a unit change in X. Also, e^{β} represents the odds ratio for $X + 1$, compared to X.

For the example, in the prior section, we can interpret the parameter for β as follows: for every unit increase in crime index, there is an $e^{0.012} = 1.012$ odds ratio (or 1.2% increase in the likelihood of a manager leaving during the year). Alternatively, we may want to look at larger increases. For example, a 100 point increase in the crime index has an $e^{0.012 \times 100} = 3.32$ odds ratio (or, to put it differently, it is 3.32 times more likely that a manager will terminate employment in a store with an increase in crime score of 100 points).

Probability modeled is managerleft=1.

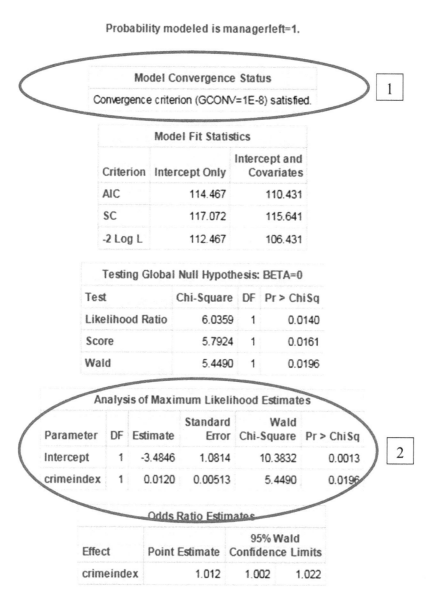

Model Convergence Status

Convergence criterion (GCONV=1E-8) satisfied.

☐ 1

Model Fit Statistics		
Criterion	Intercept Only	Intercept and Covariates
AIC	114.467	110.431
SC	117.072	115.641
-2 Log L	112.467	106.431

Testing Global Null Hypothesis: BETA=0			
Test	Chi-Square	DF	Pr > ChiSq
Likelihood Ratio	6.0359	1	0.0140
Score	5.7924	1	0.0161
Wald	5.4490	1	0.0196

Analysis of Maximum Likelihood Estimates					
Parameter	DF	Estimate	Standard Error	Wald Chi-Square	Pr > ChiSq
Intercept	1	-3.4846	1.0814	10.3832	0.0013
crimeindex	1	0.0120	0.00513	5.4490	0.0196

☐ 2

Odds Ratio Estimates		
Effect	Point Estimate	95% Wald Confidence Limits
crimeindex	1.012	1.002 1.022

Figure 11.2: SAS Output for Simple Logistic Regression

Making Predictions and Prediction Intervals

Now that the model is fitted, beyond interpreting the parameters, there may be a need to predict the probability of the outcome for an unknown case. For example, suppose that, at the beginning of the year, the human resources department wanted to know

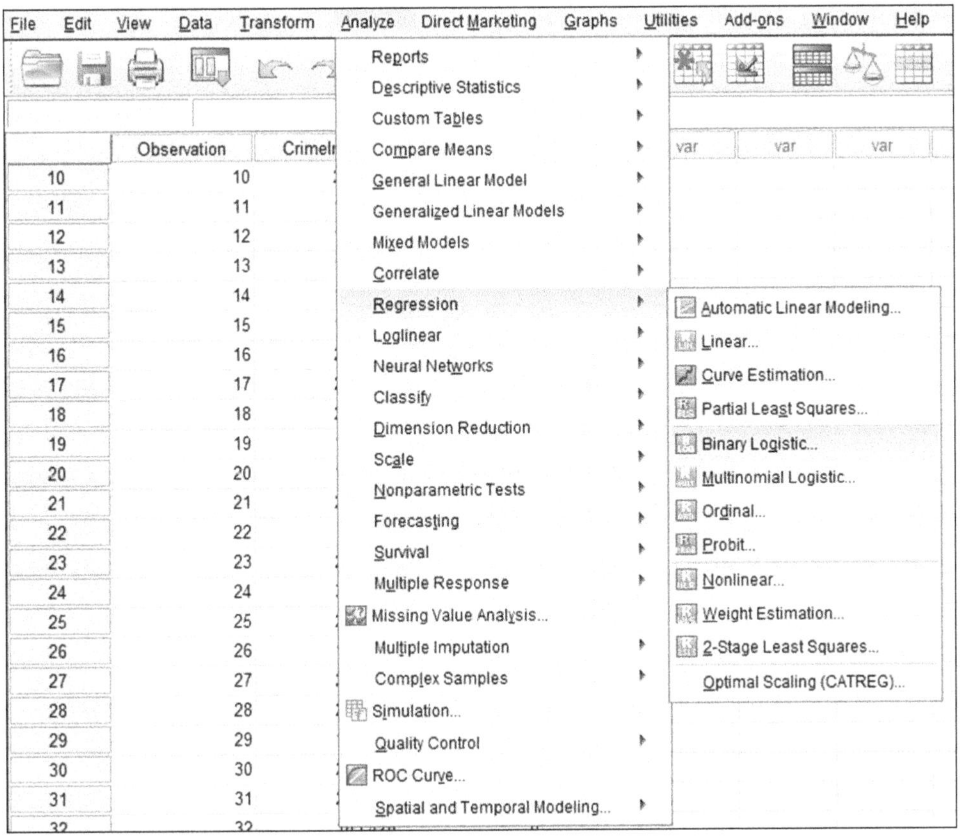

	Observation	Crimeln
10	10	
11	11	
12	12	
13	13	
14	14	
15	15	
16	16	
17	17	
18	18	
19	19	
20	20	
21	21	
22	22	
23	23	
24	24	
25	25	
26	26	
27	27	
28	28	
29	29	
30	30	
31	31	
32	32	

Figure 11.3: Running Logistic Regression in SPSS

managers that were at high risk of leaving. They could apply the model to each store to obtain a prediction and use that to determine which managers might require some type of intervention. Predictions from the logistic regression model can be made by using the logistic regression equation and plugging in the estimates. For example:

$$\hat{P}(Y = 1 | X) = \frac{e^{\hat{\alpha} + \hat{\beta}X}}{1 + e^{\hat{\alpha} + \hat{\beta}X}}$$

11.7

The values $\hat{\alpha}$ and $\hat{\beta}$ represent the estimates obtained during the model fit. So the prediction is calculated, for example, with a crime index of 200 as:

$$\hat{P}(Y = 1 | X) = \frac{e^{-3.4846 + 0.012(200)}}{1 + e^{-3.4846 + 0.012(200)}} = 0.253$$

11.8

261

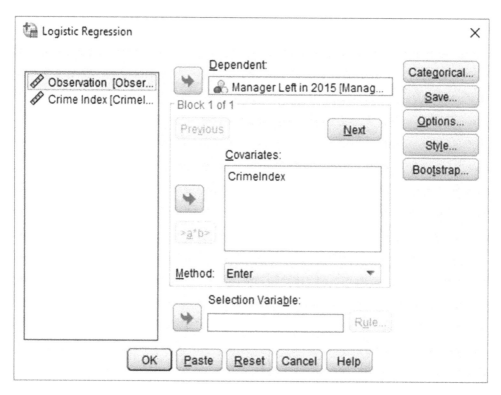

Figure 11.4: Running Logistic Regression in SPSS

This means that in a store with a crime index of 200, the manager has a 25.3% chance of leaving in the next year. Suppose further that the end user wanted confidence intervals for the prediction. While the mathematical formulas are beyond the scope of this book, most statistical software packages will produce the confidence intervals for a prediction. The following SAS code will produce a confidence interval and output predicted probabilities:

```
proc logistic data=madeupdata descending plots=ALL;
    model managerleft = crimeindex;
    output out=outpreds p=predicted_p lower=lower_conf_limit
    upper=upper_conf_limit;
run;
```

This code is the same as the code used to fit the model shown earlier in this section, with additional code in blue, which outputs the predictions as well as the lower and upper confidence limits of the predictions. In the highlighted code, "outpreds" is the

Block 1: Method = Enter

Omnibus Tests of Model Coefficients

		Chi-square	df	Sig.
Step 1	Step	6.036	1	.014
	Block	6.036	1	.014
	Model	6.036	1	.014

Model Summary

Step	-2 Log likelihood	Cox & Snell R Square	Nagelkerke R Square
1	106.431[a]	.059	.087

a. Estimation terminated at iteration number 5 because parameter estimates changed by less than .001.

Classification Table[a]

			Predicted		
			Manager Left in 2015		Percentage
	Observed		0	1	Correct
Step 1	Manager Left in 2015	0	74	1	98.7
		1	22	3	12.0
	Overall Percentage				77.0

a. The cut value is .500

Variables in the Equation

		B	S.E.	Wald	df	Sig.	Exp(B)
Step 1[a]	CrimeIndex	.012	.005	5.449	1	.020	1.012
	Constant	-3.485	1.081	10.383	1	.001	.031

a. Variable(s) entered on step 1: CrimeIndex.

Figure 11.5: Logistic Regression Output in SPSS

name of the output dataset, which can have any name chosen by the user that is allowable by SAS for a table name. The lower and upper confidence limits are named in the output dataset by the "upper=" and "lower=" keywords in the highlighted "output" statement. The names "lower_conf_limit" and "upper_conf_limit" can be replaced by anything allowable by SAS for a variable name.

Sensitivity, Specificity, Classification, and Receiver Operating Characteristics

With a binary regression model, often the desired use of the model is for classification. For example, the end user of the model will not want to know the probability that a manager will terminate employment in the next 12 months; the end user will want to know whether or not the manager intends to leave. Since the logistic regression model produces predictions between 0 and 1, we will need to convert this continuous output from 0 to 1 into a binary classification of "we predict that the manager will leave" or "we predict that the manager will stay." This is done using the following logic:

$$
\text{predicted category} = \begin{cases} \text{if prediction} > P_0, & \text{We predict that the manager will leave.} \\ \text{else} & \text{We predict that the manager will stay.} \end{cases}
$$

11.9

Choosing the value of P_0 is a balancing act. If P_0 is large, we will probably be more accurate, but too few observations may be classified as leaving. Alternatively, if P_0 is too small, we will identify many managers who may leave, but we will be less accurate. Figure 11.6 highlights the classification problem.

There are two key metrics, sensitivity and specificity, that typically identify the accuracy at each cut point for P_0. Sensitivity measures the chance that if we predict that a manager will leave, the manager will actually leave. Specificity is the opposite and measures the probability that if we say that a manager will not leave, the manager will actually not leave. Many of the software packages output a receiver operating characteristics curve, which displays the sensitivity vs. $1 -$ specificity. Figure 11.7 illustrates the receiver operating characteristics curve for the simple logistic regression example shown earlier in the chapter and is output by SAS.

Each point on the receiver operating characteristics curve corresponds to a cut point for P_0. The curve shows that any increase in sensitivity results in a corresponding

		Truth	
		Employee Will Leave	Employee Will Stay
Prediction	Employee Will Leave	Correct Classification (*a*)	Incorrect Classification (*c*)
	Employee Will Stay	Incorrect Classification (*b*)	Correct Classification (*d*)

Sensitivity = $a/(a+b)$
Specificity = $d/(c+d)$

Figure 11.6: Classification Problem

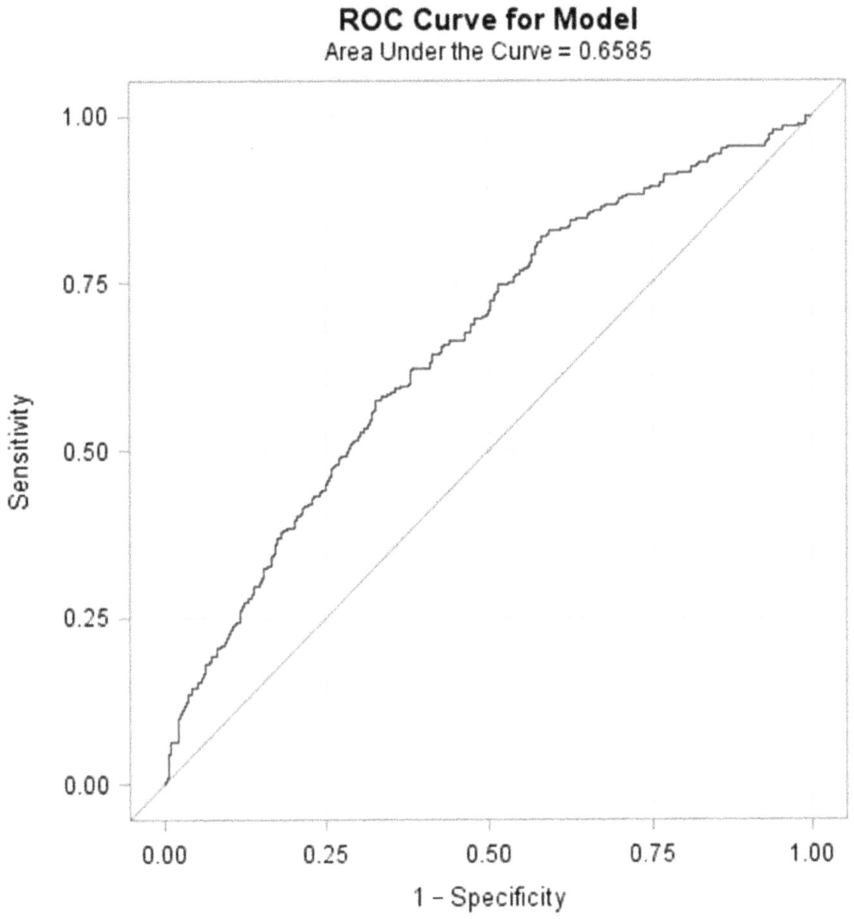

ROC Curve for Model
Area Under the Curve = 0.6585

Figure 11.7: Receiver Operating Characteristics Curve

decrease in specificity. The area under the curve represents how good a classifier the model is. A perfect classifier would have the area under the curve equal to 1.

Kolmogorov–Smirnoff Statistic

One way to measure the overall predictive power of a logistic regression model is to compute what is known as the Kolmogorov–Smirnoff statistic. The Kolmogorov–Smirnoff statistic measures the difference between two distribution functions. In this case, the two distribution functions are the distribution of the $Y = 1$ records versus the distribution of the $Y = 0$ records across the predictions. Ideally, the $Y = 1$ records will have most of the distribution on the high predictions and the $Y = 0$ records will have

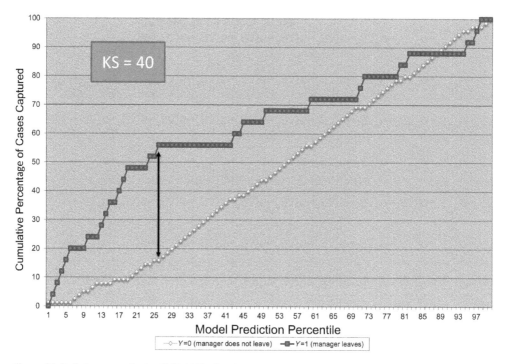

Figure 11.8: Kolmogorov–Smirnoff Statistic Graph

most of the distribution on the low predictions. Figure 11.8 shows a comparison of the distribution functions for $Y = 0$ vs. $Y = 1$.

The Kolmogorov–Smirnoff statistic represents the maximum separation between the two lines; this is 40% at the point marked on the graph at the 26th percentile of scores. The line for $Y = 1$ represents the percentage of the cases that are captured as the model predictions go from high to low. In the perfect model, we would capture all of the $Y = 1$ cases immediately and none of the $Y = 0$ cases. This would lead to a Kolmogorov–Smirnoff statistic = 100, as all of the distribution for $Y = 1$ would be shifted to the left and the distribution for $Y = 0$ would be shifted to the right.

Multiple Logistic Regression Model Structure

In this section, we make the leap from a single X to $X_1, X_2, \ldots, X_k$ in the logistic regression model. The multiple logistic regression model generalizes from the simple logistic regression model in a similar way to how the simple linear regression model generalizes to the multiple linear regression model. The following equation shows the multiple logistic regression model:

$$\ln\left(\text{odds}\left(Y = 1 \mid X_1, X_2, \dots, X_k\right)\right) = \beta_0 + \beta_1 X_1 + \beta_2 X_2 + \dots + \beta_k X_k \qquad 11.10$$

Just as with the simple logistic regression model, with a little algebra we can rearrange the model into an alternate expression, which shows the probability of $Y = 1$. This model is similar to the multiple linear regression model.

$$p(Y = 1 \mid X_1, \dots, X_k) = \frac{e^{\beta_0 + \beta_1 X_1 + \dots + \beta_k X_k}}{1 + e^{\beta_0 + \beta_1 X_1 + \dots + \beta_k X_k}} \qquad 11.11$$

SAS Example: Manager Turnover vs. Crime Score and More Variables

The following SAS code was used to simulate 1000 cases and fit a multiple logistic regression model:

```
data madeupdata2;
        ** This block of code generates 1000 random observations ****;
        do i=1 to 1000;
                crimeindex=max(200+50*rannor(12354),0);
                tenure=round(10*exp((0.5-ranuni(45671))),1);
                age = 18+round(ranuni(54321)*30,1);
                if age<30 then age_group=1;
                else if age<40 then age_group=2;
                else age_group=3;
p = 1/(1+exp(-(0.2+.005*crimeindex-.2*tenure-(age_group=2)*4-(age_
    group=3)*.8)));
                managerleft= ranbin(12345,1,p);
                output;
        end;
run;
proc logistic data=madeupdata2 descending plots=(ROC);
        class age_group/param=glm;
        model managerleft = crimeindex tenure age_group;
        output out=preds p=predval lower=lower upper=upper;
run;
```

Figure 11.9 represents the SAS output for the logistic regression.

Type 3 Analysis of Effects			
Effect	DF	Wald Chi-Square	Pr > ChiSq
crimeindex	1	5.5654	0.0183
tenure	1	37.1156	<.0001
age_group	2	13.5568	0.0011

Analysis of Maximum Likelihood Estimates						
Parameter		DF	Estimate	Standard Error	Wald Chi-Square	Pr > ChiSq
Intercept		1	-0.5471	0.4224	1.6776	0.1952
crimeindex		1	0.00348	0.00148	5.5654	0.0183
tenure		1	-0.1611	0.0264	37.1156	<.0001
age_group	1	1	0.6843	0.1942	12.4149	0.0004
age_group	2	1	0.2816	0.2065	1.8599	0.1726
age_group	3	0	0	.	.	.

Figure 11.9: SAS Output for Multiple Logistic Regression

In this example, there are three main variables. Since the third variable is a category variable with three levels, it is necessary to represent it as two different variables (age_group = 1 and age_group = 2). The third value (age_group = 3) will be part of the intercept.

The two tables in Figure 11.9 represent tests of hypothesis for the overall variables and for each specific category of the third variable. You should notice that the test results in the first results match the second results for crime index and tenure. For the categorical variable age_group, the results are different between the two tables. The first table shows the overall test for that variable which has a p value = 0.0011 (which is significant at the 1% level) and the second table shows the hypothesis test results on the two sub-levels of age_group = 1 and age_group = 2 compared with age_group = 3. While age_group = 1 is significantly different from age_group = 3, the results show that age_group = 2 and age_group = 3 are not statistically different.

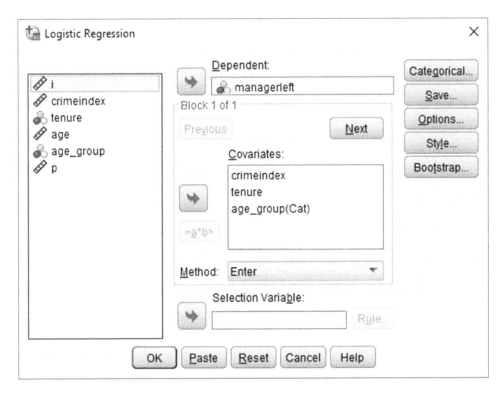

We can combine those levels (age_groups 2 and 3) at this point, since they are not statistically different, or we can continue to leave them separate if we believe that they are actually different (i.e., we are second guessing the model output and suggesting that since age_group = 1 and age_group = 3 are different, we don't want to assume that age_group = 2 and age_group = 3 are the same).

Interpreting the Coefficients

Interpreting the coefficient in the multiple logistic regression model is the same as interpreting the model coefficients in the simple logistic regression model. In logistic regression, β represents the slope of the log-odds line. In multiple logistic regression, β_i represents the slope of the line between X_i and Y, assuming all other X values are considered fixed. β_i represents the expected change in the log-odds that $Y = 1$ given a one unit change in X_i. Alternatively, e^{β_i} represents the change in odds of $Y = 1$ given a one unit change in X. Also, e^{β_i} represents the odds ratio for $X + 1$ compared with X. Just as in the simple logistic regression case, we can compare the odds ratio of $X + 100$ vs. X with $e^{100 \times \beta_i}$.

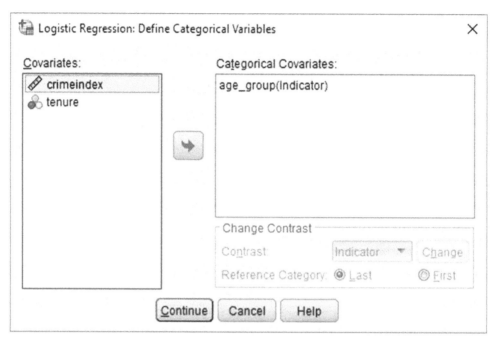

Figure 11.11: Logistic Regression in SPSS, Categorical Variable

Classification Table[a]

			Predicted		
			managerleft		Percentage Correct
	Observed		0	1	
Step 1	managerleft	0	748	2	99.7
		1	248	2	.8
	Overall Percentage				75.0

a. The cut value is .500

Variables in the Equation

		B	S.E.	Wald	df	Sig.	Exp(B)
Step 1[a]	crimeindex	.003	.001	5.565	1	.018	1.003
	tenure	-.161	.026	37.116	1	.000	.851
	age_group			13.557	2	.001	
	age_group(1)	.684	.194	12.415	1	.000	1.982
	age_group(2)	.282	.207	1.860	1	.173	1.325
	Constant	-.547	.422	1.678	1	.195	.579

a. Variable(s) entered on step 1: crimeindex, tenure, age_group.

Figure 11.12: Output from SPSS

To run the same logistic model in SPSS, you should go to "Analyze" → "Regression" → "Binary Logistic." In the window that appears, use the arrow to move the "managerleft" variable to the "Dependent" box and the three independent variables to the "Covariates" section (see Figure 11.10). For this logistic regression, you must select the "Categorical" box on the right, and move the "age_group" variable to the "Categorical Covariates" section (see Figure 11.11).

The output from SPSS is illustrated in Figure 11.12. As noted, the results are the same as those shown in SAS. Column "B" represents the coefficients and Column "Sig." the significance levels for each variable.

Conclusion

The logistic regression model is the most commonly used model for modeling outcomes with only two values. It is very popular in modeling fraud. There are many popular software packages that can fit the logistic regression model and many opportunities within loss prevention to use the model.

Exercises

1. What type of response variable is being predicted with a logistic regression model?
2. Assume the following data:
   - Group 1 has a 5% chance of winning.
   - Group 2 has a 8% change of winning.
   a. Calculate the odds of winning for Group 1 and Group 2.
   b. Calculate the odds ratio of Group 1 winning vs. Group 2 winning.
3. You have obtained the output shown in Figure 11.13 from a logistic regression model:
   a. Which variables are significant?
   b. How would you interpret the "Age" coefficient?

Variables in the Equation

Variable	B	S.E	Wald	df	Sig.	Exp(B)
Constant	1.244	1.05	10.5	1	0.001	3.4695
Age	0.11	0.005	5.2	1	0.02	1.1163
Sex	0.23	0.003	5.12	1	0.06	1.2586

Figure 11.13: Output from a Logistic Regression Model

     c. How would you interpret the "Sex" coefficient?

     d. Compute the odds ratio for a one-year increase in age.

4. What are sensitivity and specificity?

5. What is a receiver operating characteristics curve? How is it used?

6. What is a Kolmogorov–Smirnoff statistic? How is it used?

Chapter Twelve

Advanced Techniques and Machine Learning Models

All life is an experiment. The more experiments you make, the better.

—*Ralph Waldo Emerson*

Introduction

In the previous chapters, we have focused on traditional statistical modeling techniques and data analysis methods. Almost all of the problems faced by loss prevention staff members can be solved using the techniques, or variations of those techniques, described in the prior chapters. The majority of the techniques were designed when computational resources were scarcer and therefore may be more limited than their modern counterparts. As computational resources have evolved, and as statisticians and computer scientists have also evolved, new techniques have been developed to address the problem of finding more robust estimates of $g()$, the explainable portion of our model.

In this chapter, we will explore a few of the more popular advanced techniques; these include many machine learning methods, although new ones are being introduced continuously. While many of these techniques are better at estimating $g()$, they often add more complexity in explaining the relationship of each individual variable X and the outcome, Y. Since the ability to explain a model's output can often be a requirement, this may make more advanced methods more difficult to use in practice.

Neural Networks

Neural networks are one of the original machine learning methods that were developed to solve complex problems in computer science, such as character recognition and computer vision. They are appropriate for modeling a number of scenarios with one or more response variables and one or more predictor variables. Neural networks are often touted as a digital representation of the human brain. They are very good at approximating complex functions and therefore have gained popularity at modeling problems where the function $g()$, the explainable portion of the model described in Chapter 9, is not obvious. Additionally, the complexity of a neural network can be specified to be more or less complex depending on the perceived complexity of the problem.

Formulation of the Neural Network

Neural networks work by following a simple principle in mathematics that complex functions can be approximated well by a combination of simple functions. Figure 12.1 shows a common representation of a neural network.

Figure 12.1 represents a feed-forward neural network with one hidden layer and M nodes. The number of hidden layers or nodes can be varied. When the number of hidden layers is large, this is also known as deep learning. Each circle in the diagram

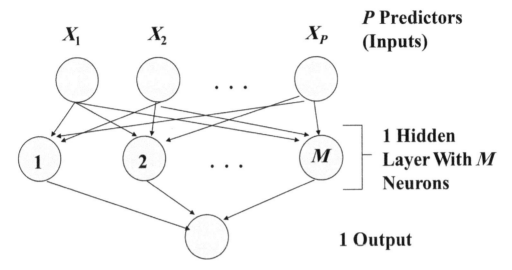

Figure 12.1: Neural Network

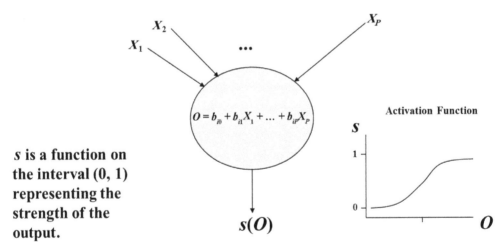

Figure 12.2: Neural Network Node

is referred to as a node; within each node, there is an activation function, which transforms the data to pass onto the next node. Figure 12.2 illustrates the detail of a node.

While the diagram is far more complex than the model for multiple linear regression, you should note that the multiple linear regression equation is shown in the center of the node. Each node will have its own linear regression equation; all of the equations will then be combined into one overall representation of $g()$. The following equation represents the diagram:

$$g(.) = \left(\pm_0 + \sum_{i=1}^{M} \pm_i s \left(\beta_{0j} + X_1\beta_{1j} + X_2\beta_{2j} + \ldots + X_k\beta_{kj} \right) \right)$$

12.1

Fitting a Neural Network

The additional complexity of the neural network model makes fitting it more complex than fitting either linear regression models or logistic regression models. Fitting any model involves finding a set of parameters (i.e., the values of α and β) that minimizes the error equation, which measures the difference between predicted values and actual values. Since the neural network has more parameters and the function we are optimizing is not as well "behaved" mathematically as either logistic regression models or linear regression models, finding the estimates can be complex.

The math involved in the estimation process is beyond the scope of this book, but you should be aware that the fitting algorithm is not as simple as the other models previously discussed in this book. The equation to minimize is the same:

$$\sum (\text{prediction}_i - \text{actual}_i)^2 = (\text{prediction}_1 - \text{actual}_1)^2 + (\text{prediction}_2 - \text{actual}_2)^2$$
$$+ (\text{prediction}_3 - \text{actual}_3)^2 + \ldots + (\text{prediction}_n - \text{actual}_n)^2$$

12.2

The difference in the estimation process is that the prediction is calculated with the neural network model for $g()$. It is actually not desirable to completely minimize the equation above and we must use a cross-validation sample, which is held out specifically to tell us how well to fit the data. The process is illustrated in Figure 12.3.

While the training data (i.e., the data used to fit the model) will have an error that is constantly reduced as the model is being fitted, the testing data error, at some point,

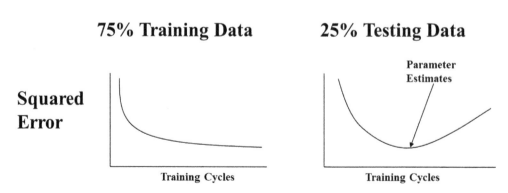

Figure 12.3: Fitting and Validating Models

will begin to increase. This means that the data is being overfit and the ability of the model to work on new data will be diminished because we are beginning to fit the error and not the true explainable portion of the data.

In this section, we show a few examples where neural networks can perform well and automatically detect the variable structure, whereas linear models would require more human intervention. Consider a case where we are trying to predict weight based on age for boys and girls. Assume that the relationship is as shown in Figure 12.4.

Clearly, there is a different slope for the line for boys and girls. If a linear regression model is fit with sex and age as predictor variables only, the change in slope will not be caught by the model automatically. A manual process will be needed that adds an interaction term, "age*sex," to the model to capture this feature. With a neural network, however, this interaction will be detected automatically.

Similarly, suppose the data shown in Figure 12.5 is presented.

The data in Figure 12.5 is clearly a curve and not a straight line and the Y-axis indicates that the response variable should be modeled on the log scale. While this one-dimensional example is easy to display, if a relationship exists between several X variables (in a multidimensional space) it will be impossible to visualize. In this case, the person fitting the model can add an X^2 term to the model and can convert the data to the log scale, but this needs to be handled manually. It also means the modeler needs to spend a substantial amount of time learning and investigating the shape of each predictor variable relative to the response variable and transforming the variables

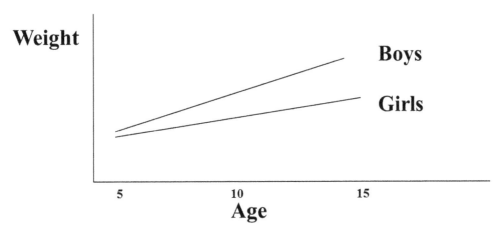

Figure 12.4: Age–Sex–Weight Relationship

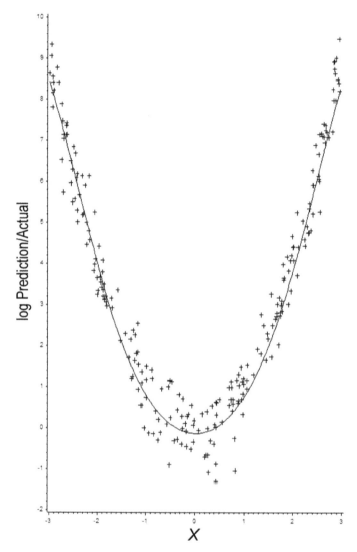

Figure 12.5: Curved Data Fit in Neural Networks

(log, squared, etc.) or including interaction terms to fit the relationship (if this is even possible to do manually). The line shown in Figure 12.5 was fit with a neural network model, which was able to detect these two hidden features automatically. In conclusion, fitting neural networks is more mathematically and computationally complex, but if the data is also complex, neural networks may be a good solution.

A dataset with one continuous input variable (X_1), one categorical input variable (X_2), and one continuous response variable (Y) will be used in this example. The dataset is shown in Figure 12.6. When $X_2 = 1$, the data follows the upward facing blue curve and when $X_2 = 2$ the data follows the downward facing orange curve.

A linear model will not be able to fit a complex function like this without significant work by the modeler. However, neural networks should be able to fit (learn) this complex function. To fit a neural network we will use Python and Scikit-learn, a popular machine learning library. Python can be downloaded and installed from https://www.python.org, while Scikit-learn can be installed from http://scikit-learn.org. The code shown in Figure 12.7 describes the process of training a neural network with a single hidden layer made up of five units (nodes). The code is commented.

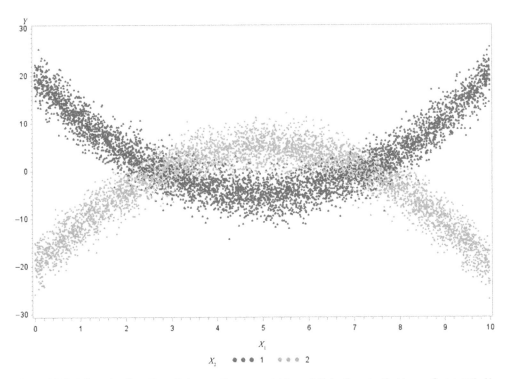

Figure 12.6: A Complex Function. X_1 is a continuous variable and X_2 is discrete (1: blue or 2: orange). Y is the response variable. The scatter plot shows the dataset with 10,000 points.

```
1    # Import libraries
2    import pandas as pd
3    from sklearn.neural_network import MLPRegressor
4
5    # Read the data
6    d = pd.read_csv('simdata.txt', sep='\t')
7
8    # Encode the categorical variable
9    d['x2_1'] = (d['x2']==1).astype('int')
10   d['x2_2'] = (d['x2']==2).astype('int')
11
12   # Create arrays for X and Y
13   X = d.loc[:, ('x2_1', 'x1', 'x2_2')].values
14   Y = d['y'].values
15
16   # Create NN with one hidden layer containing 5 units
17   nn = MLPRegressor(hidden_layer_sizes=(5,), solver='lbfgs',
18                     learning_rate_init=0.01, learning_rate='adaptive',
19                     max_iter=500, activation='tanh', random_state=5,
20                     early_stopping=True,  validation_fraction=0.25, )
21   nn.fit(X, Y)
22
23   # Make predictions using the neural network
24   pred = nn.predict(X)
```

Figure 12.7: Python Code to Train a Neural Network

Training neural networks can be challenging for two main reasons. First, neural networks are sensitive to user-selected parameters, such as number of hidden layers, number of hidden units (nodes), learning rate, or initial weights. Second, they can often overfit the data. However, when successfully trained, they can be very powerful at learning complex functions. In this example, we used 75% of the data for training and set 25% of the data aside for validation, to avoid overfitting. Figure 12.8 shows the prediction from the neural network as a solid line along with the raw data. As noted in Figure 12.8, the neural network was able to learn the underlying function extremely well.

Models Based on Classification and Regression Trees

Classification and regression trees can be used to fit models where the response variable Y is categorical (classification tree) or continuous (regression tree). The model can have one or many predictor variables X. In this section, we will first cover the simple case of a single regression or classification tree and then move on to more complex structures, which are combinations of many simple trees.

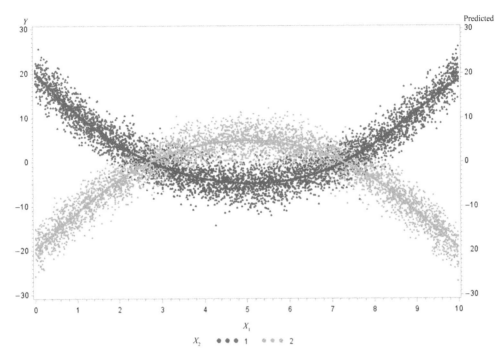

Single Classification and Regression Trees

The regression tree is typically written with a diagram, shown in Figure 12.9.

Figure 12.9 represents a classification tree, since the outcome is a categorical variable. Each endpoint is known as a leaf in the tree and each intermediate square is a node in the tree. The data presented in Figure 12.9 is from a fictitious model fitted using the problem described at the end of Chapter 11 (note that the data in this example is different from the data used in Chapter 11). In this example, we are interested in identifying the managers most likely to leave in the next 12 months. We suspect that employee tenure, employee age, and the crime rate in the area are all related to turnover. In Figure 12.10, the top level node represents the overall rate of manager turnover in the following year across all predictor variables.

In this node, we can see that a 3.6% rate of turnover is expected in the following year (based on historical data). The next level of the tree (Figure 12.11) represents a segmentation of the data by employee tenure.

This part of the tree indicates that if the data is split for employees with <1 year and ≥1 year of tenure, those with more tenure have a lower chance of leaving in the

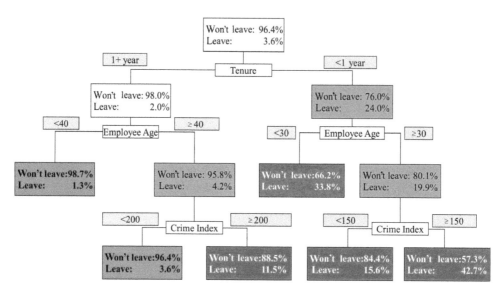

Figure 12.9: Simple Regression Tree

Won't leave:	96.4%
Leave:	3.6%

Figure 12.10: Top Node

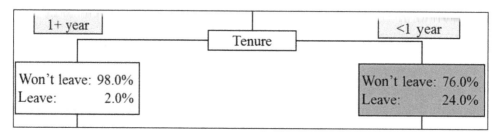

Figure 12.11: Level of Tree Based on Tenure

next year (2.0% vs. 24.0%). When the regression tree model is fitted, the cut point of 1 year would be determined by an algorithm that minimizes some mathematical function. Additionally, the choice to cut the data based on tenure first is something that is also algorithmically determined. The next level of the tree is shown in Figure 12.12.

The next level of the tree shows the individuals with low tenure (<1 year) on the right, and the individuals with high tenure (1+ year) on the left. The next variable that is segmented is employee age; note that the components on the left are split when the age is 40, but the components on the right are split at an age of 30. The ability of the tree to choose a different cut point within different sections of the tree gives more power to the predictions. The lowest portion of the tree continues by splitting employees by the crime index at their stores (see Figure 12.13).

Once again, different cut points are allowed in the two segments.

Fitting Regression and Classification Trees

The tree of Figure 12.9 is fitted using an algorithm that is designed to minimize misclassification error. There are many popular software packages for fitting tree models, such as SPSS, R, and Python.

Compare and Contrast Linear Regression Models and Regression Trees

Linear regression models attempt to fit everything with a line and will often have trouble finding shapes in the data without the user forcing in X variables that capture the shape, such as log-based transformations, or squared terms (X^2). The tree, however, can identify these shapes automatically. There is a tradeoff in that the tree will have a very nonsmooth shape and sometimes can produce predictions that are counterintuitive and unstable. This primarily comes from the fact that each leaf in the tree is estimated

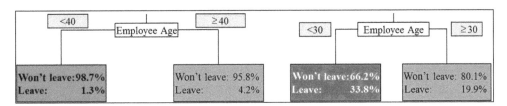

Figure 12.12: Level of Tree Based on Manager Age

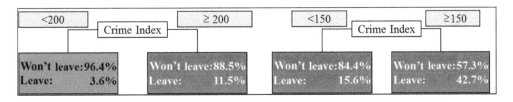

Figure 12.13: Level of Tree Based on Crime Index

only from the data within the classification of the leaf (which could be a small sample). With a linear model, the line is estimated using all of the data. Therefore, while the shape may be imperfect in a linear model, the stability of the estimate will be higher, owing to the increased sample size. The opposite is true of a regression tree. It will be better at estimating nonlinear shapes, but the estimates will be unstable, owing to the decreased sample size at each point.

While we displayed the regression tree as a node and leaf structure in Figure 12.9, there is a different way to display a tree, which can illustrate the tree's ability to handle nonlinear structures. Consider a simple linear regression model with one Y and one X variable, illustrated in Figure 12.14. Further, assume that the model is not quite appropriate, meaning that a simple linear regression model fits most of the data well but that there is clearly a curve to the data, which is not addressed with a straight line.

Figure 12.15 shows a tree fit to the same data. The tree is able to model the curvature of the data. In the next section, we introduce variations on the tree idea that combine multiple simple trees to create a better model.

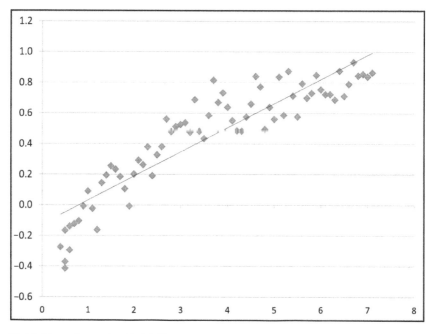

Figure 12.14: Linear Regression Model Fit

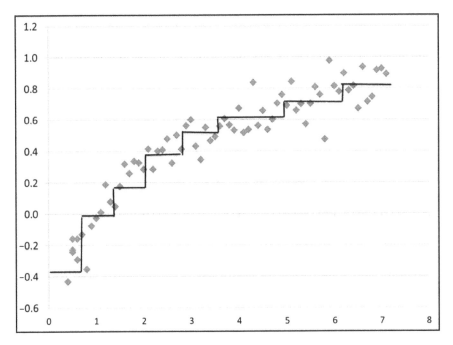

Fitting a Tree in SPSS for a Binary Outcome

Using the simulated data used for the multivariate logistic regression in Chapter 11, we will fit a tree to determine manager turnover (the dependent variable) based on employee tenure, employee age, and the crime rate in the area (the independent variables). To fit a tree, go to "Analyze" → "Classify" → "Tree" (see Figure 12.16). In the next window, use the arrow to move "managerleft" to the "Dependent Variable" section and "tenure," "age," and "crimeindex" to the "Independent Variables" section (see Figure 12.17). You can change many options in the "Criteria" and "Options" buttons on the right, such as the minimum number of cases defining a node, the level of significance required to split or merge nodes, and how to handle missing values. For the purposes of this example, we assumed that tenure was a categorical variable.

Figures 12.18 and 12.19 illustrate the tree output in SPSS. Figure 12.18 shows that although three independent variables were provided, only two were selected in the tree. The final tree is two levels deep with four terminal nodes.

The tree is first split by tenure (see Figure 12.19). You can see that SPSS determined that the most effective manner to divide tenure is to create three categories according

File	Edit	View	Data	Transform	Analyze	Direct Marketing	Graphs	Utilities	Add-ons	Window

		i		crim	Reports ▶			age_group	
1		1	67.5	Descriptive Statistics ▶		36	2
2		2	261.4	Custom Tables ▶		23	1
3		3	221.7	Compare Means ▶		48	3
4		4	231.7	General Linear Model ▶		47	3
5		5	186.7	Generalized Linear Models ▶		30	2
6		6	210.6	Mixed Models ▶		24	1
7		7	118.6	Correlate ▶		28	1
8		8	222.2	Regression ▶			
9		9	144.0	Loglinear ▶			
10		10	232.3	Neural Networks ▶			
11		11	230.3	Classify ▶ TwoStep Cluster...			
12		12	122.4	Dimension Reduction ▶ K-Means Cluster...			
13		13	253.3	Scale ▶ Hierarchical Cluster...			
14		14	167.3	Nonparametric Tests ▶ Cluster Silhouettes			
15		15	308.5	Forecasting ▶ Tree...			
16		16	103.4	Survival ▶ Discriminant...			
17		17	160.1	Multiple Response ▶ Nearest Neighbor...		18	1
18		18	250.7	Missing Value Analysis...		47	3
19		19	267.7	Multiple Imputation ▶		46	3
20		20	176.9	Complex Samples ▶		34	2
21		21	253.9	Simulation...		25	1
22		22	238.9	Quality Control ▶		23	1
23		23	163.2	ROC Curve...		28	1
				Spatial and Temporal Modeling... ▶			

to tenure: Group 1 (11, 13, 16, 14, 15), Group 2 (10 and 12), and Group 3 (7, 9, 6, 8). The turnover rate in Node 3 is 34.6% as compared with the tenure rate of 14.7% in Node 1. The next level used age to split Node 1 into Node 4 and Node 5, based on age 38 or below. Comparing the four final nodes, the tenure rate ranges from 3.6% in Node 5 to 34.6% in Node 3.

Example: Fitting Complex Functions Using a Decision Tree (in Python)

The sample dataset shown in Figure 12.6 was fitted using a simple decision tree in Python. The Python library Scikit-learn was used to fit the trees. The code is shown in Figure 12.20. While decision trees are more commonly used for classification problems, they can also be used for regression problems.

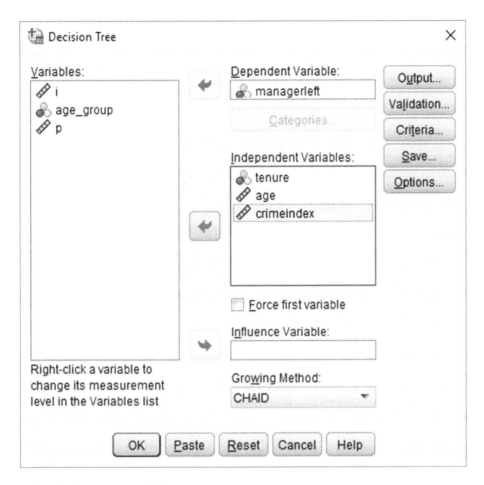

Figure 12.21 shows an example of a decision tree with just four leaf nodes, which can hence only produce four different outputs. As a result, the prediction capability is very limited for our dataset. As we increase the depth of the tree, the number of leaf nodes increases; hence, the output is more continuous. As another example, a tree of depth 3 is shown in Figure 12.22.

Figure 12.23 illustrates the precision of the tree, given increasing levels of depth. When the depth of the tree is 20, the fit to the data is very similar to that obtained by the neural networks model. Fitting trees requires a balancing act by the modeler, since very deep trees can potentially overfit the data while shallow trees cannot learn the functions very well.

Unlike neural networks, which are often referred to as black-box models, decision trees can be easily understood or explained based on the input. In the next section, we

Model Summary

Specifications	Growing Method	CHAID	
	Dependent Variable	managerleft	
	Independent Variables	tenure, age, crimeindex	
	Validation	None	
	Maximum Tree Depth		3
	Minimum Cases in Parent Node		100
	Minimum Cases in Child Node		50
Results	Independent Variables Included	tenure, age	
	Number of Nodes		6
	Number of Terminal Nodes		4
	Depth		2

Figure 12.18: SPSS Tree Output

discuss ensemble methods that can make regression trees fit the data more aggressively by creating a large number of simple decision trees and combining their individual outputs.

Ensemble Models Based on Classification and Regression Trees

In this section, we introduce two methods, which are variants on the same basic principle that a combination of many simple trees can produce a superior prediction. This combination is referred to as an *ensemble* model. The following two sub-sections discuss these two approaches.

Random Forest Models

Random forest models use a collection of simple classification or regression trees to create a more accurate overall model. Random forests are a popular machine learning method. Each classification and regression tree model is fitted on a sample of the original data selected with replacement (this process is known as resampling). When each observation is sampled, it is put back in the candidate pool and then the next observation is selected. By sampling with replacement, the same observation has a chance

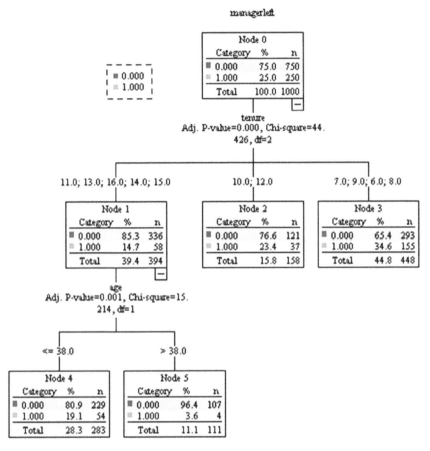

managerleft

Node 0
Category	%	n
■ 0.000	75.0	750
▨ 1.000	25.0	250
Total	100.0	1000

■ 0.000
▨ 1.000

tenure
Adj. P-value=0.000, Chi-square=44.
426, df=2

11.0; 13.0; 16.0; 14.0; 15.0

Node 1
Category	%	n
■ 0.000	85.3	336
▨ 1.000	14.7	58
Total	39.4	394

10.0; 12.0

Node 2
Category	%	n
■ 0.000	76.6	121
▨ 1.000	23.4	37
Total	15.8	158

7.0; 9.0; 6.0; 8.0

Node 3
Category	%	n
■ 0.000	65.4	293
▨ 1.000	34.6	155
Total	44.8	448

age
Adj. P-value=0.001, Chi-square=15.
214, df=1

<= 38.0

Node 4
Category	%	n
■ 0.000	80.9	229
▨ 1.000	19.1	54
Total	28.3	283

> 38.0

Node 5
Category	%	n
■ 0.000	96.4	107
▨ 1.000	3.6	4
Total	11.1	111

Figure 12.19: Final SPSS Tree

of being selected several times. This approach is also used in other areas of statistics to determine the distributional properties of sampling statistics. In the typical regression tree, the nodes are split using the optimal splits among all variables; however, in a random forest, the nodes are optimally split using only a randomly chosen subset of the *X* values (Liaw & Wiener, 2002). Once many typical regression trees are built, they are combined using a simple average, or by majority vote if it is a classification tree.

Extreme Gradient Boosting

Extreme gradient boosting is also a combination of simple regression trees, but the trees are built recursively. It is also a popular machine learning method. The first tree is built like a typical regression tree and each additional tree is built on the residuals of the

```
1    # Import libraries
2    import pandas as pd
3    from sklearn.tree import DecisionTreeRegressor
4
5    # Read the data
6    d = pd.read_csv('simdata.txt', sep='\t')
7
8    # Create arrays for X and Y
9    X = d.loc[:, ('x1', 'x2')].values
10   Y = d['y'].values
11
12   # Create the decision tree
13   tree = DecisionTreeRegressor(criterion='mse', splitter='best', max_depth=7,
14                                min_samples_split=100, min_samples_leaf=10,
15                                min_weight_fraction_leaf=0.0, max_features=None,
16                                random_state=5, min_impurity_split=1e-07, presort=False)
17   tree.fit(X, Y)
18
19   # Make predictions using the decision tree
20   pred = tree.predict(X)
```

Figure 12.20: Python Code to Fit a Decision Tree

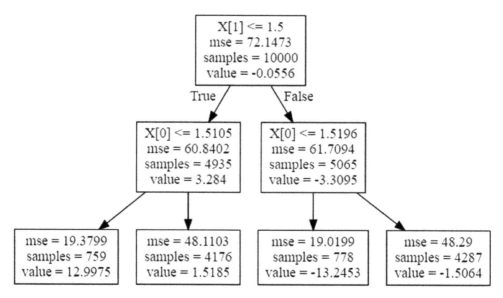

Figure 12.21: Tree of Depth 2

prior trees. This approach to modeling has proven to be very robust and is a method consistently used by the winners of many recent modeling competitions (Chen & Guestrin, 2016).

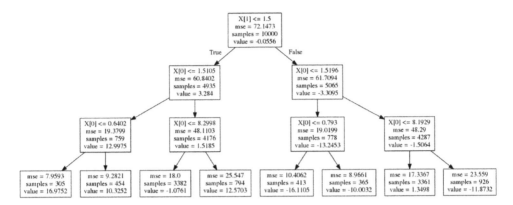

Figure 12.22: Tree of Depth 3

Example: Fitting Complex Functions Using Tree-Based Ensemble Models (in Python)

The same sample dataset shown in Figure 12.6 was fitted using a random forest regression model and an extreme gradient boosting model in Python. The Python library Scikit-learn was used for the random forest regression model while XGBoost (which can be installed from https://xgboost.readthedocs.io) was used to fit the extreme gradient boosting model. The code is shown in Figures 12.24 and 12.25.

As seen in Figure 12.26, both models perform very similarly. Both models can learn the complex function well; however, their output, unlike neural networks, is not continuous. Care should be taken when fitting these models to avoid overfitting or fitting to the noise.

For continuous outcome problems, the extreme gradient boosting method and the random forest method were able to fit the model more easily and discover the correct shape, as compared with a neural network. However, once the neural network was fitted, the model provided a better fit to the relationship. We recommend using the tree-based approaches as a benchmark to determine whether a neural network has fitted the data completely or gotten stuck in the estimation processes and not truly found an optimal set of parameter estimates.

Conclusion

In this chapter, we covered some of the newer predictive modeling approaches (many are also known as machine learning algorithms). The reader should note that while the methods can differ quite widely from traditional methods, such as linear regression

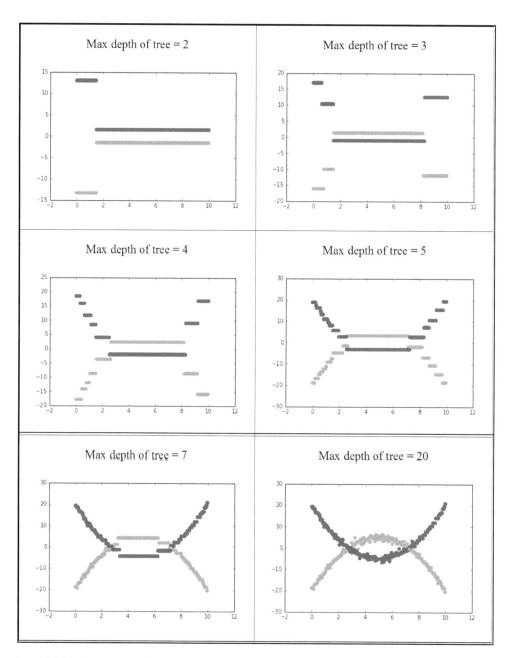

Figure 12.23: Predictions Using Trees with Different Depths

```
1    # Import libraries
2    import pandas as pd
3    from sklearn.ensemble import RandomForestRegressor
4
5    # Read the data
6    d = pd.read_csv('simdata.txt', sep='\t')
7
8    # Create arrays for X and Y
9    X = d.loc[:, ('x1', 'x2')].values
10   Y = d['y'].values
11
12   # Create the random forest regressor with 100 trees
13   forest = RandomForestRegressor(n_estimators=100, criterion='mse', max_depth=12,
14                                  min_samples_split=100, min_samples_leaf=30,
15                                  min_weight_fraction_leaf=0.0, max_features=2,
16                                  bootstrap=True, oob_score=False,
17                                  random_state=5, verbose=1, warm_start=False)
18   forest.fit(X, Y)
19
20   # Make predictions using the random forest model
21   pred = forest.predict(X)
```

Figure 12.24: Code to Train a Random Forest Regressor in Python

and logistic regression, the objective of determining a value for the explainable part of a model, $g()$, is still the same. The algorithms described in this section go beyond those traditional methods in that they are attempting to discover the relationship between $X_1, ..., X_k$ and Y without much assistance from the modeler. The attempt to learn the relationship of the predictors to the response variable automatically is a step along the path of automated relationship discovery. While we are not quite there, it is a step forward on the road to that goal.

Exercises

1. List some of the pros associated with more complex models, such as neural network models.
2. List some of the cons associated with more complex models, such as neural network models.
3. What are classification and regression trees? How are they different from each other?
4. How can you ensure that your model is not fitting "noise"?
5. When should you consider fitting these advanced models instead of the more traditional model options (for example, regression)?

```
1   # Import libraries
2   import pandas as pd
3   import xgboost as xgb
4
5   from sklearn.neural_network import MLPRegressor
6   from sklearn import cross_validation
7
8   # Read the data
9   d = pd.read_csv('simdata.txt', sep='\t')
10
11  # Encode the categorical variable
12  d['x2_1'] = (d['x2']==1).astype('int')
13  d['x2_2'] = (d['x2']==2).astype('int')
14
15  # Create arrays for X and Y
16  X = d.loc[:, ('x2_1', 'x1', 'x2_2')].values
17  Y = d['y'].values
18
19  # Split data into training and testing set
20  X_train, X_test, y_train, y_test = cross_validation.train_test_split(X, Y, test_size=0.33)
21
22  dtrain = xgb.DMatrix(X_train, y_train)
23  dtest = xgb.DMatrix(X_test, y_test)
24  dall = xgb.DMatrix(X, Y)
25
26  # Create and fit XGB model
27  param = {'bst:max_depth': 15, 'bst:eta':0.3, 'silent':1, 'objective':'reg:linear',
28           'subsample': 0.75, 'min_child_weight': 35, 'eval_metric': 'rmse'}
29  model = xgb.train(param, dtrain, evals=[(dtest,'test')],
30                    early_stopping_rounds=5, num_boost_round=20)
31
32  # Make predictions using XGB model
33  pred = model.predict(dall)
```

Figure 12.25: Code to Train an Extreme Gradient Boosting Model in Python

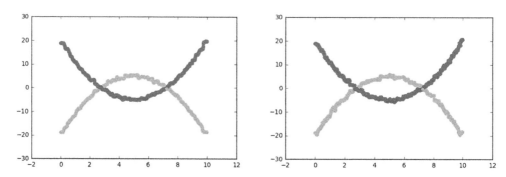

Figure 12.26: Model Fitting by Random Forest and Extreme Gradient Boosting

Chapter Thirteen

Integrating Analytics into Loss Prevention Teams

Statistics is the science of learning from experience.

—Bradley Efron

Introduction

Previous chapters of this book have addressed the methods and procedures for address-
ing specific problems for analytics and loss prevention. In this chapter, we move one

step further and describe the tools, team members, data infrastructure, and planning needed to develop an analytics environment within a retailer's loss prevention team. Most retailers today do not have a traditional analytics group within the loss prevention department. Some loss prevention teams may have one or two team members who know some analytics; some may not have any. The goal of this chapter is to create a roadmap for loss prevention teams to plan for and adopt a culture of analytics.

Analytics Infrastructure

To attack loss prevention analytics problems head on, you will need an analytics infrastructure that is central to unlocking business value from your organization's data, which is essential to making better decisions. A proper analytic infrastructure is often the difference between a successful and an unsuccessful analytics project. With the proper analytics infrastructure, analytics projects can be performed more quickly and with a higher probability of success and usability. The analytics infrastructure often refers to the staff, services, applications, utilities, platforms, software, and systems that are used for housing the data, accessing the data, preparing data for modeling and analytics, estimating models, validating models, and taking actions.

Data Infrastructure

The first step in integrating analytics is to create a data infrastructure. Without the data needed to develop models, analyze performance, and deploy solutions, there will be no foundation to build on. Lately, there has been a lot of buzz about big data. But the definition of this new area of technology is ill-defined and many struggle to understand exactly what it can accomplish. While there is a lot of hype, there definitely are new technology and greater insights buried under all of the noise. Computing data storage infrastructures have changed radically in the past 15 years and this change is good news for those wanting to do more with their data. Companies like Google, Facebook, and Yahoo have destroyed these boundaries by architecting parallel computing frameworks like Hadoop, HBase, Cassandra, Greenplum, Netezza (now IBM's PureData for Analytics), and other tools, which allow for supercomputer type power for a fraction of the cost. These environments may be overkill for your needs, but some of them are fairly low-cost solutions and should be considered.

Big data and its associated tools are allowing practitioners to solve more complex problems and to tackle traditional problems more rapidly. This will almost surely change the future of investigations and loss prevention. Just as the US National Security Agency is using massive big data infrastructures to fight terrorism, loss prevention teams should be using them to stop criminals, prevent fraud, and reduce shrink.

When Would Traditional Analytics Benefit from "Big Data" Tools?

Data preparation and processing tasks take way too long or cannot be completed at all.

You frequently make compromises on the complexity of the information you use to do your job (e.g., we can't do that, it would take hours to compute, let's do this instead).

Predictive models are only built from small samples of the data, not the entire data.

You are storing far less history than you really need (e.g., 6 months versus 3 years).

Figure 13.1: Is Your Existing Infrastructure in Need of an Upgrade?

Our recommendation is to begin today by setting the building blocks in place to build a world-class analytics infrastructure. Many have already sensed the trend toward heavier usage of data for tackling loss prevention problems and will have already taken some of these recommended steps. You will probably not start with a big data infrastructure unless you are already pretty far down the path, but see Figure 13.1 for a good barometer to tell you when you are nearing a transition point.

Computing Infrastructure

In addition to the team, you will need to have the appropriate computing infrastructure. This will be the (1) analytics software, (2) data management software, and (3) appropriate hardware (see Figure 13.1). Analytics teams, in their infancy, may cope with general analytics using Excel but as the group begins to tackle more complex problems, the group will invariably need to use a more robust statistical programing software package. There are a few options to choose from, the most common being R, SPSS, and SAS. SPSS has the advantage of being "point and click," so the user does not need to learn the specific language. However, with "point and click" comes the issue of inflexibility on various techniques. To use R and SAS, one must learn the specific coding language, but the benefits are greater flexibility and strength. Another important note is that SAS and SPSS will have license fees, while R is an open-source technology and is free. However, R may be harder to use for the beginner.

As with the analytics software, there are choices regarding data management software and hardware (Figure 13.2). Oracle, SQL Server, and MySQL are commonly used data management software tools. Netezza, Greenplum, and Hadoop's Hive are all data management infrastructures that offer more scalability for larger data projects. The retailer's IT organization typically tries to maintain only one type of data management software, so it is likely that the analytics organizational function will use the same data management software as the general organization. The more advanced the problems your functional data is tasked with solving, or the more data you have available to tackle, the more powerful hardware you will have to invest in. In our most recent infrastructure, we found it useful to have many high-powered workstations running Microsoft Windows (the Linux operating system works well too), along with the data on Hadoop and Netezza.

It is best to start out with some basic equipment that matches the immediate goals of the team and then grow from there. This does not have to be a costly venture. As the team proves their incremental value to the organization and makes a business case for themselves, additional members, tougher problems, and more advanced hardware are likely to follow.

Analytics Hardware and software

Analytics software: This will include packages like SAS, SPSS, and R. Currently, these are the most popular packages for analytics. Excel is also a good supplement to these packages, but cannot handle much data or do many complex tasks.

Data management software: This includes databases like Oracle, SQL Server, MySQL, or data warehouse environments like Netezza, Teradata, or similar.

Hardware: High-powered workstations or servers running on MS Windows or Linux operating systems are the standard for conducting basic and advanced work. Big data tools such as Hadoop, Hive, HBase, Netezza, Teradata, and the like, can bring analytics to another level of complexity.

Figure 13.2: Potential Infrastructure Needs to Support Big Data Analytics

A successful analytical infrastructure is predicated on getting the right analytics people. A successful analytics team starts with the manager. That manager is a person who has deep technical and analytical skills, excellent interpersonal skills, is accessible, is results oriented, and gives clear and direct feedback to the team.

Next, the manager will have to build the team from the starting line to having an advanced analytics infrastructure. In most retail organizations, some of these staff members and functions may already exist within different parts of the company. Some key characteristics in an analytics team member include strong analytical skills (and an advanced education in analytical methods), problem-solving skills, creativity, flexibility, programming skills, attention to detail, ability to multitask, and ability to glean insights from data. Since big data analytics is a burgeoning field, even the top data scientists are still honing their analytical skills.

Here are some of the key team members (or skills) needed for the advanced analytics function:

Team leader	This individual needs to have a business understanding of how analytics can impact the overall organization. This individual should be able to speak to the executive in business terms and translate these ideas to the team in mathematical terms.
Data experts	These individuals will know how to work with data from many different sources.
Modeling experts	These individuals can work with data (provided by the data experts) to produce and implement working models.
Communications leader	This individual can work with key stakeholders and decision makers to ensure that their needs (and those of the end user) are met in the process. The communications leader should have an understanding of the mathematical concepts and be good at developing presentations and documentation to communicate these concepts to the rest of the organization.
Project manager	This individual can remain focused on completing modeling tasks, manage meetings and communications, and be a liaison to other teams in the organization.

One person may have many of these skills and be able to function in multiple roles initially. In general, you will want a team that has all of the skills listed, but you may be able to spread these skills across a very small group of people who have several skills each.

Solutions and Areas of Focus

When going down the big data and analytics path, it is important for a practitioner to start with the basics. The following illustrates some common examples of using analytical methods and data handling to tackle problems in loss prevention. If you are not doing these already, we recommend them as a good start.

Measuring the Impact of a Loss Prevention Initiative

A large part of deriving and executing new ideas in retail operations and loss prevention involves trial and error. Someone in the organization has a good loss prevention idea, but is not sure if it will work. Then, if the idea is good enough, an executive will sponsor an in-store pilot test of the idea to determine its viability. Then the test is run and results are measured. If the results show that the test was successful (compared with nontest stores, known as the balance of the chain), the program may move ahead (see Figure 13.3). Analytics and statistics are used in a few main areas: (1) store selection, (2) structuring the test period, and (3) conducting the analysis.

Many experiments can be conducted at the store level, but how do you choose the right stores? The best general strategy for selecting stores is to use a complete randomization. This can be done as easily as putting the store list into Excel and assigning a random number to each store, and then picking the top stores for the study. Following traditional statistical approaches for designed experiments and A/B testing will go a long way in setting up the experiments so that the results are defensible. Basic comparison tests, like *t* tests and chi-square tests for independence, can help to prove the efficacy of the initiative.

Using Commonly Available Data to Find Factors Associated with Shrink

Some retailers have used the data they collect from a number of sources to find relationships between those data points and shrink using multiple regression models. These variables may include, for example, store sales, employee tenure, crime surrounding the store, the number of enhanced public view monitors or CCTVs, the presence of a security guard, the number of apprehensions, manager tenure, training programs, store

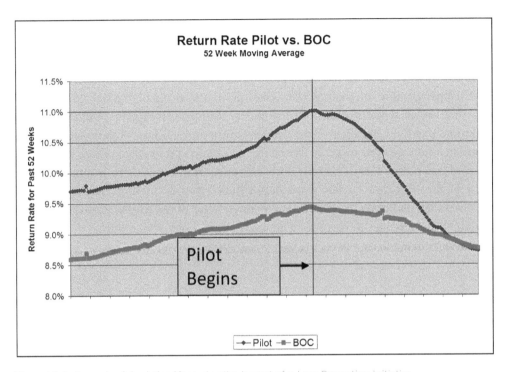

Figure 13.3: Example of Analytics Measuring the Impact of a Loss Prevention Initiative

survey results, and metrics based on point of sale data to determine which, if any, are related to shrink.

Once the data is collected, statistical analysts will fit multiple regression models to the shrink percentages using typical model-building procedures, which include cleaning the data, transforming predictor variables for optimal response, and fitting the algorithms using statistical software such as SAS or SPSS.

Using Exception Reporting Systems to Identify Fraud Cases

Most exception reporting systems (commercial or home grown) combine data from the point of sale, employee records, item files, and store files into a single system that a loss prevention professional uses to find cases. These systems are generally based on a query-based set of rules, which are historically known to identify a reasonable concentration of fraudulent and abusive individuals. Utilizing these types of systems allows investigators to identify a large number of actionable cases in a short amount of time.

Advanced Data-Based Investigations

Data handling problems are generally those where practitioners will quickly hit boundaries when dealing with loss prevention analytics. Data handling is the process that happens before an analysis even takes place and is usually tasked with bringing together lots of types of data from many data sources. Investigators will begin to ask questions that the computers or the database cannot solve. Many of these types of questions are often referred to as "N^2 problems" (*n* squared problems) because they usually involve comparing lots of records with lots of records, resulting in a squaring of the data. Figure 13.4 shows a few examples of these types of question, which may overwhelm many traditional hardware architectures. Most of the data listed would produce intermediate variables to be used in an analysis or a predictive model.

Predictive Modeling and Scoring

Everything we do generates data and, thanks to the advent of big data, hundreds of predictions from models (often called scores) are calculated for every individual based on his or her past behavior in a wide array of industries. These scores, in turn, provide a likelihood of some future behavior, which can be used to drive anything from

Examples of N^2 Problems
Finding all individuals who visited a store within 30 minutes of another customer more than 10 times.
Finding all pairs of baskets having 10+ items in common, in the same store.
Finding all combinations of Product A and Product B on the same credit card across two different transactions at two different stores.
Finding combinations of a nonreceipted return with a store credit followed by an exchange with cash to the store followed by an all cash return.

Figure 13.4: Examples of N^2 Problems

marketing decisions to banking decisions to crime prevention decisions. According to Intel, the highest value of big data is achieved through predictive modeling, which is applied using advanced techniques to predict future events and drive decisions in real time. While predictive modeling has been used in conjunction with big data to analyze trends for other markets, its application in loss prevention is just the beginning.

From a loss prevention viewpoint, predictive modeling involves performing statistical analyses that may uncover trends in the underlying risks that may indicate the likelihood of future loss. Predictive modeling anticipates future behavior and improves strategic planning. For example, it can identify how an institution can effectively and deliberately target certain fraudulent employees, high-risk locations, and high-risk products—leading to increased action via a more efficient loss prevention process.

Video Analytics

Video analytics is a unique task that is evolving rapidly. While there are some very advanced companies working on solutions in this area, there is a lot of room to advance from where we are now to large-scale video loss prevention systems.

There are a few barriers standing in the way of large-scale video deployments. First, video data is very large. Even a single day of video data for an entire chain may exceed a whole year of transactional data, and moving that over a network is costly. Second, video data is very difficult to analyze. Identifying a face in a video feed or recognizing when a product is on the counter during a transaction could take millions of calculations. Remember, a one megapixel image, which is a low-end digital camera, literally means one-million pixels. Video is many separate images collected per second. Third, there may not be a strong business case in retail to have automatic video analytics. Fourth, there is a huge privacy concern in retail where good customers may be affected by too much tracking technology.

That said, these barriers are being whittled away over time and are likely to dissolve at some point. Big data tools are nearing a cost-effective state, bandwidths are continually increasing, and computing platforms can handle the massive amounts of computations. In less than a decade, centralized video storage and analytics are likely to be the norm for loss prevention.

Putting Social Media Data to Use

There are many sources of external data, which may be useful in managing loss prevention activities. Today, most retailers utilize crime statistics to help deploy resources to stores and manage loss prevention activities. Additionally, social media data is beginning to be used by loss prevention teams to help investigate cases.

With the proliferation of social media through such services as Twitter, Facebook, and LinkedIn there has been an explosion of data available to solve a variety of problems. It is often surprising how much individuals reveal, in a very public way, about their activities. These data sources have been incorporated in investigations to support retailers' efforts to catch and prosecute serial offenders.

While there has been some use of this data, it is not being mined to its full potential and we believe there are many stones yet to be turned over. For example, if retailers could utilize social media postings in a proactive way to thwart, mitigate, and respond to crime much earlier, this would provide tremendous savings for the retailers.

Strategy for Ramping Up Analytics

We have laid out the landscape where we think the industry is now and where it is likely to go in the near future. Figure 13.5 shows a sample plan that we believe could move a loss prevention team from the basics to applying advanced analytics. This is really a start for a team and many retailers may already have many of these items in place. Of course, to be successful, the team needs to foster and encourage growth and expect a few challenges along the way. Additionally, it is critical that the team have a strong leader who can live and breathe data-based technology.

Conclusions

The use of analytics and predictive modeling is a critical component in the future of loss prevention. The ability to assess patterns in data, measure loss prevention programs, and make decisions in real time will become fundamental in solving complex issues related to customers, sales, and loss. As the criminals become more sophisticated, they will always go to areas of weakness; retailers that have not adopted an aggressive strategy for detection and prevention will be easy targets.

That said, integrating these technologies can take time and the acquisition of expertise that most loss prevention teams currently do not possess. We encourage loss prevention leaders to begin discussions, internally and with external partners, now to create an infrastructure that can bring significant value to the organization through the use of data and analytical methods.

Needs	Considerations
Staff	• Allocate investigator as team lead • Allocate IT team member (serves as data expert and systems expert) • Hire analyst(s)
Hardware and Software	• Database access to key data sources for transaction, shrink, employees, supply chain • Database server • Acquire analytics software, such as SAS, R, or SPSS • High powered workstation
Types of Problem	• Shrink modeling • Exception reporting • Measuring programs
Business Case Drivers	• Preventing fraud; stopping actual cases (examples) • Improved allocation of resources • Better programs (optimizing resources) • Improved customer service (remove restrictive policies)

Figure 13.5: Potential Considerations to Develop an Analytics Infrastructure in a Loss Prevention Department

Exercises

1. Who are the key team members to include in your analytics team?
2. Which analytics software package might you select for your organization? Why?
3. How can you assess whether your analytical infrastructure is nearing capacity?

Chapter Fourteen

Conclusion

Be able to analyze statistics, which can be used to support or undercut almost any argument.

—*Marilyn vos Savant*

Loss prevention teams are charged with the task of keeping people safe and reducing internal and external theft, while not negatively impacting business operations or sales. We contend that a key ingredient in a successful loss prevention approach is analytics. The focus of this book is to provide you and your team with helpful examples and insight into using data and analytics to determine root causes of shrink and to apply more science to the day-to-day act of loss prevention. Simply "putting out fires" does not solve the root causes of shrink; therefore, this book is intended to provide ways to assess risk and loss before it happens. Additionally, this book provides ways to explain and predict shrink beyond just gut feelings.

This book is a vital resource for loss prevention personnel, retail organizations, students, and anyone interested in research and analytics. This handbook gathers information on several topics, as it is related to loss prevention and analytics. It covers basic topics from variable distributions to correlations, as well as more advanced topics, such as logistics regression modeling and neural networks, and puts it all into a criminological framework to form a complete picture of the basic elements of loss prevention. This handbook was designed in a successive fashion, so that you can first learn the basics of statistics. Then it builds on the foundation of statistics with hypothesis testing moving to the importance of data cleaning and checking for assumptions and finally to building and assessing statistical models to examine shrink.

The emphasis of this book is on the importance of leveraging data to make better decisions in your organization. More specifically, the emphasis is on developing models and using them to predict shrink or store risk in the future based on past data. The material in this book will help you compile data, examine data, prepare data, model data, and convey statistical results.

This book provided many examples of analyzing shrink data using multiple software packages. We assumed that not every organization has access to expensive statistical packages, so we provided modeling examples in Excel as well. As can be seen, the results obtained in Excel are also congruent with the results from SPSS and SAS. Although Excel is limited, compared with some of the more expensive statistical packages, it still provides a great tool for analyzing and modeling data.

We argue that sound data modeling can be instrumental in helping explain and prevent shrink. The information in this book is important because it provides a tool that can help many loss prevention teams move from gut feeling reactions to sound decision making. This book can be used to save money by allocating resources in ways that are supported by data and analytics. Loss prevention teams deal with all aspects of the business from sales to loss. Being able to uncover reasons for low performing stores is vital in finding solutions and saving money.

Broader implications of this book could include other types of data modeling in the retail industry and criminal justice. For example, retail organizations may want to use the methods in this book to predict customer attrition, customer retention, or trends in sales. Also, data modeling techniques derived from this book could aid in predicting future crimes or when geographic areas will have an increase in crime (e.g., hotspots).

An important aspect to remember with any modeling and analytical project is to check your data for assumptions. Make sure that you clean and assess your data for outliers, as they can change the accuracy of your model. Make sure to validate your model before you deploy it to determine its predictive accuracy. Lastly, optimize and repeat.

Follow-up research should include real-world examples of shrink modeling and decisions that were made based on the results of shrink modeling. Future discussions on shrink modeling and predictive analytics for retail could include some other data sources, such as facial recognition and video analytics. Other topics that were beyond the scope of this book could include k^{th} nearest neighbors and Bayesian networks.

One key point we would like to end with is this: don't deal with just the symptoms in your organization; determine the causes and be proactive. As the science of data analytics continues to grow and benefit many different business sectors, we recommend that you begin to grow your data science team. For the authors, it has been a combined 40+ years working on data and analytics and we are pleased to share this book with you, and hope that you can benefit from analytics.

Appendix A

Common Statistical Distributions

In this section, we provide the common values for some typical statistical distributions that have been covered in this book.

X	Pr(x < X)	X	Pr(x < X)	X	Pr(x < X)	X	Pr(x < X)	X	Pr(x < X)
0.00	0.5000	0.60	0.7257	1.20	0.8849	1.80	0.9641	2.40	0.9918
0.01	0.5040	0.61	0.7291	1.21	0.8869	1.81	0.9649	2.41	0.9920
0.02	0.5080	0.62	0.7324	1.22	0.8888	1.82	0.9656	2.42	0.9922
0.03	0.5120	0.63	0.7357	1.23	0.8907	1.83	0.9664	2.43	0.9925
0.04	0.5160	0.64	0.7389	1.24	0.8925	1.84	0.9671	2.44	0.9927
0.05	0.5199	0.65	0.7422	1.25	0.8944	1.85	0.9678	2.45	0.9929
0.06	0.5239	0.66	0.7454	1.26	0.8962	1.86	0.9686	2.46	0.9931
0.07	0.5279	0.67	0.7486	1.27	0.8980	1.87	0.9693	2.47	0.9932
0.08	0.5319	0.68	0.7517	1.28	0.8997	1.88	0.9699	2.48	0.9934
0.09	0.5359	0.69	0.7549	1.29	0.9015	1.89	0.9706	2.49	0.9936
0.10	0.5398	0.70	0.7580	1.30	0.9032	1.90	0.9713	2.50	0.9938
0.11	0.5438	0.71	0.7611	1.31	0.9049	1.91	0.9719	2.52	0.9941
0.12	0.5478	0.72	0.7642	1.32	0.9066	1.92	0.9726	2.54	0.9945
0.13	0.5517	0.73	0.7673	1.33	0.9082	1.93	0.9732	2.56	0.9948
0.14	0.5557	0.74	0.7704	1.34	0.9099	1.94	0.9738	2.58	0.9951
0.15	0.5596	0.75	0.7734	1.35	0.9115	1.95	0.9744	2.60	0.9953
0.16	0.5636	0.76	0.7764	1.36	0.9131	1.96	0.9750	2.62	0.9956
0.17	0.5675	0.77	0.7794	1.37	0.9147	1.97	0.9756	2.64	0.9959

(Continued)

X	Pr(x < X)	X	Pr(x < X)	X	Pr(x < X)	X	Pr(x < X)	X	Pr(x < X)
0.18	0.5714	0.78	0.7823	1.38	0.9162	1.98	0.9761	2.66	0.9961
0.19	0.5753	0.79	0.7852	1.39	0.9177	1.99	0.9767	2.68	0.9963
0.20	0.5793	0.80	0.7881	1.40	0.9192	2.00	0.9772	2.70	0.9965
0.21	0.5832	0.81	0.7910	1.41	0.9207	2.01	0.9778	2.72	0.9967
0.22	0.5871	0.82	0.7939	1.42	0.9222	2.02	0.9783	2.74	0.9969
0.23	0.5910	0.83	0.7967	1.43	0.9236	2.03	0.9788	2.76	0.9971
0.24	0.5948	0.84	0.7995	1.44	0.9251	2.04	0.9793	2.78	0.9973
0.25	0.5987	0.85	0.8023	1.45	0.9265	2.05	0.9798	2.80	0.9974
0.26	0.6026	0.86	0.8051	1.46	0.9279	2.06	0.9803	2.82	0.9976
0.27	0.6064	0.87	0.8078	1.47	0.9292	2.07	0.9808	2.84	0.9977
0.28	0.6103	0.88	0.8106	1.48	0.9306	2.08	0.9812	2.86	0.9979
0.29	0.6141	0.89	0.8133	1.49	0.9319	2.09	0.9817	2.88	0.9980
0.30	0.6179	0.90	0.8159	1.50	0.9332	2.10	0.9821	2.90	0.9981
0.31	0.6217	0.91	0.8186	1.51	0.9345	2.11	0.9826	2.92	0.9982
0.32	0.6255	0.92	0.8212	1.52	0.9357	2.12	0.9830	2.94	0.9984
0.33	0.6293	0.93	0.8238	1.53	0.9370	2.13	0.9834	2.96	0.9985
0.34	0.6331	0.94	0.8264	1.54	0.9382	2.14	0.9838	2.98	0.9986
0.35	0.6368	0.95	0.8289	1.55	0.9394	2.15	0.9842	3.00	0.9987
0.36	0.6406	0.96	0.8315	1.56	0.9406	2.16	0.9846	3.05	0.9989
0.37	0.6443	0.97	0.8340	1.57	0.9418	2.17	0.9850	3.10	0.9990
0.38	0.6480	0.98	0.8365	1.58	0.9429	2.18	0.9854	3.15	0.9992
0.39	0.6517	0.99	0.8389	1.59	0.9441	2.19	0.9857	3.20	0.9993
0.40	0.6554	1.00	0.8413	1.60	0.9452	2.20	0.9861	3.25	0.9994
0.41	0.6591	1.01	0.8438	1.61	0.9463	2.21	0.9864	3.30	0.9995
0.42	0.6628	1.02	0.8461	1.62	0.9474	2.22	0.9868	3.35	0.9996
0.43	0.6664	1.03	0.8485	1.63	0.9484	2.23	0.9871	3.40	0.9997
0.44	0.6700	1.04	0.8508	1.64	0.9495	2.24	0.9875	3.45	0.9997
0.45	0.6736	1.05	0.8531	1.65	0.9505	2.25	0.9878	3.50	0.9998
0.46	0.6772	1.06	0.8554	1.66	0.9515	2.26	0.9881	3.55	0.9998
0.47	0.6808	1.07	0.8577	1.67	0.9525	2.27	0.9884	3.60	0.9998
0.48	0.6844	1.08	0.8599	1.68	0.9535	2.28	0.9887	3.65	0.9999

(Continued)

X	Pr(x < X)	X	Pr(x < X)	X	Pr(x < X)	X	Pr(x < X)	X	Pr(x < X)
0.49	0.6879	1.09	0.8621	1.69	0.9545	2.29	0.9890	3.70	0.9999
0.50	0.6915	1.10	0.8643	1.70	0.9554	2.30	0.9893	3.75	0.9999
0.51	0.6950	1.11	0.8665	1.71	0.9564	2.31	0.9896	3.80	0.9999
0.52	0.6985	1.12	0.8686	1.72	0.9573	2.32	0.9898	3.85	0.9999
0.53	0.7019	1.13	0.8708	1.73	0.9582	2.33	0.9901	3.90	1.0000
0.54	0.7054	1.14	0.8729	1.74	0.9591	2.34	0.9904	3.95	1.0000
0.55	0.7088	1.15	0.8749	1.75	0.9599	2.35	0.9906	4.00	1.0000
0.56	0.7123	1.16	0.8770	1.76	0.9608	2.36	0.9909		
0.57	0.7157	1.17	0.8790	1.77	0.9616	2.37	0.9911		
0.58	0.7190	1.18	0.8810	1.78	0.9625	2.38	0.9913		
0.59	0.7224	1.19	0.8830	1.79	0.9633	2.39	0.9916		

Table of Common Values from the t Distribution

Degrees of Freedom	Pr(T < t)				
	0.900	0.950	0.975	0.990	0.995
1	3.0777	6.3138	12.7062	31.8205	63.6567
2	1.8856	2.9200	4.3027	6.9646	9.9248
3	1.6377	2.3534	3.1824	4.5407	5.8409
4	1.5332	2.1318	2.7764	3.7469	4.6041
5	1.4759	2.0150	2.5706	3.3649	4.0321
6	1.4398	1.9432	2.4469	3.1427	3.7074
7	1.4149	1.8946	2.3646	2.9980	3.4995
8	1.3968	1.8595	2.3060	2.8965	3.3554
9	1.3830	1.8331	2.2622	2.8214	3.2498
10	1.3722	1.8125	2.2281	2.7638	3.1693
11	1.3634	1.7959	2.2010	2.7181	3.1058
12	1.3562	1.7823	2.1788	2.6810	3.0545
13	1.3502	1.7709	2.1604	2.6503	3.0123
14	1.3450	1.7613	2.1448	2.6245	2.9768

(Continued)

Degrees of Freedom	Pr(T < t)				
	0.900	0.950	0.975	0.990	0.995
15	1.3406	1.7531	2.1314	2.6025	2.9467
16	1.3368	1.7459	2.1199	2.5835	2.9208
17	1.3334	1.7396	2.1098	2.5669	2.8982
18	1.3304	1.7341	2.1009	2.5524	2.8784
19	1.3277	1.7291	2.0930	2.5395	2.8609
20	1.3253	1.7247	2.0860	2.5280	2.8453
21	1.3232	1.7207	2.0796	2.5176	2.8314
22	1.3212	1.7171	2.0739	2.5083	2.8188
23	1.3195	1.7139	2.0687	2.4999	2.8073
24	1.3178	1.7109	2.0639	2.4922	2.7969
25	1.3163	1.7081	2.0595	2.4851	2.7874
30	1.3104	1.6973	2.0423	2.4573	2.7500
40	1.3031	1.6839	2.0211	2.4233	2.7045
50	1.2987	1.6759	2.0086	2.4033	2.6778
60	1.2958	1.6706	2.0003	2.3901	2.6603
70	1.2938	1.6669	1.9944	2.3808	2.6479
80	1.2922	1.6641	1.9901	2.3739	2.6387
90	1.2910	1.6620	1.9867	2.3685	2.6316
100	1.2901	1.6602	1.9840	2.3642	2.6259

Table of Common Values from the Chi-Square Distribution

Degrees of Freedom	Pr(X < x)				
	0.900	0.950	0.975	0.990	0.995
1	2.7055	3.8415	5.0239	6.6349	7.8794
2	4.6052	5.9915	7.3778	9.2103	10.5966
3	6.2514	7.8147	9.3484	11.3449	12.8382
4	7.7794	9.4877	11.1433	13.2767	14.8603
5	9.2364	11.0705	12.8325	15.0863	16.7496

(Continued)

Degrees of Freedom	Pr(X < x)				
	0.900	0.950	0.975	0.990	0.995
6	10.6446	12.5916	14.4494	16.8119	18.5476
7	12.0170	14.0671	16.0128	18.4753	20.2777
8	13.3616	15.5073	17.5345	20.0902	21.9550
9	14.6837	16.9190	19.0228	21.6660	23.5894
10	15.9872	18.3070	20.4832	23.2093	25.1882
11	17.2750	19.6751	21.9200	24.7250	26.7568
12	18.5493	21.0261	23.3367	26.2170	28.2995
13	19.8119	22.3620	24.7356	27.6882	29.8195
14	21.0641	23.6848	26.1189	29.1412	31.3193
15	22.3071	24.9958	27.4884	30.5779	32.8013
16	23.5418	26.2962	28.8454	31.9999	34.2672
17	24.7690	27.5871	30.1910	33.4087	35.7185
18	25.9894	28.8693	31.5264	34.8053	37.1565
19	27.2036	30.1435	32.8523	36.1909	38.5823
20	28.4120	31.4104	34.1696	37.5662	39.9968
21	29.6151	32.6706	35.4789	38.9322	41.4011
22	30.8133	33.9244	36.7807	40.2894	42.7957
23	32.0069	35.1725	38.0756	41.6384	44.1813
24	33.1962	36.4150	39.3641	42.9798	45.5585
25	34.3816	37.6525	40.6465	44.3141	46.9279
30	40.2560	43.7730	46.9792	50.8922	53.6720
40	51.8051	55.7585	59.3417	63.6907	66.7660
50	63.1671	67.5048	71.4202	76.1539	79.4900
60	74.3970	79.0819	83.2977	88.3794	91.9517
70	85.5270	90.5312	95.0232	100.4252	104.2149
80	96.5782	101.8795	106.6286	112.3288	116.3211
90	107.5650	113.1453	118.1359	124.1163	128.2989
100	118.4980	124.3421	129.5612	135.8067	140.1695

Akers, R.L. (2000). *Criminological Theories: Introduction, Evaluation, and Application.* 3rd ed. Los Angeles, CA: Roxbury Publishing Co.

Baxter, D.N. (2014). *Who is Taking the Shirt off Your Back? A Multi-Method Analysis of Theft at a Specialty Retailer.* Ph.D. Thesis. Indiana University of Pennsylvania. Indiana, PA, USA.

Bellur, V.V. (1981). Shoplifting: can it be prevented? *Journal of the Academy of Marketing Science.* **9**(2):78–87.

Brantingham, P.L. & Brantingham, P.J. (1995). Criminality of place: crime generators and crime attractors. *European Journal on Criminal Policy and Research.* **3**:1–26.

Brantingham, P.L. & Brantingham, P.J. (2008). Crime pattern theory. In: R. Wortley & L. Mazerolle (eds.). *Environmental Criminology and Crime Analysis.* pp. 78–94. Cullompton, UK: Willan.

Brasier, L.L. (2015). Man's scam turned home depot thefts into gift cards. *USA Today Network.* October 6, 2015. http://www.usatoday.com/story/news/nation-now/2015/10/06/home-depot-thief-gift-cards/73441386/

Cantrell, V. & Moraca, B. (2015). *Organized Retail Crime Survey.* Washington, DC: National Retail Federation. https://nrf.com/resources/retail-library/2015-organized-retail-crime-survey

Chen, C.X. & Sandino. T. (2012). Can wages buy honesty? The relationship between relative wages and employee theft. *Journal of Accounting Research.* **50**:967–1000.

Chen, T. & Guestrin C. (2016). XGBoost: a scalable tree boosting system. In: *Proceedings of the ACM SIGKKD International Conference on Knowledge Discovery and Data Mining. KDD'16.* August 13–17, 2016. San Francisco, CA.

Clarke, R.V. (1983). Situational crime prevention: its theoretical basis and practical scope. In: M. Tonry & N. Norris (eds.). *Crime and Justice: An Annual Review of Research.* vol. 4. pp. 225–256. Chicago, IL: University of Chicago Press.

Clarke, R.V. (1997). *Situational Crime Prevention: Successful Case Studies.* 2nd ed. Albany, NY: Harrow and Heston.

Clarke, R.V. (1999). *Hot Products: Understanding, Anticipating, and Reducing Demand for Stolen Goods.* Police Research Series, Paper 112. London, UK: UK Home Office.

Clarke, R.V. (2005). Seven misconceptions of situational crime prevention. In: N. Tilley (ed.). *Handbook of Crime Prevention and Public Safety.* Portland, OR: Willan Publishing.

Clarke, R. & Cornish, D. (1985). Modeling offenders' decisions: a framework for research and policy. *Crime and Justice.* **6**:147–185.

Clayton, M. (2005). Is black-market baby formula financing terror? *The Christian Science Monitor.* June 29, 2005. http://www.csmonitor.com/2005/0629/p01s01-usju.html

Cohen, L.E. & Felson, M. (1979). Social change and crime rate trends: a routine activity approach. *American Sociological Review.* **44**:588–608.

Cornish, D. & Clarke, R.V. (1986). Introduction. In: D. Cornish & R.V. Clarke (eds.). *The Reasoning Criminal.* pp. 1–16. New York, NY: Springer-Verlag.

Cornish, D.B. & Clarke, R.V. (2003). Opportunities, precipitators and criminal decisions: a reply to Wortley's critique of situational crime prevention. In: M. Smith & D.B. Cornish (eds.). *Theory for Situational Crime Prevention: Crime Prevention Studies.* vol. 16. pp. 41–96. Monsey, NY: Criminal Justice Press.

Cozens, P. (2008). Crime prevention through environmental design. In: R. Wortley & L. Mazerolle (eds.). *Environmental Criminology and Crime Analysis.* Devon, UK: Willan Publishing.

Cozens, P., Saville, G., & Hillier, D. (2005). Crime prevention through environmental design (CPTED): a review and modern bibliography. *Property Management.* **23**(5):328–56.

Crowe, T. (2000). *Crime Prevention Through Environmental Design: Applications of Architectural Design and Space Management Concepts.* 2nd ed. Oxford, UK: Butterworth-Heinemann.

Cullen, F.T., Agnew, R., & Wilcox, P. (2014). Situational crime prevention. In: F.T. Cullen, R. Agnew, & P. Wilcox (eds.). *Criminological Theory: Past to Present.* pp. 480–481. New York, NY: Oxford University Press.

Dragland, Å. (2013). Big Data, for better or worse: 90% of world's data generated over last two years. *ScienceDaily.* May 22, 2013. https://www.sciencedaily.com/releases/2013/05/130522085217.htm

Dupont, W.D. & Plummer, W.D. (1998). Power and sample size calculations for studies involving linear regression. *Controlled Clinical Trials.* **19**(6):589–601.

Eck, J., Clarke, R.V., & Guerette, R. (2007). Risky facilities: crime concentrations in homogeneous sets of establishments and facilities. In: G. Farrell *et al.* (eds.). *Imagination for Crime Prevention: Essays in Honor of Ken Pease, Crime Prevention Studies.* vol. 21. pp. 225–264. Monsey, NY: Criminal Justice Press.

Farrington, D.P., Bowen, S., Buckle, A., Burns-Howell, T., Burrows, J., & Speed, M. (1993). An experiment on the prevention of shoplifting. In: R.V. Clarke (ed.). *Crime Prevention Studies*. vol. 1. pp. 93–119. Monsey, NY: Willow Tree Press.

Felson, M. (2002). *Crime and Everyday life.* 3rd ed. Thousand Oaks, CA: Sage Publications.

Felson, M. (2006). *Crime and Nature.* Thousand Oaks, CA: Sage Publications.

Felson, M. & Cohen, L. (1980). Social change and crime rate trends: a routine activity approach. *Human Ecology and Crime.* **8**(4): 389–406.

Finklea, K.M. (2012). *Organized Retail Crime*. CRS Report to Congress. Washington, DC: Congressional Research Service.

Gottfredson, M.R. & Hirschi, T. (1990). *A General Theory of Crime.* Stanford, CA: Stanford University Press.

Hayes, R. & Downs, D.M. (2011). Controlling retail theft with CCTV domes, CCTV public view monitors, and protective containers: a randomized control trial. *Security Journal.* **24**(3): 237–250.

Hayes, R., Johns, T., Scicchitano, M., Downs, D., & Pietrawska, B. (2011). Evaluating the effects of protective keeper boxes on 'hot product' loss and sales. *Security Journal.* **24**(4): 357–369.

Hayes, R., Downs, D.M., & Blackwood, R. (2012). Anti-theft procedures and fixtures: a randomized controlled trial of two situational crime prevention measures. *Journal of Experimental Criminology.* **8**(1): 1–15.

Hollinger, R.C. & Clarke, J.P. (1983). *Theft by Employees.* Lexington, KY: Lexington Books.

Hollinger, R. & Langton, L. (2005). *2004 National Retail Security Survey.* Gainsville, FL: University of Florida.

Hollinger, R.C. & Adams, A. (2007). *National Retail Security Survey.* Gainesville, FL: University of Florida.

Jack L. Hayes International, Inc. (2016). *28th Annual Retail Theft Survey.* Wesley Chapel, FL: Jack L. Hayes International, Inc. http://hayesinternational.com/news/annual-retail-theft-survey/

Liaw, A. & Wiener, M. (2002). Classification and regression by randomForest. *R News.* **2/3**:18–22

Miller, C.I. (2005). *Organized Retail Theft: Raising Awareness, Offering Solutions.* p. 17. Washington, DC: National Retail Federation Foundation.

Moraca, B., Hollinger, R., & Cantrell, V. (2015). *The 2015 National Retail Security Survey.* Washington, DC: National Retail Federation and Gainesville, FL: University of Florida. https://nrf.com/resources/retail-library/national-retail-security-survey-2015

Moraca, B., Hollinger, R., & Cantrell, V. (2016). *The 2016 National Retail Security Survey.* Washington, DC: National Retail Federation and Gainesville, FL: University of Florida. https://nrf.com/resources/retail-library/national-retail-security-survey-2016

Nagin, D.S. & Paternoster, R. (1993). Enduring individual differences and rational choice theories of crime. *Law and Society Review.* **27**:467–496.

National Association of Shoplifting Prevention. (2006). www.shopliftingprevention.org/

Nelson, D. & Perrone, S. (2000). Understanding and controlling retail theft. *Trends & Issues in Crime and Criminal Justice.* no. 152. Canberra, Australia: Australian Institute of Criminology.

Petrossian, G.A. & Clarke, R.V. (2014). Explaining and controlling illegal commercial fishing: an application of the CRAVED theft model. *British Journal of Criminology.* **54**:73–90.

Prabhakar, H. (2012). *Black Market Billions: How Organized Retail Crime Funds Global Terrorists.* Upper Saddle River, NJ: FT Press.

Reynald, D.M. (2011). Factors associated with the guardianship of places: assessing the relative importance of the spatio-physical and socio-demographic contexts in generating opportunities for capable guardianship. *Journal of Research in Crime & Delinquency.* **48**:110–142.

Shiode, S., Shiode, N., Block, R., & Block, C. (2015). Space-time characteristics of micro-scale crime occurrences: an application of a network-based space-time search window technique for crime incidents in Chicago. *International Journal of Geographical Information Science.* **29**(5):697–719.

Smith, C. & Patterson, G. (1980). Cognitive mapping and the subjective: geography of crime. In: D. Georges-Abeyie & K. Harries (eds.). *Crime: A Spatial Perspective.* New York, NY: Columbia University Press.

Smith M.J. & Clarke R.V. (2012). Situational crime prevention: classifying techniques using 'good enough' theory. In: B.C. Welsh & D.P. Farrington (eds.). *The Oxford Handbook of Crime Prevention.* pp. 291–315. New York, NY: Oxford University Press.

Speights, D. (2014). *Big Data—Turning the Tide on Fraud and Shrink.* Irvine, CA: The Retail Equation Inc.

Speights, D. & Hilinski, C. (2005). *Return Fraud and Abuse: How to Protect Profits.* Irvine, CA: The Retail Equation Inc.

Speights, D. & Hanks, C. (2014). *How the Science of Statistics Creates Profitable Solutions in Retail Loss Prevention.* Irvine, CA: The Retail Equation Inc.

Speights, D., Downs, D., & Raz, A. (2012). Shrink Exposed: New Studies Show Return Rate Impacts Shrink. *LP Magazine.* LPPortal.com

Speights, D., Downs, D., & Raz, A. (2016). How a strict retail return policy can decrease revenue and return rates. *LP Magazine.* February 13, 2017. http://losspreventionmedia.com/insider/retail-industry/how-a-strict-retail-return-policy-can-decrease-revenue-and-affect-return-rates/

Sutton, A., Cherney, A., & White, R. (2008). *Crime Prevention: Principles, Perspectives and Practices.* Cambridge, UK: Cambridge University Press.

Index

Page numbers in *italics* refer to figures. Page numbers in **bold** refer to tables.

For Product Safety Concerns and Information please contact our EU
representative GPSR@taylorandfrancis.com
Taylor & Francis Verlag GmbH, Kaufingerstraße 24, 80331 München, Germany